Christology and Atonement

Christology and Atonement

A Scotistic Analysis

Guus H. Labooy

LEXINGTON BOOKS/FORTRESS ACADEMIC
Lanham • Boulder • New York • London

Published by Lexington Books/Fortress Academic
Lexington Books is an imprint of The Rowman & Littlefield Publishing Group, Inc.
4501 Forbes Boulevard, Suite 200, Lanham, Maryland 20706
www.rowman.com

86-90 Paul Street, London EC2A 4NE, United Kingdom

Copyright © 2024 by The Rowman & Littlefield Publishing Group, Inc.

All rights reserved. No part of this book may be reproduced in any form or by any electronic or mechanical means, including information storage and retrieval systems, without written permission from the publisher, except by a reviewer who may quote passages in a review.

British Library Cataloguing in Publication Information Available

Library of Congress Cataloging-in-Publication Data

Names: Labooy, G. H., 1959– author.
Title: Christology and atonement : a scotistic analysis / Guus H. Labooy.
Description: Lanham : Lexington Books, Fortress Academic, [2024] |
  Includes bibliographical references and index. | Summary: "This scotistic study in
  analytical theology presupposes Conciliar Christology and aims at a more profound
  understanding of two vital and connected Christian doctrines: Christology and
  atonement. Guus H. Labooy describes Duns Scotus's analysis of the incarnation and
  defends penal substitution with the aid of Scotus's analytical tools"—Provided by
  publisher.
Identifiers: LCCN 2023043724 (print) | LCCN 2023043725 (ebook) |
  ISBN 9781978713598 (cloth) | ISBN 9781978713604 (epub)
Subjects: LCSH: Atonement. | Duns Scotus, John, approximately 1266-1308.
Classification: LCC BT265.3 .L336 2024 (print) | LCC BT265.3 (ebook) | DDC
  234/.5—dc23/eng/20231213
LC record available at https://lccn.loc.gov/2023043724
LC ebook record available at https://lccn.loc.gov/2023043725

♾️ The paper used in this publication meets the minimum requirements of American
National Standard for Information Sciences—Permanence of Paper for Printed Library
Materials, ANSI/NISO Z39.48-1992.

Contents

Preface	vii
Introduction	1

PART I: THE COHERENCE OF THE INCARNATION: A SCOTISTIC ANALYSIS — 7

Chapter 1: Preliminary Considerations: The Trinity	9
Chapter 2: The Hypostatic Union	23
Chapter 3: Stepped Characterisation	41
Chapter 4: Two Intellects	57
Chapter 5: Two Wills	73
Chapter 6: Supralapsarian Christology	93

PART II: THEORY OF ATONEMENT: AN ANALYSIS WITH SCOTISTIC TOOLS — 105

Chapter 7: Scotus on Atonement	107
Chapter 8: The Meaning of the Passion, an Exegetical Excursion	125
Chapter 9: The Coherence of Penal Substitution	131
Chapter 10: Vicarious Penance: A Synthesis with Scotistic Tools	147
Glossary	163

Bibliography	165
Index	175
About the Author	179

Preface

The setting of this systematic study is the Church, in which I am a local pastor. The Church which, as McGuckin so incomparably said, is 'the community that celebrates the joy of the Trinity, as the nearness of the transcendent Father, the Lordship of the humble Saviour, and the concreteness of the ineffable Spirit.' Concentrating on the doctrines of Christology and atonement, this systematic study contemplates the central panel of this triptych, 'the Lordship of the humble Saviour.'

Stemming from an intellectual milieu increasingly hostile to religion, my Shepherd found me in my early twenties and brought me back to his flock. Perhaps the condescending environment of my youth predisposed me to a rather apologetic attitude, a discipline broadly akin to Anselm's motto 'faith seeking understanding.' Step by step, my zeal developed from wanting to prove why Christianity is true into desiring to more deeply understand the mysteries of the church. No one inspired me more on this journey than Antoon Vos. In countless fervent tutorial moments, he enkindled in me a keen interest in analytic theology and in the 'subtle doctor' Duns Scotus (1266–1308) in particular. This led to my PhD in the science-religion debate (2000) in which I tried to integrate Scotistic analytic tools in the debate on the then current neurobiological developments in psychiatry—a field dear to me due to my erstwhile medical background.

The first part of this book comprises various topics concerning the incarnation. Since my conversion to Christianity, I have been awestruck when thinking of the incarnation, the belief that God became man in Jesus Christ. I have worshipfully reflected upon this central tenet of Christian faith ever since, and I never found such a compelling analysis of the incarnation as that of Scotus—I had the privilege to become acquainted with it within the inspiring environment of the John Duns Scotus Research Group.[1] The wish to share

---

1. N. den Bok, M. Bac, A. Beck, K. Bom, G. Labooy, H. Veldhuis, and A. Vos, 'More than Just an Individual. Scotus's Concept of Person from the Christological Context of Lectura III 1,' *Franciscan Studies*, no. 66 (2008): 169–96.

viii *Preface*

this analysis of the incarnation, of the 'hypostatic union,' forms a key motive for writing this book. Not that truth is a structure of analytically refined doctrines; truth is a living person, the Lord Jesus Christ. That is palpable in Scotus's texts as well, and several chapters of this book bear witness of that: his theology is, eventually, *'love seeking understanding.'*

This theme of love is, if possible, still more central in the second part of this study on atonement. The Messiah dying for our sins is perhaps the storm centre of the confrontation between Christian faith and the secular intellectual mindset. I will argue, for exegetical reasons, that all the current models of atonement are complementary. None of them should be discarded and neither should 'penal substitution'—or 'vicarious penance' as I call it. The account of vicarious penance I defend is shaped with the decisive aid of Scotus's analytical tools, though Scotus himself, as I will maintain, was not an advocate of vicarious penance. Hence, standing on his shoulders, now with regard to his analytical apparatus and especially his innovative meta-ethical framework, I will defend a complementary view of atonement which also includes vicarious penance. Thus, it is honey from the rock (Psalm 81: 17).

I have used Bernard of Chartres's image: I am like a dwarf on the shoulders of the giant Duns Scotus—while not pretending that I see further. But I also want to thank some contemporary 'giants' to whom I am deeply indebted, like the members of the Scotus Research Group back then: Martijn Bac, Andreas Beck, Nico den Bok, Klaas Bom, Eef Dekker, Antoon Vos, and the late Henry Veldhuis; then Richard Cross from whose eminent work I have greatly profited. And Maarten Wisse, with whom I wrote two journal articles corresponding to two of the present chapters. Also, my friends Arjan Plaisier and Dolf te Velde, who both coread the first version; Kees Lavooij and Bert van Veluw for our numerous conversations; Egbert Bos who kindly encouraged me with his advice; and Peter Simpson whose translations of Scotus on the internet were very helpful to me. I translated Scotus's complicated texts myself,[2] but again, standing on the shoulders of others! I am also very grateful to my parishes for their support and to the Protestant Church of the Netherlands, which facilitates study for its pastors.

This book is mainly targeted at postgraduate students of philosophy and theology and upward—as long as they are endowed with a certain keenness for analytical theology. Finally, my hope in writing this book is to share 'subtle' apologetic tools to further enkindle the joyful awareness of 'the Lordship of the humble Saviour.'

Guus H. Labooy, *Verbi Divini Minister*

---

2. Except for those on the hypostatic union (chapter 2): those translations stem from the Scotus Research Group as a whole.

Introduction

This study in analytical theology presupposes Conciliar Christology and aims at a more profound understanding of two vital and connected Christian doctrines: Christology and atonement. Of course, I will not start from scratch; instead, I will take the humble role of a dwarf on the shoulders of giants. And among all our giant sages, one deserves to be named especially: the 'doctor subtilis' Duns Scotus (1266–1308). He is my principal guide because his analysis of the incarnation is groundbreaking and his analysis of the atonement yields many insights which can be fruitfully applied to the modern debate on atonement.

As regards methodology, conceptual analysis is essential in this book. The reader will scent the originally Augustinian motto 'credo ut intelligam,' 'I believe in order to understand.' This attitude decisively prospered due to Anselm of Canterbury (1033–1109) and became characteristic for all the medieval schoolmen—and far beyond, well into the eighteenth century. Only after the French Revolution, an anomalous rift occurred between faith and philosophy, a divorce which expressed itself institutionally as well. However, the significance for philosophy of Anselm's maxim parallels the significance of space exploration for the development of technology in general: in order to investigate theological topics like the Trinity and the incarnation, the schoolmen further developed and enriched entire philosophical disciplines like, for example, logic and meticulous conceptual analysis. Yet all this richness of argumentation was not intended 'to replace faith with rational proof, as if it were something better, but to provide an insight into what exactly the person of faith already believes.'[1]

---

1. Peter Adamson, *Medieval Philosophy*, first edition, *A History of Philosophy without Any Gaps*, volume 4 (Oxford; New York: Oxford University Press, 2019), chap. 8.

2 *Introduction*

CHAPTER 1: PRELIMINARY CONSIDERATIONS: THE TRINITY

As a preliminary, I dwell on the Trinity, because the analysis of the incarnation requires a precise definition of what a divine 'Persona' is. For the incarnation is about a divine Persona, the Word, assuming the human nature. And this medieval Trinitarian concept of a 'Persona' has a different meaning than our modern concept of a person—I therefore, throughout this study, use the Latin 'Persona' to indicate this specific medieval meaning. Equipped with a more sophisticated definition of Persona or of the Greek equivalent 'hypostasis,' we proceed to our actual topic: the coherence of Christology.

CHAPTER 2: THE HYPOSTATIC UNION

The Council of Chalcedon states that the Word as the second Persona of the Trinity became 'truly God and truly man.' In this formula, the Council watched over two insights which are essential to the Christian faith: firstly, the Word must be the single 'bearer' of both the divine and the human nature. Or, as the creed states it: 'no division, no separation' between the natures. For if the natures remained in fact separated, then God did not really become man, the divine and the human nature actually being 'divided' over two distinct 'bearers.' Accordingly, the creed requires that both natures are united in only one divine Persona or hypostasis, a union traditionally called the 'hypostatic union.' Secondly, the creed demands the integrity of these two natures—no 'confusion or change' of them. For if the human nature is changed in the incarnation, then surely God became *something*, but not like us *a human being*; hence the second creedal demand that the two natures must remain *unaltered* in their union. These two conciliar tenets, though essential for Christian faith, seem to be contrary. If that would be the case, we could only salvage Christian faith by shrouding it in the wrong kind of 'mystery,' that of venerating contradictions. I will describe Scotus's meticulous account of the hypostatic union which is uniquely successful in combining these two demands.

CHAPTER 3: STEPPED CHARACTERISATION

The creeds hold that all the properties of Christ's human nature can be applied to the Word. However, this yields the problem of 'Christological predication.' Because when we say that Jesus died for our sins, the Word is characterised

Introduction 3

by this too: thus, the eternal Word died for our sins. However, this generates a plain contradiction, for the Word cannot die! Now the creeds already had a way of dealing with this: they differentiated between 'as regards his Godhead' and 'as regards his manhood.' So as regards his manhood, He died for us, but as regards his Godhead, He is everlasting. I call these phrases 'qua-propositions.' However, these qua-propositions are philosophically contested. Following Marilyn McCord Adams, I contribute to the defence of qua-propositions by probing their metaphysical backbone. This constitutes, I think, a small but fresh contribution to the debate.

CHAPTER 4: TWO INTELLECTS

If the Word assumed a human nature, Christ must have a human soul and body. Now the soul has two powers, intellect and will. But as the divine essence has an intellect and will too, there are in Christ two intellects and two wills, just as Conciliar Christology confirmed. I reflect on this immense mystery, partly by means of a metaphor, partly by reaping the benefit of Scotus. What impressed me in these medieval texts, not least because of the significance for spirituality, is that we moderns tend to shape Christ's human intellect in the image of our intellectual deficiencies and limitations, while for the schoolmen it was the other way around: they shaped the general human intellect in the image of Christ's glorious beatific vision! That is, our human intellect in its restored, eschatological bliss.

CHAPTER 5: TWO WILLS

God not only gracefully perfects Christ's intellect, but He also perfects his human will through grace and fruition. As regards his human will, I examine a series of interrelated difficulties: the relation between the divine and the human will; the distinction between the *causal* and the *predicative* aspects of agency; what human freedom in general is; the point that being assumed in itself does not affect the scope of freedom for that human will; and the concordance between Christ's freedom and, respectively, his foreknowledge, his inability to sin, and the perpetuity of his beatific status. In all of this, I persistently stand on Scotus's shoulders.

4   *Introduction*

CHAPTER 6: SUPRALAPSARIAN CHRISTOLOGY

As a hinge between the two main parts of this study, we reflect on the view—dearly held by Scotus—that even if Adam did not sin, the Word would have assumed a human nature. Hence, the need for redemption because of Adam's fall is no longer the *primary* reason for the assumption of the human nature. In other words, the reason for the incarnation is 'explanatory prior' to the fall ('supralapsarian'). For according to Scotus, prior to anything else, God wants the predestination of Christ to the highest glory, because He wants others to share in his glory and love. Only in the next instant, the incarnation is also used to redeem. I portray how the primacy of love of this 'supralapsarian Christology' pervades Scotus's whole thought.

CHAPTER 7: SCOTUS ON ATONEMENT

As regards atonement, I begin by posing a historical research question: What is Scotus's view on atonement? I argue that he endorses a nonpenal view that depends on Christ's meritorious, substitutionary, and supererogatory acts of righteousness. Christ offers satisfaction for our trespasses by the meritorious quality of his goodness, not by the vicariously endured punishment of our badness. I further verify this assessment of Scotus's view by examining his thought on penance, an adjacent issue which casts additional light on atonement. A further feature of Scotus's view on atonement is his persistent criticism of Anselm's necessitarian analysis. In sharp contrast to Anselm, Scotus argued that it is not necessary that the redemption was done by a God-man. Anselm famously reasoned that God had *necessarily* to become man, in order to fulfil 'what only a true God could do and only a true man was obliged to do.' Yet Scotus refutes this necessity and this results in a radically different perception of the field of possibilities for God's actions: a shift from moral necessity stemming from God's nature to freedom stemming from God's will; a shift towards nonnecessitarian meta-ethics.

CHAPTER 8: THE MEANING OF THE PASSION, AN EXEGETICAL EXCURSION

Because an Anselmian deductive proof of the necessity of the incarnation and the atonement is thus blocked, we have to rely on historical evidence and hence on exegesis instead. And exegesis is exactly what Scotus did too: when asking what caused the passion, Scotus gives an *exegetically* established

Introduction 5

answer: 'the passion of this man was for the sake of justice.' His exegesis was, however, not extensive—to be polite. Therefore, I emulate Scotus's exegetical clue and insert this exegetical excursion. Relying on historical research on first-century Judaism, I defend a complementary standpoint on atonement which, among other aspects like the important 'Christus-Victor' view, encompasses a penal substitutionary aspect as well.

CHAPTER 9: THE COHERENCE OF PENAL SUBSTITUTION

I now return to an analytic question: Can penal substitution, or what I also call 'vicarious penance,' withstand critical scrutiny? Is it conceptually coherent to punish someone who does not deserve that? And, if so, is it just? Several scholars, both scholastic and contemporary, have argued that you can only punish someone if there is 'deservedness.' But in the case of an innocent person, there is no deservedness; consequently, substitutionary punishment is *logically* impossible. In this dilemma, it proves crucial that the rightful demand of an analytic unity of punishment and deservedness does not logically imply *personal* deservedness. For it could also be, I argue, *representative* deservedness. I conclude, therefore, that penal substitution, as evidenced by scripture, is not contradictory. Moreover, I briefly trace the crucial role of the relevant Scotistic analytic apparatus in Reformed scholasticism, which, perhaps more than any other tradition, intensively dealt with all the conceptual intricacies of penal substitution.

CHAPTER 10: VICARIOUS PENANCE: A SYNTHESIS WITH SCOTISTIC TOOLS

I finally pull together the threads of the preceding chapters on atonement. Firstly, as compared to Anselm, Scotus offered a radically different perception of the field of possibilities for God's moral actions (as I already said, see chapter 7). This is of decisive importance to avoid the impression that satisfaction is about a blind, mechanistic process of meting out punishment. It is central to a theology of love. Next, because God acts in a perfect way, ends are willed before means. This implies that God's wish to reward his children with everlasting life in his presence is the *basis* of God's redeeming acts and He then provides the means for that as well: He *bestows* meritoriousness on suitable acts of the elect. Praiseworthy works are not autonomously generated by us; kindled by the Spirit they are graciously *accepted* by God as meritorious in order to properly reward us. They are not a man-made *sufficient condition* for election but a God-made *necessary condition* for election. To further understand penal substitution, Scotus's analysis of penance proves very helpful (see chapter 7). For it is there that medievals focused on the topic of punishment. Although Scotus himself remained silent about penal substitution, his meticulous analysis of punishment within the context of penance forms an important contribution to the analysis of vicarious penance. Thus equipped, I provide a systematic account of Christ's atoning work, focussing on vicarious penance.

PART I

The Coherence of the Incarnation

A Scotistic Analysis

Chapter 1

Preliminary Considerations

The Trinity

1.1: TO THE FATHER, THROUGH THE SON, IN THE HOLY SPIRIT

In this chapter, I provide an outline of some important features of the Trinity, because Trinitarian conceptual and ontological decisions figure prominently in Christology. The Triune God concerns the inner life and worship of the church. For the church essentially is 'the community that celebrates the joy of the Trinity, as the nearness of the transcendent Father, the Lordship of the humble Saviour, and the concreteness of the ineffable Spirit.'[1] Hence, the Trinity is a mystery in which we are to be inaugurated. We are invited to come 'to the Father, through the Son, in the Holy Spirit.' Invited to participate, with all the angels and saints, in love, worship, and joy. Trinitarian theology—and indeed theology proper—without this anchorage in worship is void: like Adam and Eve in the garden of Eden, we would then hide for God's radiant presence behind a fence of speculation and rationality.

Throughout this book, this anchor in worship is essential to me. It reminds us of Scotus, whose view of the ultimate end of theology was not theoretical but *practical*: to love God above all else. Hence, notwithstanding his enormous intellectual oeuvre, theology was a *practical* science for Scotus.[2] And let me quote Scotus's fellow Franciscan Bonaventure, who, in the prologue of *The Soul's Journey into God*, 'invites the reader to the groans of prayer through Christ crucified,' so that he not believe that

---

1. John Anthony McGuckin, *The Orthodox Church: An Introduction to Its History, Doctrine, and Spiritual Culture* (Malden, MA; Oxford: Blackwell Pub. Ltd, 2008), 122.

2. Ludger Honnefelder, 'Philosophische Reflexion als Medium theologischer Einsicht im Rahmen der Christologie des Johannes Duns Scotus,' in *Wie beeinflusst die Christusoffenbarung das franziskanische Verständnis der Person?*, ed. Herbert Schneider, Veröffentlichungen der Johannes-Duns-Skotus-Akademie für Franziskanische Geistesgeschichte und Spiritualität Mönchengladbach 16 (Kevelaer: Butzon und Bercker, 2004), 76.

10 *Chapter 1*

> reading is sufficient without unction,
> investigation without wonder,
> observation without joy,
> work without piety,
> knowledge without love,
> understanding without humility,
> endeavour without divine grace,
> reflection as a mirror without divinely inspired wisdom.[3]

Imbued with the tradition of faith seeking understanding, Bonaventure here magnificently captures the relation between devotion and theological investigation. This needs to be said first, because Trinitarian thought and, more broadly, analytical theology, are often charged with erecting lifeless doctrines, static systems to idolatrously *pin down* God. Let me, therefore, underline that we cannot fathom God, we cannot rationally *grasp* him. According to the Christian tradition, God is incomprehensible, He is infinitely beyond the reach of our human finite intellectual capacities. Yet this does not exclude all knowledge of him, just as it does not entail that all our concepts are blind.[4] Our limited understanding is rather *a building block* of his true incomprehensibility:[5] He is incomprehensible to us, but we only become aware of that by means of our limited understanding. Just as only a deeper knowledge of physics enables us to realise that we cannot comprehend the Big Bang, so our limited knowledge of God enables us to worship his incomprehensible glory and majesty. Without any knowledge of him, the true Christian kind of incomprehensibility would collapse; it would be reduced to an elusive state of just not knowing anything at all. This would perhaps conduce us to a Neo-Platonist kind of mysticism, ancient or modern;[6] it would, however, fail to make us bend our knees before the God of Abraham, Isaac, and Jacob. Whereas that is, ultimately, the 'Sitz im Leben' of Trinitarian thought: as the conceptual marrow of liturgy and worship, it reflects our journey *to the Father, through the Son, in the Holy Spirit.*

Obviously, I here just offer a cursory description of a Conciliar, Scotistic view of the doctrine of the Trinity, without further arguing for it. I just briefly inform the reader which specific Trinitarian choices compose the background of this book.

---

3. Bonaventura, Ewert H. Cousins, and Ignatius C. Brady, *The Soul's Journey into God*, The Classics of Western Spirituality (Mahwah, NJ: Paulist Press, 1978), 55.

4. Behind this loom huge differences between Aristotle and the Christian tradition: not everything we can denominate is comprehensible. Duns Scotus: 'Ut mihi videtur, haec propositio falsa est quod 'nihil potest nominari a nobis magis proprie quam intelligatur.' *Lect.* I, d. 22, §2.

5. Epistemically spoken, not ontologically.

6. See G. H. Labooy, '"Duns Scotus" Univocity: Applied to the Debate on Phenomenological Theology,' *International Journal for Philosophy of Religion; Dordrecht* 76, no. 1 (August 2014): 53–73, http://dx.doi.org.vu-nl.idm.oclc.org/10.1007/s11153-014-9443-8.

1.2: ECONOMIC AND ESSENTIAL ASPECTS OF TRINITY

Let me start by briefly sketching the origin of Trinitarian thought. It arose out of the incomprehensible encounter with Jesus Christ, both before and after the resurrection.[7] This man somehow seemed to be identical with God, for He seemed to be worthy of the Name of God, 'השם' (ha Sjem); and hence, worthy of being venerated as divine. This was astonishing because it arose within the strict monotheistic context of Judaism. And, secondly, this encounter with Jesus was not that of a neutral onlooker: worshipping him as Lord was itself driven by the Holy Spirit, poured out at Pentecost. So, the Christian faith was, right from the start, Trinitarian. It was Trinitarian at the creedal, hymnal, and baptismal level. Yet theological reflection could not but lag behind: only in the fourth century, Trinitarian thought matured, connected with names such as Athanasius and the Cappadocians.[8] This ongoing theological reflection was driven by the need for clarification: How is it possible that on this man 'is bestowed the name which is above every name' (Phil. 2)? Doesn't this inevitably lead to di-theism? In the first attempts at clarification, it was alleged that the Word, the Logos, had become man and that the Logos was God's intelligence, his rational thought. Such an endeavour, having its roots in John's prologue, enabled the apostolic fathers to tentatively explain that God the Father and the redeeming Son are essentially one.

Until now, we approached the Trinity from the so-called *economic* viewpoint. We thereby observe the Trinity as manifest in the 'economy,' that is, in 'the ordered process of His self-disclosure.'[9] There, in this realm of God's intercourse with his creation, the three-ness of the one God leaps into the eye: יהוה the Lord, Jesus his Messiah, and his Holy Spirit. And these three, we confess, are one: they share one and the same divine nature. However, John's 'In the beginning was the Word, and the Word was with God, and the Word was God' sparked a further question: Is God also intrinsically Trinitarian? Apart from all his deeds towards his creation? This is called the *essential* or *intrinsic* viewpoint. Hence two levels of envisioning the Trinity: as regards its *essential* and as regards its *economic* aspect. I prefer this 'aspect-language' because talk of 'the economic Trinity' and 'the essential Trinity' could suggest that there are two separate Trinities. However, there is but one Trinity: the economic Trinity *is* the essential Trinity freely communicating

---

7. See Richard Bauckham, *Jesus and the God of Israel: God Crucified and Other Studies on the New Testament's Christology of Divine Identity*, (Colorado Springs: Paternoster, 2008); Larry W. Hurtado, *Lord Jesus Christ: Devotion to Jesus in Earliest Christianity* (Grand Rapids, MI: Eerdmans, 2005).

8. J. N. D. Kelly, *Early Christian Doctrines*, fifth revised edition (London: A & C Black, 1985), 255–63.

9. Kelly, 104. In patristic Greek, the 'economy' is the divine providential management of the entire creation, including the mission of the Son and the outpouring of the Spirit.

12   *Chapter 1*

itself outwardly. And this communicating process implies that we are invited to share in it, as Jesus prays: 'As you, Father, are in me and I am in you, may they also be in us, so that the world may believe that you have sent me' (John 17: 21).

Talk about 'the essential aspect of the Trinity' does not imply that the economic aspect is somehow less important because it is *not* essential. Here we must distinguish between two meanings of 'essential': in colloquial language, 'essential' often means 'important' or 'crucial.' Its technical meaning, though, is that a property of x is essential if x could not be x without it. Being a human being is an essential property for Daniel, for instance. Equally, being Triune is essential for God: God is Triune regardless of whether He creates or not. By contrast, an accidental property for x is a property x does not need in order to be x, like, for instance, Daniel being loyal to God. Now because creation is not necessary but a free divine gift instead, the economic Trinity cannot be an essential property of God in this *technical* sense. If that were the case, the creation would be necessary, like in Greek thought. Yet the creation and its redemption are not unimportant! God's love outpouring itself into his creation is the summit of beauty, love, and glory.

1.3: BONAVENTURE'S MONO-PERSONAL VIEW OF THE TRINITY

Today, there are two leading views of the Trinity: the social Trinity and the Augustinian or 'mono-personal' view of the Trinity. In the first 'social' type, the three divine (in Latin) 'personae' tend to acquire person-like characteristics, so the Trinity becomes a kind of 'social' Trinity of three subjects. This social model contributed significantly to the resurgence of Trinitarian thought in the latter half of the twentieth century. Its provenance was projected back to the Greek Cappadocian fathers, thus creating a polarity between the 'Western' Augustinian and the typically 'Eastern' or social view. This East-West disjunction theory, though, is increasingly criticised in recent scholarship because of overdrawing the Cappadocians: a real social Trinity cannot be found in their work.[10] However, the social Trinity is undoubtedly anticipated in the twelfth century in the work of Richard of Saint Victor. He set out to explore the possibilities of a more personal relationship between the persons of the Trinity, but still did not contribute to them a 'will' in the

---

10. For a critical stance on this social interpretation of the Cappadocians, see Lewis Ayres, *Nicaea and Its Legacy: An Approach to Fourth-Century Trinitarian Theology* (Oxford; New York: Oxford University Press, 2004); Kelly, *Early Christian Doctrines*, 263–69; Sarah Coakley, *God, Sexuality and the Self: An Essay 'on the Trinity'* (Cambridge; New York: Cambridge University Press, 2013).

Preliminary Considerations 13

modern sense of the word. The subsequent century retreated from this path, because of the emerging inconsistencies.[11]

The Augustinian view could be called the 'single-perfect-Mind' view or the 'mono-personal' view—'personal' in its modern sense, not in its medieval sense. I will return to this important semantic point shortly. Augustine compared the essential Trinity to three human mental features: memory, intellect, and love. As the Logos theory showed (chap. 1.2), this view predates Augustine: it is prefigured already in the second century.[12] Scholastics like Bonaventure, Thomas, and Duns Scotus further developed this Augustinian lead. This view is magnificently reflected in Bonaventure's *The Soul's Journey into God*. Here Bonaventure invites us to see the Trinitarian God through ourselves as through an image: 'to see through a mirror in an obscure manner' (1 Cor. 13: 12). I will take his lead:

> Enter into yourself, then, and see
> that your soul loves itself most fervently;
> that it could not love itself unless it knew itself,
> nor know itself unless it remembered itself,
> because our intellects grasp only what is present to our memory.
> From this you can observe, that your soul has a threefold power.
>
> These powers lead us to the most blessed Trinity itself
> in view of their order, origin and interrelatedness.
> From memory, intelligence comes forth as its offspring,
> since we understand when a likeness which is in the memory
> leaps into the eye of the intellect in the form of a word.
> From memory and intelligence love is breathed forth as their
> mutual bond.
> These three—the generating mind, the word and love—are in the
> soul
> as memory, understanding and will,
> which are consubstantial, coequal and coeval, and interpenetrate
> each other.
> If, then, God is a perfect spirit,
> he has memory, understanding and will;
> and he has the Word generated and Love breathed forth,
> which are necessarily distinct since one is produced by the other
> —not in order of essence, not in order of accident, therefore in order
> of persons.[13]

---

11. Nico den Bok, *Communicating the Most High: A Systematic Study of Person and Trinity in the Theology of Richard of St. Victor (1173)*, Bibliotheca Victorina 7 (Paris: Brepols, 1996).

12. Kelly, *Early Christian Doctrines*, 107–8.

13. Bonaventura, Cousins, and Brady, *The Soul's Journey into God*, pts. 1 and 5.

14   *Chapter 1*

A captivating passage in its blissful unity of analysis and contemplation. In this passage, the mono-personal or Augustinian view emerges. Here we cannot enter into the extensive debates between social and Augustinian trinitarianism. My favourite tradition though is this Augustinian view. My reservations as regards social trinitarianism are succinctly caught in this quotation: 'Conceptions of the Trinity as the communion of three divine subjects tend to empty the notion of subject of all content (which cannot refer to an individual being having its own free will), or else tend to tritheism (referring to three individual beings each having their own free wills).' Fortunately, I think that a substantial part of the social Trinitarian language and motives can be integrated and safeguarded in the mono-personal view. I will return to this point.

1.4: SCOTUS ON THE IMAGO DEI

Scotus follows Augustine and Bonaventure as regards this mono-personal view of the Trinity and its image, the human soul.[14] He first examines the view of Augustine in book X of *De Trinitate*, namely the image as '*memoria, intelligentia* and *voluntas*.' Judging this model to be troublesome for several reasons,[15] Scotus prefers the other image of the Trinity, also provided by Augustine, the view of the image as '*mens, notitia et amor*' in book IX.[16] The concept 'mens' is difficult to translate, for 'mind,' the obvious candidate, refers for us to the whole mind, not to just one aspect of it. For Scotus, however, 'mens' especially pics out the aspect of *fecundity*, which resides in a *habitual yet not actual* kind of knowing and willing.[17] Hence 'mens,' with this double fecundity which yields knowledge and love, is for Scotus the proper term (*Lect.* I, d3, p3, q4, §444–46). According to him, the human soul as 'mens,' knowledge, and love mirrors the Father, the Son, and the Holy Spirit. For greater clarity, I prefer to speak of the image of the Trinity as *origin, knowledge,* and *love*. The term 'origin' captures Scotus's focus on fecundity quite well and the use of the term 'mind' is problematic because of the aforementioned reason.

---

14. *Lect.* I, d3, p3, q4: *De Imagine.*

15. Picking out 'memoria' as the first term of the image of the Trinity is problematic because the third term, loving, is not produced by 'memoria,' so Scotus argues. In the Trinity, the Word and the Spirit are both produced, as we will shortly see. In this image of the Trinity though, the 'voluntas' is not produced, but, as Duns reasons, it has only the act of intelligence as a 'conditio sine qua non' (*Lect.* I, d3, p3, q4, §441).

16. See also *Lect.* II, d25, §75–6.

17. Here the medieval distinction between 'first act' (the habitual aspect) and 'second act' (the acting itself) is operative.

Preliminary Considerations 15

1.5: BASIC TRINITARIAN TERMINOLOGY

The basic Trinitarian formula states that there is one divine substance in a Trinity of persons, Father, Son, and the Holy Spirit. Trinitarian thought always took great pains to analyse what those 'persons' exactly are and how they are related to each other. Let us first take some time to rehearse the basic Trinitarian terminology. In Greek, the fundamental Trinitarian formula became one 'ousia,' three 'hypostaseis.' This was rendered into Latin as 'una substantia, tres personae.' To be precise: 'hypostatis' was actually rendered as 'suppositum' in Latin, a supposit, but a supposit *of a rational nature* is a 'persona.' Now 'ousia' and 'substantia' can loosely be translated by the modern 'essence' or 'nature'; but what is a 'hypostasis' and what is its Latin counterpart 'persona,' a supposit in a rational nature? On the traditional medieval understanding, 'persona' is a very technical term. It connotes for instance 'incommunicability' and 'independence.' I will further describe it shortly (chap. 1.8).[18] For now, however, it is apparent that there is a fundamental difference with the meaning of the *modern* concept of a person. Therefore, from now on, I use 'person' for the ordinary modern concept of a person and 'persona' (or the Latin plural 'personae') for this distinct medieval sense. And when I refer to God, I capitalise the terms. Hence, in sum:

Persona =	the concept in its Trinitarian sense, predicated of a divine Persona
Person =	the concept in its *modern* sense, predicated of God
persona =	the concept in its medieval sense, predicated of humans[19]
person =	the concept in its *modern* sense, predicated of human beings

Equipped with these terminological distinctions, we can express the mono-personal or 'single-perfect-Mind' view without a blatant contradiction:

Three Persons are one Person   —involves a contradiction
Three Personae are one Person —involves no contradiction

This last sentence involves no contradiction because the concepts are *not* univocal: they have a different sense, just like 'persona' and 'person' said of humans. In the following chapter, I will show that Christ is a human *person* without a human persona—the famous *anhypostatic union* of the Word with the individual human nature.

---

18. For a more precise definition, see Timothy Pawl, *The Incarnation*, Cambridge Elements (Cambridge: Cambridge University Press, 2020), chap. 2.1.

19. I do not claim univocity between Persona and persona, but the two concepts are similar enough to justify this terminological similarity; see chap. 2.7.

16   *Chapter 1*

1.6: AN ILLUSTRATION OF THE
MONO-PERSONAL VIEW

I once developed an illustration of the mono-personal view of the Trinity for the communities I served. Imagine, Malcolm had a lovely daughter named Ann. However, Ann got leukaemia when she was four years old. It turned out that her father Malcolm was the only relative with exactly the right bone marrow for a transplant. So Malcolm gave part of his marrow to save the life of his daughter. Luckily, she recovered. While further maturing, Ann always felt that her father was a beautiful person: she sensed his love in everything he did—not least of course that he gave his bone marrow for her—and she just wanted to become as good a person as he.

This little story provides us with a helpful image of the Trinity: Malcolm acts in three distinct ways on the life of his daughter. He begets her, saves her, and inspires her. Nevertheless, he is the same person, one and the same Malcolm. Just like that, God acts in three distinguishable ways on his creatures—the 'economic' level: He creates them, redeems them and inspires them. Nevertheless, He is one and the same God. Hence, this story resembles the mono-personal Augustinian view: just like Malcolm is one person, the Trinitarian God is one Person (constituted by three Personae).

Someone acquainted with Trinitarian theology would perhaps remark that this story echoes a view called 'modalism': the view that the three Personae eventually do not differ. Reminiscent of the classic meaning of 'persona' as a mask in a play, modalism holds that the Personae are just three different modes in which the one God acts '*ad extra*,' acts 'economically,' but apart from this external activity his three-ness is illusory. The Triad is but a mask. Essentially, the Father and Son are just names for one and the same Godhead. Hence, the protagonists of modalism were willing to defend that you could equally say that the Father became flesh and suffered on the cross.[20] This consequence of modalism was always marked as heretic. But the view defended here clearly steers clear from modalism, because in the Augustinian 'single-perfect-Mind' view the three Personae really differ. Let us examine this in more detail.

1.7: THE THREE PERSONAE AND THE
TWO INTERNAL PRODUCTIONS

As already discussed, I speak of the triad of *origin, knowledge*, and *love* as an image of the Trinity. The origin somehow *produces* the latter two, knowledge

---

20. Kelly, *Early Christian Doctrines*, 119–26.

Preliminary Considerations

and love. We thus arrive at another central concept in Trinitarian thought, the 'internal productions.' There are two kinds of internal productions: to beget and to proceed. As the Athanasian Creed puts it: 'The Father is made of none; neither created nor begotten. The Son is of the Father alone; not made, nor created, but begotten. The Holy Ghost is of the Father and of the Son; neither made, nor created, nor begotten, but proceeding.'

But what exactly is the difference between these two productions 'begotten' and 'proceeded'? We therefore observe the human mind as an image of the Trinity. In a human mind, one could distinguish two and only two essential internal productions: a fountain produces *thoughts* and the same fountain, while using these thoughts, produces *acts*. Or, to put it differently, a mind is characterised by knowing and willing—or loving. In the Godhead, there are two internal productions too: an origin produces all the divine *thoughts*, and the same source, using these thoughts, produces all the divine *acts*. According to Scotus, we cannot reduce the will to an intellectual phenomenon, because the will has a two-way capacity (chapter 5). It can avow or not avow an object, whereas the intellect is produced 'naturally': there is only a one-way relation to its natural goal. The intellect just knows its object, yet the will is capable of avowing an object or not, choosing it or not: a two-way capacity. Therefore, the two productions traditionally called 'begetting' and 'proceeding' are really distinct. To sum up: these are the uniquely identifying properties[21] of the *Personae*:

Father,	*Son, Word,*	*Holy Spirit*
made of none,	begotten,	proceeded
origin,	knowing,	loving
origin,	thought,	act
origin,	one-way,	two-way capacity

These three together constitute the one divine perfect Mind, the triune God. Because of the distinctness of the productions, modalism is ruled out. Incidentally, equipped with these distinctions, it is possible to give a purely logical answer to a vexed issue between East and West: the 'filioque.' Do the Father *and* the Son (filioque) produce the Spirit? On a strictly logical level and presupposing this view of the Personae, the answer must be affirmative: loving an object presupposes knowing it. Hence indeed 'filioque.'

---

21. Is the distinctness of the Personae constituted by their relations or by an absolute property of each? Later in his life, Scotus argued that the relation theory was preferable to the absolute-property theory; see Richard Cross, *Duns Scotus*, Great Medieval Thinkers (Oxford: Oxford University Press, 1999), 65–67. I do not have to decide on this issue.

18   *Chapter 1*

Regrettably, however, that an analytic topic like this became wound up with issues of church polity.[22]

What is the object of these divine thoughts and acts? First of all, God himself: God knows and loves himself. And He does so rightly: this love is most perfect and beautiful. Social trinitarianism is critical of this eminence of divine self-love; I will return to this topic in due course. And, secondly, God knows and wills and thus creates all external things. The Dutch theologian and Victorine scholar Nico den Bok put all this very succinctly like this:

> The *Father* is God as He is the origin of all there is, firstly of his own ideas. And of all what He can create and do on the basis of that.

> The *Son* is God as He knows himself and the whole creation. And then also God as He makes himself known in creation by assuming a human face and redeeming humanity.

> The *Spirit* is God in his fervent will towards the good that He acknowledges and chooses, God in his love for himself and his creation. A love, which He then also pours out into creation, in the hearts of men.[23]

This quotation brings out that it is three times one and the same God, just like in my story of Malcolm: the three Personae share in the *same* divine essence and each is God—though God in a different mode, three participial modes of divine existence: the originating mode, the knowing/revealing mode, and the fulfilling mode. But these three different participial exemplifications of God's existence cannot be compared to just roles 'ad extra,' they are not just masks towards his creation, there is also an *essential* Trinitarian aspect. For two really *distinct* productions constitute the indelibly distinct features of the three Personae.[24]

An important objection at this point is that the language of 'production' seems to entail subordination. The concept of 'production' seems to lead us towards Neo-Platonism or Arianism, the view that the Son is not of the same essence as the Father: He is not 'consubstantial' but ontologically subordinated. This was exactly what the protagonists of modalism feared. However, these two divine internal productions are eternal: 'there was no time that

---

22. Many orthodox connect the 'filioque' with the rise of papal power to the detriment of conciliar authority. See McGuckin, *The Orthodox Church*, 166–73; Cross, *Duns Scotus*, chap. 5.

23. In A. J. Plaisier, red., *Om een persoonlijk God*, serie Utrechtse cahiers 1 (Zoetermeer: Boekencentrum, 2006), 46. My translation.

24. For the relation of these productions to the acts of the divine essence, see Richard Cross, *Duns Scotus on God*, Ashgate Studies in the History of Philosophical Theology (Aldershot: Ashgate, 2005), chap. 16.

Preliminary Considerations 19

the Son was not.'[25] Due to this co-eternal aspect, any form of Neo-Platonic *subordination* between the Personae is ruled out, for there is an *eternal* production and all three Personae share the same divine essence. Quoting Bonaventure again: 'memory, understanding and will are *consubstantial, coequal* and *coeval.*'

1.8: FURTHER REFINEMENT OF THE CONCEPT OF PERSONA

The concept of Persona is a key concept in Christology, for it is the second Persona of the Trinity, the Word, that assumes the human nature and the human nature itself has no human persona. So what is a Persona—or a persona—more exactly? We already know that it is seen as the 'hypostasis' or 'supposit' of a rational nature. But this term 'supposit' was in need of further clarification. According to Scotus, a supposit connotes *incommunicability*. Consequently, the Personae, as supposits of rational nature, are marked by 'incommunicability.' However, this incommunicability is difficult to pin down. Let me start by clarifying the positive term: communicability. A nature like 'being human' is communicable to numerous entities: all those individuals share in the same nature. Likewise, the divine essence is communicable, for it is communicated to the three Personae: they all share in the one divine nature. Now the concept of 'Persona' is defined by the denial of this, by *incommunicability*.[26] Thus, it is attributed, and attributable, to only one.[27] Hence, it closely resembles an individual property like 'being Daniel,' which is also attributable to only one, namely Daniel. Accordingly, the Persona of 'being the Father' is attributed, and attributable, to only one, namely the Father. Next, a supposit implies *independence*. So a supposit of a rational nature, a Persona, cannot depend on something else, it cannot be *sustained* by something else. This last aspect will be further clarified within the context of the incarnation (chap. 2.5).

In sum, one can say that, broadly speaking, the medieval tradition conceived the divine Personae as *incommunicable, independent modes of being of the divine rational essence*: the one Godhead as originating, as knowing and as loving; Father, Word, and Holy Spirit. In the next chapter, I will demonstrate that especially this aspect of *independence* of the concept of

---

25. See also Oliver Crisp's defence of this eternal production in Oliver Crisp, *The Word Enfleshed: Exploring the Person and Work of Christ* (Grand Rapids, MI: Baker Academic, 2016), 1–18.

26. See Cross, *Scotus on God*, chap. 12; see also Pawl, *The Incarnation*, chap. 2.1.

27. Bok, *Communicating the Most High*, 219.

20 *Chapter 1*

Persona—and persona—fits neatly into the analysis of the Word's anhypostatic assumption of the human nature.

1.9: 'OPERA AD EXTRA INDIVISA SUNT'

I already spoke of God's works 'ad extra,' his external actions. An important Trinitarian formula concerns these external operations: 'opera ad extra indivisa sunt.' God's acts towards objects external to himself are undivided as regards the three Personae; the three Personae share *one and the same* thoughts and acts.[28] This maxim figured prominently in the writings of the Cappadocians: 'we are obliged to infer unity of nature from the identity of activity.'[29] It thus formed a shield against the thread of tritheism and, handed down by Augustin, this rule became an indelible part of the tradition. The dictum secures that all external divine actions are to be ascribed to the level of the divine Triune essence, not to just one of the Personae. External actions like creating or recreating are the work of the one divine essence; the three participial modes of the Personae share in those actions, distinguishably yet undividedly. Clearly, creating a tree or converting Paul is not the work of an isolated *mode*—that's a category mistake. That is not to deny that a specific mode like 'originating' has its own proper effects: perhaps we could tentatively say that the *originated* aspect of a tree belongs clearly to the Father; the aspect of being *understandable* to the Word; the aspect of being *loved* to the Spirit. This would clarify why the *Word* assumes the human nature and not the Father or the Spirit: because the Word is God in his knowing mode and, after the creation, the Word is God in his *revealing* mode. Revealing, that is, letting *others* know. So each mode somehow corresponds to its appropriate creational aspect, although entering into the specifics here lies beyond the aim pursued.[30] In accordance with tradition I only contend that an external action like 'converting Paul' is not the work of an *isolated* participial divine mode of being, supposedly the Spirit in this case. That would ascribe to the third Persona the status of a Person, which it is not. Persons like Paul or God do things, isolated modes of being however do not. These category mistakes are provoked by the conflation of biblical language and the more *precise* language of later Trinitarian concepts. Biblical terms like 'the Father' or 'the Spirit' do not *precisely* refer to the Personae of later Trinitarian theology,

---

28. What lies behind this is the intricate point of the distinction between the notional and essential acts; see Cross, *Scotus on God*, chap. 16; see for an illuminating mid-position Williams, 'Unity of Action.'

29. Kelly, *Early Christian Doctrines*, 266.

30. See also, yet slightly different I think, Cross, *Duns Scotus*, 124–25.

Preliminary Considerations 21

simply because that realm of more sharply defined concepts did not exist in biblical times.

In sum, I argue that the formula 'opera ad extra indivisa sunt' protects us from committing a category mistake: persons act, participial modes as such do not. We will time and again see how important this maxim is in Scotus's analyses.

1.10: INTEGRATION OF SOCIAL TRINITARIAN MOTIVES

I will now try to integrate some gems of social Trinitarian thought. An often-heard objection concerns the alleged 'individualistic' nature of the Augustinian mono-personal view. It is argued that God thus becomes a solitary, loveless Deity. In what follows I will argue that this portrayal is stained by our human projections. However, that does not mean that positive motives of social trinitarianism should not be preserved. I think of God as a fullness of dynamic love, as mutual giving, as mutually emptying oneself in loving the other. How can we integrate these legitimate intents in the mono-personal view of the Trinity?

To begin with, in medieval thought, God has to be the highest perfection of love. And this perfection implies loving oneself by oneself. For this divine self-love is not contaminated by egocentrism or loneliness. His self-love just exemplifies the deepest truth that what is most high and most lovable must be loved *first* and to the *highest degree* and *for its own sake*. This equally explains why we humans cannot prioritise self-love: we are not the highest nor the most lovable and our proper centre lies outside ourselves in God. Hence, we cannot project our charges connected with human self-centeredness on God. That the origin of everything primarily loves himself as the fountain of all perfect happiness is exactly the *guarantee* of ultimate righteousness and joy for the entire universe. For 'God is light and in him there is no darkness at all' (1 John 1).

And exactly because He abundantly loves himself, this perfect love tends to the *sharing* of love with others. This 'sharing of love' captures a central motive of social Trinitarian theology; it is also operative in Richard of Saint Victor's Trinitarian thought. His Trinitarian explorations, as said, foreshadowed modern social Trinitarian sensibilities. Richard, being sensitive to the increased sense of intersubjectivity in the twelfth century, tried to 'integrate a core of social trinitarianism into the early twelfth-century Trinitarian consensus which was implicitly mono-personal.'[31] He sought for a co-lover (condiligens) *within*

---

31. Bok, *Communicating the Most High*, 465.

22   *Chapter 1*

the essential Trinity. According to Den Bok, however, the inner tensions of this endeavour caused the thirteenth century to retreat from this path. Bonaventure, Aquinas, and Scotus all bear witness to this thirteenth-century consensus of a mono-personal Trinitarian view. Nonetheless, just like Bonaventure and Scotus, we can apply the concept of a 'co-lover' that propelled the Ricardian enterprise to the *economic* realm: for it is true, real love seeks a co-lover.[32] If applied to the essential Trinity, all kinds of tensions arise, both in Richard and in modern social trinitarianism. But still, love by its very nature freely tends to a co-lover. Therefore, the highest form of love in God, which has itself both as its source and object, tends to a co-lover. It is possible to detect two economic fulfilments of this tendency: firstly, in Christ God elects an individual human nature which He assumes in order to let it supremely share in his love towards Himself. Now an individual human nature perfectly and maximally shares in God's love for himself. But then a wider circle of lovers emerges: God shares his love with other humans. As it is worded in Ephesians 1: 'He chose us in Christ before the foundation of the world to be holy and blameless before him in love.' Thus, the Holy Spirit endows us with the right dispositions to personally love him as his co-lovers, *to the Father, through the Son, in the Holy Spirit.* God is loved by others, first by the human nature in Christ in the unity with His own deepest self, then by a multitude of other co-lovers, through himself, the Holy Spirit. This forms an 'economic' rendering of a core motive of social Trinitarian thought: love seeks to be shared with others. Yet this motive is vindicated on the *economic* level, not on the essential Trinitarian level. I return to this essentially Dionysian theme in the chapter on supralapsarian Christology (chap. 6).

Tailored to our goal of exploring the coherence of the incarnation, I thus offered a cursory description of a broadly Scotistic doctrine of the Trinity. In sum, Scotus is a proponent of the Augustinian mono-personal view of the Trinity—which is in fact quite hospitable to social Trinitarian motives. I distinguished two different key concepts, Person and Persona (and person and persona), and I tried to describe in greater detail what a divine Persona exactly is. In line with Scotus, I see the divine Personae as *incommunicable and independent modes of being of the divine essence*: one and the same Godhead as originating, as knowing and as loving. This understanding of the Trinity and, more specifically, of Persona—and persona—is presupposed in the rest of this book. We are thus properly prepared to investigate the coherence of Christology.

---

32. Nico den Bok, 'Eén ding is noodzakelijk,' in *Geloof geeft te denken: opstellen over de theologie van Johannes Duns Scotus*, ed. Andreas J. Beck and H. Veldhuis, Scripta Franciscana 8 (Assen: Koninklijke Van Gorcum, 2005), 245–51.

Chapter 2

The Hypostatic Union

And the Word became flesh and lived among us, and we have seen his glory, the glory as of a father's only son, full of grace and truth.

—John 1: 14 (NRSV)

2.1: THE CREED OF CHALCEDON

Let me begin our systematic enquiry with the Christological creed of Chalcedon (AD 451). In line with Chalcedon, Jesus Christ is said to have two natures, both the divine and the human nature. Here is the decisive part of the confession of Chalcedon, together with some crucial Greek terminology:

> Following, then, the holy fathers, we all with one voice teach that we should confess that our Lord Jesus Christ is one and the same Son, the Same[1] perfect in Godhead, and the Same perfect in manhood, truly God and truly man, the Same (consisting) of a rational soul and a body; consubstantial (*homoousios*) with the Father as to his Godhead, and the Same consubstantial with us as to his manhood; like us in all things except sin; begotten of the Father before all ages as to His Godhead, and in the last days, the Same, for us and for of our salvation, of Mary the Virgin, *Theotokos*[2] as to his manhood; One and the same Christ, Son, Lord, Only-begotten, made known in two natures (*physai*) (which exist) without confusion, without change, without division, without separation; the difference of the natures being by no means removed because of the union, but rather the property of each being preserved, and (both) concurring into one Person (*prosopon*) and one *hypostasis*—not parted or divided into two Persons (*prosopa*), but one and the same Son and Only-begotten, the divine Word (*Logos*), the Lord

---

1. This capitalisation (mine) renders the Greek 'autos,' which is repetitively used to emphasise that both divine and human properties are predicated of the *same* subject.

2. Meaning God-bearer or Mother of God.

24   *Chapter 2*

Jesus Christ; even as the prophets from of old and Jesus Christ Himself have taught us about Him and the creed of our fathers had handed down.

This Conciliar Christology is thoroughly rooted in Trinitarian thought. I described the Trinitarian core premises in the previous chapter: there is supposed to be one divine substance with three subsisting divine Personae, the Father, Son, and the Holy Spirit. Now the Chalcedonian creed states that the Son, the second Persona, assumed the human nature and thus was 'truly God and truly man.' And he is made known 'in two natures without confusion, without change, without division, without separation.'[3] So this second divine hypostasis or Persona seems to be the single 'bearer' of the human nature— a Persona, again, is a hypostasis of a rational nature (chap. 1.5). Thus, both natures are united in only *one divine hypostasis*; hence the traditional idiom of the '*hypostatic union*.'[4] The human nature has no hypostasis or persona of its own: when assumed by the Word the human nature is 'anhypostatic.' The hypostasis in Christ comes from God's side: it is the divine Word or Logos.

2.2: TWO CHALCEDONIAN
BOUNDARIES: THE 'FAMOUS FOUR'

These terms and formulas perhaps evoke the impression of cold, barren rationalism. Historically though, this estimation is flawed, for it misjudges the genre. The fathers produced these formulas as 'witnesses to the Word and not as scholars.' And 'their grasp of the content of their expressions is more intuitive than speculative.'[5] Rather than offering a scholarly analysis of the content of key concepts, the Chalcedonian fathers confessed the faith. To express and preserve it, they set up two critical boundaries. First of all, the two natures must each remain complete and must retain their distinctive properties. This is expressed by the first half of the formula of the 'famous four': '*without confusion, without change.*' A clear example of a transgression of this first boundary is 'monophysitism,' of which Apollinaris of Laodicea is the classic representative.[6] His 'Alexandrian' monophysitism goes something like this: the one and single bearer of the unity is supposed to be the divine Logos, the divine Mind, the divine Word, which wrapped itself in the clothes of the human flesh. Consequently, this was dubbed a 'Word-flesh' Christology.

---

3. Kelly, *Early Christian Doctrines*, 341.

4. By forging new creeds, the early church made the meaning of central terms like *hypostasis* congeal: due to their new creedal function, the terms developed new senses.

5. Alois Grillmeier, *Christ in Christian Tradition. From the Apostolic Age to Chalcedon (451) [Vol. 1]*, second edition, 1975, 545. 'To a Christian of the time, the formal terms of Chalcedon did not sound so formal as they might seem to a theologian of the nineteenth or twentieth century.'

6. Grillmeier, 153–344.

The Hypostatic Union

Thus, the human nature is changed, even 'decapitated': there is no human mind or soul. Consequently, this Alexandrian approach is unacceptable in the light of Chalcedon, because it does not meet the first demand: '*without confusion, without change.*' Historically speaking, this first demand stood at the centre of the fourth-century Christological debate.

The second demand was destined to be the typical endeavour of the fifth century: we must ensure that the union is *real*.[7] Somehow there has to be a *single* bearer of both natures. This is secured by the second part of the famous four: '*without division, without separation.*' In the Chalcedonian formula, this task is given to 'hypostasis,' in Latin the 'Persona.' With this second demand, *characterisation* is at stake (see chap. 3): if Jesus weeps at Lazarus's grave, does this really *characterise* the eternal Word too?[8] Is the unity between the Word and the human nature tight enough to secure this? If not, if the Word is not itself truly *characterised* by the human properties, acts, and passions, the logical consequence is that the sense of 'incarnation' is watered down. This is the perennial difficulty for the followers of Nestorius of Constantinople, the antagonists of the Alexandrian party.[9] Nestorians rightly strive to preserve the integrity of each of the two natures, but by doing so they run the risk of losing the union. For if Jesus must have had a complete human nature, it seems that the Word did not *itself become* man; it merely was present near or in this man, just as with the prophets. The Word and Jesus remain 'two,' they don't become numerically 'one.' There is '*division and separation.*' If you stress, however, the unity, then you put the integrity of the two natures in jeopardy, generating '*confusion and change.*' This is the Chalcedonian dilemma.[10] Just as Grillmeier stated:

> Chalcedon sought to discover the solution of just *one* disputed question: *how* the confession of the '*one Christ*' may be reconciled with the belief in the '*true God and man,*' '*perfect in Godhead, perfect in manhood.*'[11]

---

7. Think, for example, of Leontius of Byzantium (c. 485–c. 543); see Brian E. Daley SJ, 'Nature and the "Mode of Union": Late Patristic Models for the Personal Unity of Christ,' in *The Incarnation: An Interdisciplinary Symposium on the Incarnation of the Son of God*, ed. Stephen T. Davis, Daniel Kendall, and Gerald O'Collins (Oxford; New York: Oxford University Press, 2002), 164–96.

8. Adams, *Christ and Horrors*, 123–38.

9. Alexandrians scoffed at Nestorians in this vein: 'how can they say that the Word entered into a holy man, just as He entered into the prophets, and not that He became man, taking his body from Mary'? Kelly, *Early Christian Doctrines*. When I use the labels of 'Nestorianism' and 'monophysitism' we should not identify these tags with Syrian Nestorians and Monophysite Copts: their history and dogma are far too rich to justify that, and, moreover, the collisions of the past were dominated by misapprehensions.

10. There was an alternating movement like a pendulum, Kallistos Ware observes: Kallistos Ware, 'Christian Theology in the East 600–1453,' in *A History of Christian Doctrine*, ed. Hubert Cunliffe-Jones (Edinburgh: Clark, 1978), 189.

11. Grillmeier, *Christ in Christian Tradition*, 545.

26   *Chapter 2*

At Chalcedon, the fathers reached a solution at the level of confession, of bearing witness.[12] They left the exact meaning of the crucial terms unspecified.[13] This was left to another era: subsequent systematic reflection tried to probe further into the exact meaning of 'hypostasis.' What does it precisely mean when we say that Christ doesn't have a human hypostasis or persona, only a divine Persona? What exactly *is* this divine Persona which assumed the human nature 'without confusion, without change, without division, without separation'? And if Christ lacks a human persona, how on earth persists his human nature 'without confusion, without change'? But if we, on the other hand, therefore ascribe a human persona to Christ, how on earth is that persona seamed to the divine Persona 'without division, without separation'? In brief, how do we navigate between the Scylla of Apollinarism and the Charybdis of Nestorianism?

2.3: INCIPIENT REFINEMENTS: THE *SUMMA HALENSIS*

Though Chalcedon itself wasn't known in the Latin West until the thirteenth century, still its kernel, as transmitted by, for example, Boethius (d524) and John of Damascus (d749), pervaded the Christological debate of the early Middle Ages. Further exploration of this issue, though, was left to later medieval scholastics. A natural point of departure for a brief description of this development is Lombard (1100–1160): 'Peter Lombard laid out the three main opinions on the hypostatic union that were evidently circulating at the time he wrote his celebrated book of the *Sentences*, which date to around 1150.'[14] These three were the *assumptus homo* theory, the *subsistence* theory, and the *habitus* theory. Among historians, there is much debate as to the precise interpretation of each of these views. For our purpose, we do not need to enter into the specifics of these debates.[15] Eventually, the second view, the

---

12. This appraisal of the genre of Chalcedon seems to me more historically accurate than a purely 'linguistic' or 'regulatory' view over against an ontological view. Thus also Sarah Coakley, 'What Does Chalcedon Solve and What Does It Not? Some Reflections on the Status and Meaning of the Chalcedonian "Definition",' in *The Metaphysics of the Incarnation*, ed. Anna Marmodoro and Jonathan Hill (Oxford: Oxford University Press, 2011), 143–63.

13. Daley SJ, 'Nature and the "Mode of Union",' 194: "Beyond this, however, the Greek Fathers we have been considering rarely attempt to 'look inside' the hypostasis of Jesus or anyone else, and offer us little clue as to the peculiar ontological status or psychological character of any hypostasis within itself."

14. Lydia Schumacher, *Early Franciscan Theology: Between Authority and Innovation* (Cambridge, UK; New York: Cambridge University Press, 2019), 185.

15. Richard Cross, 'Homo Assumptus in the Christology of Hugh of St Victor: Some Historical and Theological Revisions,' *The Journal of Theological Studies* 65, no. 1 (1 April 2014): 62–77, https://doi.org/10.1093/jts/flu002.

The Hypostatic Union 27

subsistence theory, won the day.[16] According to Lydia Schumacher, a first more thorough analysis of this second view can be found in the Parisian thirteenth-century *Summa Halensis* (1240s), which comprises a teamwork of first-generation Franciscans among which John of la Rochelle and Alexander of Hales were most prominent—hence 'Summa Halensis.'

In the *Summa*'s reflection on the incarnation, we find several important building blocks which reappear in Scotus: (1) the *subsistence* theory which sees the union as somehow a composition of the divine and human nature in the one Persona of the Word. To explicate this unity-in-duality further, one refers to the relation between *substance* and *accident*. The human nature relates to the Word like an accident is related to its substance.[17] And (2) the exact analysis of the hypostatic union is accomplished by trying to differentiate between an individual human nature and a human persona: being an individual human nature does not necessarily imply having a human *persona*. Hence, the Word can assume an individual human nature yet without the necessary implication of assuming a human persona. This, of course, prevents the existence of two (P)personae in Christ, one divine and one human, which would have led to Nestorianism. This all is enlivened by (3) the metaphor of *grafting* the human nature upon the divine Word. To my knowledge, Scotus does not mention this appealing metaphor of grafting, but he integrates the other two building blocks and ameliorates the earlier analyses decisively. The result is a consistent analysis of the hypostatic union, commended by Richard Cross in unmistakable terms:

> Scotus's account of the hypostatic union is perhaps the most sophisticated to emerge from the middle ages, and is among the most philosophically astute defenses of orthodox Christology there is. Anyone who wants to take the complete humanity of the incarnate Word seriously, and who agrees with the medieval belief that this nature must—like any other human nature—be individuated independently of any union with the Word, will want to look at Scotus's subtle account of such a union very closely.[18]

---

16. It said that 'The Word, who was eternally a simple Person, became a composite Person at the Incarnation, possessing his divine as well as a human nature, entailing a body and soul.' Schumacher, *Early Franciscan Theology*, 188.

17. The comparison with an accident is in fact more broadly medieval, though Aquinas rejected it; see Cross, *The Metaphysics of the Incarnation*, 51–136. Scotus *Ord.* III, d1, p1, q1, §14–16 and §44–47.

18. Cross, *Duns Scotus*, 125–26.

28   *Chapter 2*

2.4: SUBSTANCE AND ACCIDENT

To this account I now turn. Scotus's analysis of the hypostatic union indeed exploits the analogy to the relation of substance and accident.[19] I suppose we all have at least an intuitive grasp of substance and accident—or to use more current technical language: essential and accidental properties (chap. 1.2).[20] Substances are things like 'Socrates' or 'Bonfire'—a famous Dutch jumping horse. Accidents are things that somehow 'inhere in' or 'depend on' substances: Socrates is white and Bonfire is vigorous. The whiteness of Socrates is said to 'inhere in' or to 'depend on' the substance 'Socrates.' Scotus, following the *Summa Halensis*, exploits this analogy: just like Socrates's whiteness depends on the substance 'Socrates,' so the human nature depends on the eternal Word.

This account is what philosophers call 'metaphysical': it is in terms of the most basic 'furniture' of our world, about accidents, substances, properties, relations, and so on. Despite the lack of unanimity in metaphysics, I must provisionally specify some standard terms which I will use. As I said before (chap. 1.2), a property of x is essential if x could not be x without it. For example, God could not be God without his knowledge. By contrast, an accidental property of x is a property x does not need to have in order to be x. Hence, having assumed the human nature is an accidental property of God, because He does not cease to be God if the human nature is not assumed.

There has been an enormous development in metaphysics. Aristotle called 'objects' like Socrates in fact 'primary substances' and 'being human' a secondary substance. The modern distinctions are different and more precise: I use the distinction between a common nature or 'kind-nature' and the individual essence of things or the 'individual-nature.' Or, as the medievals like Scotus would say, the difference between *haecceitas* and *quidditas*, *this-ness* and *what-ness*. In this study, I presuppose these ontological distinctions of 'kind-nature' and 'individual-nature.' Hence, everything whatsoever has a unique, individual *this-ness* and a general *what-ness*: Daniel has as

---

19. Literature on the Christology of Duns Scotus: Richard Cross, *The Metaphysics of the Incarnation: Thomas Aquinas to Duns Scotus* (Oxford: Oxford University Press, 2002); N. den Bok, M. Bac, A. Beck, K. Bom, G. Labooy, H. Veldhuis, and A. Vos, 'More than Just an Individual. Scotus's Concept of Person from the Christological Context of Lectura III 1,' *Franciscan Studies*, no. 66 (2008): 169–96; on www.dunsscotus.com: A. Vos, H. Veldhuis, G. Labooy, E. Dekker, K. L. Bom, N. W. den Bok, A. J. Beck, and J. M. Bac: John Duns Scotus, 'The possibility of the incarnation.' Lectura distinction III question 1, Latin Text and English Translation.

20. The two by no means coincide. Modern systems aim at developing subtler ontological tools. For instance, world-indexed properties are always essential, even if they are accidental in their non-world-indexed mode: like 'being snub-nosed in W.' See, for example, Alvin Plantinga, *The Nature of Necessity* (Oxford: Oxford University Press, 1974), 62–65; I do not enter into these ontological subtleties, although I presuppose them throughout.

The Hypostatic Union   29

individual-nature his 'Daniëlitas' and as kind-nature the human nature. For the sake of brevity, this must suffice.

2.5: THE RELATION OF DEPENDENCE

Just like an accident depends on its substance, so the individual human nature depends on the Word, the second Persona (hypostasis) of the Trinity. Thus, the relation of dependence attains some intuitive content. For it is not *causal* dependence that is at stake: obviously, all creatures are for their existence causally dependent on God. Such a dependence relation would not be distinctive for Christ. Nor is it *psychological* dependence: it has nothing to do with the mind or feelings or so, some kind of emotional dependence. Instead, the relation of dependence could be named 'metaphysical': like the relation of an accidental property to its substance as a kind of 'bearer.'[21]

One can readily see why this accidentality fits in: accidental properties, unlike the essential ones, are not essential to their bearer. If the human nature had been an essential property of the Godhead, it would have been part of God's essence and, consequently, it was no longer created![22] Therefore, the relation between the human nature and the divine Word is pictured as the relation between a substance and an *accident*.

This remains, however, an analogy. For there is something peculiar here: the accident in question is *itself* a substance, like most medievals said. Here one could indeed think of the appropriateness of the metaphor of grafting: a branch with both a specific kind-nature *and* an individual 'this-ness' is grafted upon a stem from another kind-nature. Likewise, the human nature, depending accidentally on the divine, is itself a substance. It has a *kind-nature*, namely the human nature, and an *individual-nature*, namely being this man Jesus.[23] In contemporary literature, this view is called a 'com-positionalist metaphysics' of the incarnation.[24]

---

21. Scotus, *Ord.* III, d1, p1, q1, §§14, 15, 16; *Lect.* III, d1, §1, §§20, 21. See also R. Cross, 'Vehicle Externalism and the Metaphysics of the Incarnation: A Medieval Contribution,' in *The Metaphysics of the Incarnation*, ed. Anna Marmodoro and Jonathan Hill (Oxford: Oxford University Press, 2011), 186–87.

22. This is a difficulty for a part-whole or mereological Christology—Aquinas's way of analysing the incarnation. See Cross, *The Metaphysics of the Incarnation*, 51–76.

23. On a general level, medieval philosophers extensively debated this metaphysical point. The leading question is this: what individuates accidental properties? Are they necessarily individuated by the substances in which they inhere, or are they individuated independently of their substance? Scotus argues for the latter option: an accident is an object individuated independently of its substance. Cross, 33–50.

24. Jonathan Hill, 'Introduction,' in *The Metaphysics of the Incarnation*, ed. Anna Marmodoro and Jonathan Hill (Oxford: Oxford University Press, 2011); Crisp, *The Word Enfleshed*; Timothy Pawl, *In Defense of Conciliar Christology: A Philosophical Essay*, Oxford Studies in Analytic Theology (Oxford; New York: Oxford University Press, 2016), 30–47.

30   *Chapter 2*

Currently, though, the view that Jesus did not have a human this-ness, a human individuality, is gaining some support.[25] Karl Barth, though, is not among them, although it is sometimes attributed to him.[26] Obviously, this view comes to the fore when the meaning of 'hypostasis' is interpreted as having individuality. Because then, 'anhypostatically' assuming the human nature means having no human principle of individuality. It is argued that Christ's individuality as a human being comes from *God's* side and constitutes the union. He alone has no principle of individuality from the human side. Yet a heavy price is thus paid, for the Word assumes the human nature 'without confusion and change'; hence, is our individuality, our being *this* man or *this* woman, no longer part of really being human? Furthermore, our human individuality is not assumed and, consequently, not saved, as the famous dictum goes. Moreover, it perhaps even implies that general natures really exist separately—an ontology which is difficult to swallow.

2.6: PERSONA AS A RELATIONAL PROPERTY

Before we can proceed with the analysis of the hypostatic union, I must add some more technical tools. Philosophers are used to distinguishing between what they call 'monadic' and 'relational' properties. Monadic properties do not involve relations. Take for instance Socrates's being white. Relational properties do: Jim being taller than Bruce. Or James is Susan's brother. Here Susan has a *relational* property: having James as her brother. And in modern logic, the denial of having a property x is seen as a property too. '*Being the father of Jesus*' is a relational property Joseph has. But, as it is an accidental property, he could have had the denial of that property, namely '*not being the father of Jesus*.' This is a property we all share, and, if you think in terms of biological parenthood, there are fair reasons to think that in that narrow biological sense Joseph had this negative property too.[27] To sum up: there is a distinction between monadic and relational properties. And the negation of a property F is also seen as a property.

---

25. A. van de Beek, *Lichaam en Geest van Christus: de theologie van de kerk en de Heilige Geest*, Spreken over God, 2.2 (Zoetermeer: Uitgeverij Meinema, 2012), 19; a source for the view that Cyril of Alexandria defended this is, besides Loofs, unquestionably Adolf von Harnack, *Lehrbuch Der Dogmengeschichte*, vol. II (Darmstadt, 1964), 351. There, highlighted in bold, we read that Cyril 'ausdrücklich verwirft die Ansicht, in Christus sei ein individueller Mensch vorhanden gewesen.' Perhaps Pannenberg depends on Harnack, see W. Pannenberg, *Grundzüge Der Christologie* (Gütersloh, 1964), 298; however, following Grillmeier, I think Harnack reads too much into the text; see Grillmeier, *Christ in Christian Tradition*, 414–17 and 473–83.

26. See Karl Barth, *Die Kirchliche Dogmatik*, vol. I/2 (Zollikon, 1939), 163–65; see also Pannenberg, *Grundzüge Der Christologie*, 295–301, 325.

27. G. H. Labooy, 'The Historicity of the Virginal Conception. A Study in Argumentation,' *European Journal of Theology* 13, no. 2 (2004): 91–101.

The Hypostatic Union 31

Now we can proceed: *being dependent on the Word* is an accidental and relational property Jesus has. *Not being dependent on the Word* is a relational property all ordinary humans have in common. This denial of dependence on the Word, this *being independent*, is, according to Scotus, the distinctive meaning of 'persona' as predicted of humans. Having a human persona means being such an *independent* person. Jesus has no human persona because He is not independent, He alone is dependent on the divine Word, the second Persona of the Trinity. Jesus is anchored in God, or *grafted on the divine stem*, using the imagery of the *Summa Halensis*. While all the others stand on their own and therefore have a human persona, Jesus is grafted on the Word.

That is the distinctive meaning of 'persona,' according to Scotus: being independent. It does not coincide with individuality, nor with being a person or having a rational soul. It is *beyond* all that: it is the *independence* of an individual human nature, the *independence* of a human person.[28] Hence, a human 'persona' is, by definition:

the independence of an individual human nature.

This is key to avoid Nestorianism. Crisp expressed the central Christological predicament in a condensed way: 'how to block the inference from human nature to human personhood?'[29] This is the central Christological dilemma generated by the Councils. The Councils demand that Jesus has an individual human kind-nature just like we do: 'without confusion, without change.' But what if being an individual human nature implies being a human persona, along Boethius's definition of being a persona: *an individual substance of a rational nature*? Then, obviously, the nature-personhood inference cannot be blocked. Jesus would have a human persona *because* He is an individual human being. But that implies that there are two personae in Christ, one divine, one human. And hence Nestorianism, because there would be no hypostatic *union*, no single 'bearer' of both natures in one Persona. However, this dreaded nature-personhood inference is clearly invalid if we employ

---

28. Van Driel argues: 'The "what" who is doing the loving is the human nature, the "who" who is doing the loving is the second person of the Trinity.' Or, similarly: 'person and nature relate to each other as "who" relates to "what." When we meet the incarnate One, we meet a human "what," the one we engage is a divine "who."' See Edwin Chr van Driel, 'God and God's Beloved: A Constructive Re-reading of Scotus's Supralapsarian Christological Argument,' *The Heythrop Journal* 63, no. 5 (September 2022): 999–1000, https://doi.org/10.1111/heyj.14132. However, this seems to involve an equivocation of Scotus's sense of 'persona' and the modern 'person' taken as a 'who.' Scotus, in accordance with Chalcedon, acknowledges that in Christ there is no human persona, but he would argue that there nevertheless is a human person (in the sense of 'a who'). 'Persona' means for him: the *independence* of a 'who.'

29. Oliver Crisp, 'Compositional Christology without Nestorianism,' in *The Metaphysics of the Incarnation*, ed. Anna Marmodoro and Jonathan Hill (Oxford: Oxford University Press, 2011), 58–59. See exactly the same predicament listed among the 'cons' by Scotus, *Ord.* III, d1, p1, q1, §§7, 22, 31. And in *Lect.* III, d1, q1, §7.

32 *Chapter 2*

Scotus's sense of a human persona. Because then an individual human nature could be independent or dependent. If it has independence, it indeed would be a human persona; yet if it is dependent, it has no human persona! Because only an *independent* individual human nature counts as a human persona.[30] Jesus is an individual human nature, is a *human* person, but as He depends on the Word, He has no *human* persona. He has a divine Persona. Having no *human* persona, He is indeed 'anhypostatically' linked to the divine Word, 'grafted' onto the Word: there is only one hypostasis or Persona in Jesus, the divine one.

Modern logic helps to further clarify this. It is stated that Aristotle reduced relational properties to monadic ones: his logic did not allow for the distinctive character of relational properties.[31] The historic accuracy of this claim is not what counts here: I use 'Aristotelian' as a label for a logic that, unlike modern logic, reduces dyadic or 'two-place' properties (Rxy) to monadic ones (Fx). In that case, Jim's being taller than John is reduced to something in Jim and John: Jim's tallness, John's smallness. Likewise, a property like *being dependent on the Word* is reduced to monadic properties too. Therefore, in Aristotelian logic, the assumed human nature has a monadic property, instrumental in establishing the incarnation, which all other human beings lack.[32] This, however, threatens to violate the Chalcedonian boundaries, because the human nature in Christ is professed to be 'without confusion or change.' But if a dyadic property is a category in its own right, then there is no difference between Jesus and us as regards instrumentally relevant *monadic* properties. He only has this distinctive relational property of *being dependent on the Word*, whereas we have the property of *not being dependent on the Word*.[33]

---

30. *Ord.* III, d1, p1, q1, §35. And in *Lect.* III, d1, q1, §37.

31. 'Thus, if Socrates is similar to Theaetetus (i.e., resembles him with respect to some quality), this is not to be explained by an entity to which Socrates and Theaetetus are somehow jointly attached (namely, the dyadic or two-place property, being-similar-to). On the contrary, it is to be explained by a pair of accidents, one of which inheres in Socrates and relates him to Theaetetus, and the other of which inheres in Theaetetus and relates him to Socrates.' Jeffrey Zie Brower, 'Medieval Theories of Relations,' in *The Stanford Encyclopedia of Philosophy* (winter 2015 edition), ed. Edward N. Zalta, http://plato.stanford.edu/archives/win2015/entries/relations-medieval/. It seems, however, that a dyadic analysis of relations is necessary for our purpose but not yet sufficient for it: a change in a dyadic relation still presupposes a change in one or both the end-terms. Like all medievals, Scotus is eager to minimize the amount of change in the foundation of the relation, that is, in the Word. His theory of relations is too complex and technical for us here. See, for example, Peter King on 'third-mode relations' in Peter King, 'Scotus on Metaphysics,' in *The Cambridge Companion to Duns Scotus*, ed. Thomas Williams, Cambridge Companions to Philosophy (Cambridge, UK; New York: Cambridge University Press, 2003), 318.

32. It could still be an accidental property.

33. See further Bok et al., 'More than Just an Individual.'

2.7: DIVINE AND HUMAN PERSONA

I now briefly relate this result to the analysis of the Trinity, the three divine Personae. Is this anthropological concept of 'persona' somehow similar to the *Trinitarian* concept of a Persona? In the previous chapter I said that, according to the scholastics, apart from their incommunicability, the divine Personae are 'independent.' They are *independent modes of being of the one divine spiritual essence*. Hence, Jesus is also independent, but not as a human being, but as the Son of God, the Word. There is, however, a difference between these two concepts, because the three Personae are also *unable* to depend, which implies that they are *necessarily* independent.[34] So there is a conceptual similarity between a divine Persona and a human persona, but there is no univocity, because a divine Persona is a *necessarily* independent mode of being but a human person is only an *accidentally* independent mode of being, for he or she *could have been* dependent on the Word.

A further difference is that each human being has *one* human persona—except Jesus. The divine substance, however, has three Personae. Hence, as regards this, there rather is a contrast between God and his image, which, as almost anything of these divine matters, far exceeds my understanding. Along with the scholastics I can only say to my amazement: in God there are three Personae and one substance; in Christ there is one Persona, the Word, and three substances: the divine, the soul, and the body.

2.8: CHARACTERISATION

According to Scotus, Jesus's human nature is dependent on the Word, whereas we are independent. Scotus further analyses this dependence relation. He claims that an ordinary aspect of the dependence relation of accidents does not occur in the hypostatic union: accidents *inform* their substances. For instance, white 'informs' the primary substance Socrates. Consequently, Socrates has a certain potentiality that can be actualised by this accident. The divine Word, however, cannot be informed by the addition of the human nature. For that would imply that the divine Word had a 'potentiality' that was to be actualised by the incarnation. This runs counter to the strong medieval conviction that God is pure act: nothing can be added to his fullness and richness of being. According to Scotus, however, another general aspect of accidental relations must not be discarded: accidents are regarded

---

34. See further Cross, *Duns Scotus on God*, chap. 12.

34   *Chapter 2*

as *truth-makers*, they *denominate* their bearers.[35] Or, as McCord Adams calls it: they *characterise* their bearers. Scotus highlights this crucial point too, in his typically dense and abstract style: 'substance is formally denominated and said to be such as the accident is, insofar as the accident is united with it and is the end term of dependence of that union which is that of an accident related to a subject.'[36] Or, less abstract: we say that Socrates is white, because of the whiteness of his skin, an accidental property of Socrates. Just so, the human nature has to be a truth-maker for the Word. If the human nature is born of the Virgin Mary, this characterises the Word too. This warrants that we say that the eternal Word is born of the Virgin Mary; the renowned hallmark of orthodoxy, Mary is '*theotokos.*' And since the human nature died for our sins, the Word is characterised by this too: the eternal Word died for our sins. Or, more precisely, the eternal Word *qua man* died for our sins. In the next chapter, I will investigate this subject of characterisation further, using 'qua-propositions.'

In sum, as a human being assumed by the Persona of the Word, Christ has the divine nature, because the Word shares in the divine nature. We confess, therefore, along Chalcedon, that 'our Lord Jesus Christ is one and the same Son, the Same perfect in Godhead, and the Same perfect in manhood, truly God and truly man.'

2.9: PRONE TO BE INCARNATE?

There is yet another topic to be addressed. Thus far I argued that Jesus is fully human and yet He is truly grafted on the Word. But is being assumed by the Word to be reckoned as somehow an ideal? Remember that being independent is an *accidental* property. This means that we all essentially have the possibility of being adopted by the Word: instead of being independent, we could have been dependent on the Word. Of course, it did not happen and it only occurred in the case of Jesus, but still, there is this ontological possibility common to all of us. Scotus labels this the '*potentia obedientialis*' of the creation. We are all—also in this very narrow and specific sense—'capax Dei.' Now is this possibility also a *propensity*? Is there something in the human nature that somehow *longs* to be united to the Word? Note that I do not mean the spiritual union bestowed by the Holy Ghost, I intend the *hypostatic union.* Is there a tendency to be united like that? Are we all prone to be

---

35. *Ord.* III, d1, p1, q1, §15. For a discussion whether these two aspects can be separated from each other; see Cross, *The Metaphysics of the Incarnation*, 124–28.

36. *Lect.* 3, d1, q1, §21: 'sed substantia formaliter denominatur et dicitur esse talis quale est accidens, prout accidens unitur ei et terminat dependentiam illius unionis quae est accidentis ad subiectum.'

The Hypostatic Union 35

incarnate as a kind of finality which inheres in our human nature? If so, this would imply that in ordinary humans this tendency is frustrated, whereas in Christ it is fulfilled.

Pondering this question, Scotus compares the dependence relation with the relation between a soul and its body. Like most scholastics, Scotus thinks that a soul has two distinct ways of being dependent on the body. First, there is the question of whether it *actually* depends. In ordinary life it does, but when the soul is separated from its body, it doesn't—in the state after death and before the resurrection. Next, the medievals contend that a soul longs for the body: it has *dispositional* dependence—quite contrary to Plato who assumed that the body is a prison for the soul. Using this example of souls, Scotus draws attention to two distinct kinds of dependence: actual and dispositional dependence. Which kind of (in)dependence holds for human personae? We already know that, according to Scotus, being a human persona implies not being actually dependent. But maybe such independent personae have still a dispositional dependence? That they have an innate, teleological propensity to be dependent on the Word? Scotus answers that to be a human persona connotes having actual *and* dispositional independence.[37] Hence, we all just have the ontological openness, the mere possibility to be united to the divine Word; there is however no *tendency* or *propensity* to be united—a creaturely tendency that is then consequently frustrated in ordinary humans. Of course, Jesus is our ideal, as regards his love for the Father, as regards his perfect fulfilment of the *Shema*. As regards the incarnation though, Jesus is only our friend and brother, *not* our ideal. Being merely human is good enough, for that is how we were created. There is no innate propensity in us which is truncated by not being assumed by the Word. Of course, the Spirit must fulfil us, we must fully resemble Him, but that is enough. Being fully human is being the brother or sister—or friend (John 15)—of Jesus Christ. That is '*tov meood*,' very good.

2.10: NO EXPLANATORY POWER?

In a later publication Cross critically remarks that this Scotistic solution of the hypostatic union 'lacks much explanatory power'; Nestorianism is ruled out 'by fiat.'[38] Not as regards the analogy of an inhering accident, but as regards the view that a human persona is a negation, that is, the negation of

---

37. *Pace* Adams, *Christ and Horrors*.

38. Cross, 'Vehicle Externalism and the Metaphysics of the Incarnation,' 188, 199; see Cross, *The Metaphysics of the Incarnation*, 308–9. Here Cross strongly argues that negation theories are not metaphysically flawed.

36   *Chapter 2*

dependence. Is such a negation-property not just an ingenious trick to avoid Nestorianism?

Yet I would argue that Scotus's view is an *analytic discovery*. And as such, it has what could loosely be called 'explanatory power.' So what is discovered? *That a certain feature of our human nature is after all not essential but accidental*. Essential parts of our metaphysical structure are having a kind-nature and an individual essence: being human and having 'this-ness.' These two taken together were always automatically regarded to be tantamount to having a human persona. Now Scotus, driven by Chalcedonian demands, discovered that that is not the case. Because being a human persona is not a logical corollary of having a human kind-nature and an individual essence, it is a *further fact*. For it could also be that an individual human nature is not independent but dependent on the second divine Persona. Accordingly, the independent existence of a human nature—having a human persona—is a further fact and an accidental feature, not an analytic consequence of being an individual human nature. I count that as an analytic discovery capable of further illuminating the incarnation and, along with that, the entire reality.

2.11: INSTRUMENTALITY

In search for alternative strategies to surmount Nestorianism, Cross explores the Thomistic idea that just as an instrument like a knife could be regarded as an extended part of me, so the human nature, being an instrument for the Word, becomes an extended part of the Word. 'The body *extends itself* to include the knife; the Word *extends himself* to include the human substance.'[39] But what makes the instrument the same subsisting thing as the one who uses it? Obviously, *being-an-instrument-of* is in itself not sufficient for being one and the same subsisting thing. Clearly, my scissors are not one with me. The required unity is explained in two ways: firstly, by the comparison with an external vehicle necessary for prolonged existence, like for instance a dialysis machine. Just as this 'external organ' is, like a normal kidney, one subsisting thing with the patient because it guarantees his life, so the human nature is one subsisting thing with the Word because it ensures God's human life. And, secondly, by the relation of *efficient causality*: just like the human soul directs its body as its instrument, so the Word directs the human nature as its instrument.

I think that the first condition of 'guaranteeing life' could be squared with Scotus's just depicted view: with due care, such instrumentality does not contradict the Scotistic view of an accident inhering in its divine substance

---

39. In Cross, 'Vehicle Externalism and the Metaphysics of the Incarnation,' 190.

The Hypostatic Union

(see chap. 2.5).[40] The second demand, however, that of efficient causality, seems to cause more difficulty. If efficient causality is a necessary condition for turning an instrument into a part of the one who uses it, the Chalcedonian demand that the human nature remains unchanged is in danger. For if the human nature is thus causally driven by the Word, it seems that the man Jesus is the only human being without free will. Wouldn't that result in him being like a puppet on a string?[41] One route of escape is, apparently, to opt for a compatibilist account of free will in general.[42] This is indeed the contemporary default position in the Philosophy of Mind—a discipline equally devoted to the default position of materialism. Elsewhere I have contended that both are mistaken.[43] However, if we opt, with Scotus, for a noncompatibilist account of human free will (chap. 5.3), the causal-efficiency demand is, I fear, bound to impair a decisive feature of the human nature. This becomes apparent in the following conclusion. Speaking about the human desires in Christ, Cross says:

> All that the view requires is that the *choice* between the desires is made by the divine person. The case contrasts nicely with that of the blessed. In the blessed, God is the causal explanation of the *desires*, not of the choice between them; in Christ, the desires can arise in the normal way; the *choice* is made by the second person of the Trinity.[44]

It is true, Cross argues that Christ's human nature only *accidentally* lacked free will, due to the incarnation: in this situation, because of efficient causality, it just cannot *exercise* its autonomous will. Later on, I will focus on this challenging issue of the human free will in Christ (chap. 5.9). For the moment, however, I doubt whether this strategy preserves the sameness of Christ's human free will in a robust enough sense.

But there is perhaps even a greater obstacle connected with the demand of efficient causality as a way to secure that the instrument is the same subsisting

---

40. For instance, instrumentality could contradict Scotus's demand that the accident does not *inform* the divine substance to which it inheres. This needs to be fleshed out.

41. The same question as regards Brian Leftow, 'The Humanity of God,' in *The Metaphysics of the Incarnation*, ed. Anna Marmodoro and Jonathan Hill (Oxford: Oxford University Press, 2011), 20–44; Anna Marmodoro, 'The Metaphysics of the Extended Mind in Ontological Entanglements,' in *The Metaphysics of the Incarnation*, ed. Anna Marmodoro and Jonathan Hill (Oxford: Oxford University Press, 2011), 205–27; see also Hill, 'Introduction,' 14: 'But if Christ's human body and soul are the instrument of his divine mind, it is hard to explain how they can be said to have any will or agency of their own.'

42. Compatibilism is the view that free will is compatible with determinism. Free will only requires the *experience* of acting freely.

43. G. J. de Ridder and R. van Woudenberg, 'Een Scotistisch argument voor dualisme,' *Tijdschrift voor Filosofie* 72, no. 3 (2010); G. H. Labooy, 'Antwoord aan Jeroen de Ridder en René van Woudenberg,' *Tijdschrift voor Filosofie* 72, no. 3 (2010): 557–80.

44. Cross, 'Vehicle Externalism and the Metaphysics of the Incarnation,' 201.

38 *Chapter 2*

thing as the one who uses it: it puts the dictum that the divine external operations are undivided in jeopardy (chap. 1.9). Because if efficient causation carries the burden of the hypostatic union, that efficient causation must be caused solely by the Word, not by the divine nature, because the hypostatic union depends on the Word, not on the divine nature.[45] But the 'opera ad extra indivisa sunt' (chap. 5.5).[46]

2.12: TO SUM UP

As I delineated, the history of Christology is characterised by two perennial pitfalls: Nestorianism and monophysitism. Nestorians gave full weight to the completeness of Christ's humanity, but doubts remained whether they were capable of accounting for the one-ness of Christ—exactly the metaphysical task of the hypostatic *union*. Does the divine nature really *assume* the human nature and make it its *own*, or does it only come nearby, without a real union? Conversely, monophysitism gave full weight to the union: the divine nature thoroughly assumes a human nature. But this tended to harm the completeness of the human nature.

The benefits of Scotus's analysis are straightforward: by using a strictly relational property of dependence for the analysis of the union between the Word and the human nature, Scotus is capable of giving full weight both to the union and to the completeness of both natures. He pinpoints the distinctive feature of our ordinary individual human nature solely in the negation of a relational property. Ordinary people are independent, whereas Christ is dependent on the Word. And remember the specific content of this dependence: think of the analogy to the substance-accident relation. As whiteness inheres in Socrates, so the individual human nature of Christ depends on the Word. The individual human Jesus is just as intimately the Word's own, as Socrates's whiteness is his whiteness: in either case just one subsisting thing. Let me try to sum up everything as condensed as possible:

---

45. See for instance *Lect.* III, d17, q1, §15–16: 'Non tamen Verbum habet specialem elicitionem respectu actus volendi [meant is of the human nature] magis quam Pater vel Spiritus Sanctus.'

46. There are other ways to avoid Nestorianism. I cannot discuss them all. A recent and quite influential solution is the line Leftow and Crisp take, following the famous 1,001 cats example of Peter Geach: 'Tibbles the cat.' The upshot of this Tibbles example is: 'given a set of parts composing at time t a member of a natural kind (e.g. a cat), no subset of that set composes at t a member of the same natural kind.' Applied to the incarnation: Jesus's 'human nature never composes a human person distinct from God the Son because no person can have a person as a proper part.' See Crisp, *The Word Enfleshed*; and Crisp, 'Compositional Christology without Nestorianism,' 58–59. The weakness of this solution concerns its applicability. One could pose this question: certainly, the 'cat-premise' is true, but in the case of the incarnation we are confronted with one Person with two mind-gifted natures. This very extraordinary case seems to defy the applicability of the premise. So this strategy runs the risk of begging the question.

The Hypostatic Union 39

- For the relation between the human nature and the Word, Scotus exploits the analogy to the relation of accident and substance. The individual human nature depends on the Word, just like David's ginger hair (an accidental property) depends on David (a primary substance).
- Such a relation between an accident and its substance is a 'metaphysical' kind of dependence, no creational (bringing into existence) or psychological dependence.
- We distinguish between 'persona' and 'person' (and, applied to the divine, between Persona and Person). We use 'person' in its modern sense: an individual human nature. We use 'persona' in a technical, Scotistic sense: 'persona' means *the independence* of such an individual human nature.
- Jesus as an individual human nature *depends on the Word* like an accident on its substance.
- Ordinary individual human natures are characterised by the *negation* of this relational property: *they are independent.* They stand on their own.
- They therefore have a human persona. Jesus however, has no such human 'persona.'
- Jesus has no human persona, but a divine Persona—the second Persona of the Trinity (which is in its turn also independent, but necessarily so).
- Jesus is also independent, not as a human being, but as the Son of God, the Word.
- The Chalcedonian demand (no division, no separation) is met: there is indeed just one (divine) Persona in Jesus Christ, and there is no human persona (the hypostatic union).
- Like all accidents, the human properties characterise the Word: they count as truth-makers. Just as David is 'a ginger,' so the Son of God gave his human life on the cross.
- The human nature has a capacity for being assumed, but not a propensity towards that goal.
- The other Chalcedonian demand of the integrity of the two natures (without confusion, without change) is also met: due to the divine Persona of the Word He is fully divine; meanwhile Christ is a complete individual human nature. The only difference with us is that He is 'grafted' into the Word, like a branch grafted into the cultivated olive tree.

I endorse this Scotistic view as a coherent analysis of the hypostatic union. Fully respecting the 'four borders' of Chalcedon, this analysis helps to explain why the incarnation is not incoherent. It doesn't seek to comprehensively understand the mystery of the incarnation as expressed by Conciliar Christology, yet this Scotistic analysis helps us to ward off the critical

40 *Chapter 2*

question of whether we might not confuse the worship of true divine splendour with the idolatrous veneration of contradictions.

This description already encompassed the semantic level, for I said: *the human properties characterise the Word, they count as truth-makers.* Let us now turn to this topic: predication in Christology. Both topics are, in fact, hierarchically interwoven as reality and *speaking about* reality. The sequence of these two chapters displays this hierarchy.

Chapter 3

Stepped Characterisation

3.1: THE COHERENCE PROBLEM

St. Augustine beautifully preached the following breathtaking lines, its to-and-fro rhythm each time augmenting the awe and adoration:[1]

> The Maker of man became Man
> that He, Ruler of the stars, might be nourished at the breast;
> that He, the Bread, might be hungry;
> that He, the Fountain, might thirst;
> that He, the Light, might sleep;
> that He, the Way, might be wearied by the journey.[2]

Or is it perhaps true what John Hick said: 'Orthodoxy has never been able to give this idea any content. It is . . . as devoid of meaning as to say that this circle drawn with a pencil on a paper is also a square.'[3] This is a fundamental problem for Conciliar Christology: 'how can one and the same person, the Second Person of the Trinity, be both God and man? For being God implies having certain attributes, perhaps immutability, or impassibility, whereas being human implies having apparently inconsistent attributes.'[4] One way of dealing with this coherence problem is to invoke the so-called 'qua-propositions': 'dividing the predicates between the two natures, such that some predicates apply to the person in virtue of the divine nature, and

---

1. This chapter is a reworked version of G. H. Labooy, 'Stepped Characterisation: A Metaphysical Defence of qua-Propositions in Christology,' *International Journal for Philosophy of Religion* 86, no. 1 (August 2019): 25–38, https://doi.org/10.1007/s11153-019-09698-y.

2. *Sermones* 191: 1, https://www.dec25th.info/Augustine%27s%20Sermon%20191.html.

3. John Hick, ed., *The Myth of God Incarnate* (London: SCM Press, 1977), 178.

4. Timothy Pawl, 'A Solution to the Fundamental Philosophical Problem of Christology,' *Journal of Analytic Theology* 2, no. May (2014): 61–85; see also Pawl, *The Incarnation*, chap. 7.

42   *Chapter 3*

some in virtue of the human nature.'[5] This chapter is a contribution to this approach.[6] I will take the lead of the late Marilyn McCord Adams, who contributed to the defence of qua-propositions by probing their metaphysical backbone, for as she puts it, *'semantics presupposes metaphysics.'*[7] As regards metaphysics, the 'compositionalist' metaphysics of the previous chapter is presupposed. The Word assumes an *individual* human nature and the relation between the Word and the individual human nature is seen as in some way similar to the substance-accident relation. Using this ontology, I will further elaborate on Adams's solution using the concept of 'stepped characterisation': the human properties first characterise the human nature and, in the next step, this individual human nature characterises the Word.

Firstly, I will provide an introduction to the 'qua-propositions,' including a discussion of a major difficulty connected to them. Next, I will outline the medieval analysis of qua-propositions, followed by an account of Adams's analysis that explores the functioning of qua-propositions in their ontological setting. Then, elaborating on Adams's proposal, I will develop the concept of stepped characterisation against its ontological background. Finally, returning to the initial topic, I will apply the concept of stepped characterisation to the semantics of qua-propositions.

3.2: AN INTRODUCTION TO QUA-PROPOSITIONS

The coherence problem is inextricably bound up with the very heart of Conciliar Christology. How is it possible that the Divine Word, the second Persona of the Trinity, is characterised by the properties of the human nature—traditionally called the 'communicatio idiomatum'? I use 'to characterise' as follows: if an essential or accidental property F characterises an entity x it is true that x is F. The scholastics frequently use 'denominate' to express this and there is an obvious resemblance with the modern use of 'is a truth-maker of.'[8] Resuming, how is it possible that the Divine Word is *characterised* by the human properties? Properties like 'gave his life as a ransom' or 'is passible'? How can the impassible Word be passible? In the Chalcedonian creed—and likewise in earlier doxological formulae—we find a way of handling this:

---

5. Cross, *The Metaphysics of the Incarnation*, 192.

6. Richard Cross, 'The Incarnation,' in *The Oxford Handbook of Philosophical Theology*, ed. Thomas P. Flint and Michael Rea, Oxford Handbooks (Oxford; New York: Oxford University Press, 2011), 452–75; Hill, 'Introduction.'

7. Marilyn McCord Adams, *Christ and Horrors: The Coherence of Christology*, Current Issues in Theology (Cambridge, UK; New York: Cambridge University Press, 2006).

8. Cross, *The Metaphysics of the Incarnation*, 35.

Stepped Characterisation

begotten from the Father before the ages as regards His Godhead, begotten from the Virgin Mary as regards his manhood . . .[9]

'As regards his Godhead,' 'as regards his manhood,' that's the way the problem of Christological predication was always handled in sermons, creeds, and hymns. Other expressions are 'in virtue of' or 'qua.' I assume that all these semantic tools are equivalent and I call them 'qua-propositions': 'Christ qua God is not created,' 'Christ qua man is created.' The use of these qua-propositions is contested, for instance by Morris, Cross, and Pawl,[10] though many other contemporary philosophers defend them, like Geach, Sturch, Swinburne, Stump, Adams, and Gorman.[11]

A frequent objection against the qua-propositions is that they are merely a way of covertly ascribing the same contradictory properties to one subject. For:

> 1 The Word *qua Divine* is not created entails that the Word is not created
>
> And   2 The Word *qua human* is created entails that the Word is created
>
> Thus: 3 The Word is not created and the Word is created.

(3) contains a contradiction and, therefore, qua-propositions are merely a tool to conceal this; just 'muddying the waters,' as Morris contends.[12] Now (3) only stands if (1) and (2) are valid. It must be true that

1. 'The Word *qua Divine* is not created' entails 'the Word is not created'
2. 'The Word *qua human* is created' entails 'the Word is created.'

Only then the claim of merely obscuring inconsistency is justified. Consequently, the validity of the inference from 'qua' to 'unqualifiedly' is at stake here:

x *qua G* is *F* entails x is *F.*

---

9. The Greek: κατὰ τὴν θεότητα, κατὰ τὴν ἀνθρωπότητα.

10. Thomas V. Morris, *The Logic of God Incarnate* (Ithaca: Cornell University Press, 1987); Cross, *The Metaphysics of the Incarnation*; Pawl, *In Defense of Conciliar Christology.*

11. Peter Thomas Geach, *Logic Matters*, 1, California paperback print (Berkeley, CA: University of California Press, 1980); R. L. Sturch, 'God, Christ and Possibilities,' *Religious Studies* 16, no. 1 (March 1980): 81–84, https://doi.org/10.1017/S0034412500011999; Richard Swinburne, *The Christian God* (Oxford [England]; New York: Clarendon Press; Oxford University Press, 1994), 197; Eleonore Stump, 'Aquinas' Metaphysics of the Incarnation,' in *The Incarnation: An Interdisciplinary Symposium on the Incarnation of the Son of God*, ed. Stephen T. Davis, Daniel Kendall, and Gerald O'Collins (Oxford; New York: Oxford University Press, 2002), 197–218; Adams, *Christ and Horrors*; Michael Gorman, 'Christological Consistency and the Reduplicative Qua,' *Journal of Analytic Theology* 2 (2014): 86–100.

12. Morris, *The Logic of God Incarnate*, 46–55.

44 *Chapter 3*

In the original Latin this was called the '*secundum quid ad simpliciter*' infer-ence. Because I use the name 'qua-propositions,' I prefer to call it the '*qua ad simpliciter*' inference. Many advocates of qua-propositions try to somehow show that these *qua ad simpliciter* inferences are not always valid.

Having obtained an initial insight into the topic, I now press ahead: can we find an answer to the previously mentioned objection by analysing how qua-propositions work? How do we have to 'read' qua-propositions?

3.3: QUA-PROPOSITIONS: AN INVENTORY

Along with Duns Scotus and medieval thought more generally, I will dis-tinguish three different analyses of qua-propositions: (1) the *reduplicative* analysis, (2) the *specificative* analysis, and (3) qualifying the *predicate* term.[13]

The first one, the reduplicative analysis, only explains why a certain predi-cate is properly applied to the subject.[14] With the qua-clause, we point to the *reason* of the applicability. Take 'Christ qua man is possible.' The qua-clause only serves to explain why possibility is ascribed to Christ, while it does not in any way *qualify* the grade or manner of the applicability. Therefore, the reduplicative analysis *itself* is of no help in blocking potential Christological contradictions.[15] The *qua ad simpliciter* inference is still valid, entailing the contradiction that 'Christ is not created and Christ is created.'

According to the specificative analysis, the qua-clause qualifies the *sub-ject* term in $x = F$ qua H. It 'redirects' the subject term. Instead of picking out the whole, it picks out the H-part of x. A standard medieval example is the Ethiopian. In 'the Ethiopian is white qua teeth,' the subject term is *redirected*: it no longer stands for the Ethiopian but for his teeth.[16] Thus, the danger of contradiction is removed, for the *qua ad simpliciter* inference is now no longer valid. For 'the Ethiopian is white qua teeth' does not entail that the Ethiopian is white. However, this welcome result comes at a cost: now the whole, the Ethiopian, is no longer *characterised* by 'white.' That would mean, in the case of the incarnation, that the human nature does not character-ise the Word, because the subject term is redirected and no longer stands for

---

13. Cross, 'The Incarnation,' 455–57; Adams, *Christ and Horrors*, 128–38; Cross, *The Metaphysics of the Incarnation*, 192–205; Allan Bäck, 'Scotus on the Consistency of the Incarnation and the Trinity,' *Vivarium* 36, no. 1 (1998): 83–107; Pawl adds another strategy, modifying the copula: Pawl, *In Defense of Conciliar Christology*, 117–51.

14. *Ord.* III, d11, q2, §48: accipiendo 'secundum quod' proprie ut est nota reduplications sive nota inhaerentiae predicati ad subjectum.

15. Scotus speaks of the 'ratio formalis,' the 'formal reason' of the inherence of the predicate; Cross, *The Metaphysics of the Incarnation*, 194. See further Scotus *Ord.* III, d11, q2, §46–47.

16. Scotus, *Ord.* III, d11, q2, §46: 'propositio cum tali determinatione distrahente esse vera, et non sine ea'; the difference with a merely reduplicative sense is a newly added 'distracting determination.'

Stepped Characterisation 45

the Word but for the human nature. Therefore, Adams rightly contends: 'the specificative interpretation threatens to remove contradiction at the expense of characterisation, for it is not generally true that a property truly predicable of one part is truly predicable of another part of the whole of which it is a part.'[17] Likewise, Richard Cross remarks that the specificative analysis seems to be wedded to a mereological Christology.[18] A mereological analysis is a part-whole analysis. It threatens the Chalcedonian demand that the Word can be characterised by the human nature as well. Scotus tries to remedy this in numerous ways, for instance by giving the example of a heart in relation to the health of an animal. The heart is a *primary indicator* as regards health, which makes this example much more promising than that of the Ethiopian.[19] As Scotus says: 'We can say that the animal is unqualifiedly healthy because his heart is healthy.' Nevertheless, in this specificative analysis, the qua-clause still redirects the subject-term by picking out a certain *part* of the whole. This will persistently hamper characterisation.

The third analysis holds that qua-propositions qualify the *predicate* term. Scotus gives this example: 'The Ethiopian qua teeth is white' means 'The Ethiopian is white-toothed.' Transferred to Christological predication: 'Christ *qua* human is born from the Virgin Mary' means 'Christ is a Virgin-Mary-born-man.' Or Cross's example:

1 Christ qua man is passible
Means: 2 Christ is a passible-man.

Next, it is argued that (2) 'Christ is a passible-man' does not entail 'Christ is passible.' Thus, our desideratum is fulfilled: the *qua ad simpliciter* inference is invalid and the contradiction with 'Christ is impassible' doesn't arise. And yet, because the subject-term is by no means redirected, the characterisation-problem doesn't arise either: both 'is a passible-man' and 'is impassible' unambiguously refer to one and the same subject, the Word.

True as this is, some serious difficulties remain, because this strategy threatens the Chalcedonian demand that the assumed human nature is the same as ours.[20] For if, as Scotus states, 'Christ is a passible-man' does not entail 'Christ is passible,' then *being a passible-man* is not an instance of

---

17. Adams, *Christ and Horrors*, 131.

18. Cross, *The Metaphysics of the Incarnation*, 197–202. See also *Ord.* III, d11, q2, §53–54.

19. The difference is: the heart (Scotus uses 'thorax') 'denominat totum (the health of the animal), quia denominat ipsum sicut natum est ipsum denominare.' This holds not for the teeth of the Ethiopian. *Ord.* III, d11, q2, §53.

20. Scotus raises another doubt: that syncategorematic statements do not qualify the predicate; see *Ord.* III, d11, q2, §48. Pawl also raises a general ontological objection: if predicates are modified by a nature, then it's no longer true that 'humans and dogs are mammals.' Because 'Fido is a mammal-qua-dog and no human is a mammal-qua-dog.' Pawl, *In Defense of Conciliar Christology*, 133.

46 *Chapter 3*

being passible. But then Chalcedon is endangered: Christ's way of being passible is different from ours.[21] This goes against the predicative analysis.

The conclusion seems to be that qua-propositions are plagued by considerable philosophical difficulties. So let's explore their metaphysical backdrop, following the lead of Adams, because 'semantics presupposes metaphysics.'

3.4: ADAMS: SEMANTICS
PRESUPPOSES METAPHYSICS

Outlining Adams's metaphysical defence of qua-propositions, I will start with the basic metaphysical assumption that *everything owns its own nature essentially*. You cannot get rid of your own nature without ceasing to exist. Socrates can't cast off his humanity, and neither Bucephalus his horse-nature. This is what the Aristotelian concept of primary substance is about. However, as Adams states:

> Aquinas, Scotus and Ockham concede that Aristotle not only captures the way things for the most part are. He gives a correct analysis of the metaphysical default position: apart from Divine intervention, individual substance natures will be primary substances and no creature has the power to subject them to (make them ontologically dependent upon) anything else. But they reasoned that the case of the Incarnation reveals something about individual substance natures that Aristotle was in no position to know.[22]

In other words, Christian faith eventually yielded this pivotal metaphysical revolution: something can *acquire* a second individual nature. The scholastics of course agreed that everything whatsoever has its *own* nature essentially— what Adams termed as 'Aristotle's correct metaphysical default position.' But in addition to this essential nature, something can *contingently* acquire a second nature. Thus, the Word can acquire a second nature, an individual human nature. As I showed in the previous chapter, Scotus compared the relation between the Word and such an individual human nature with the substance-accident relation. The human individual nature *depends* on the Word like an accident on its substance. As Socrates's whiteness depends on Socrates and is, therefore, *his* whiteness, so the individual human nature depends on the Word and is, therefore, *its* human nature: the Word can be characterised (denominated) by the human nature.

This ontology carries important semantic implications. According to Adams, the fact that the two natures are owned differently—one essentially,

---

21. Cross, *The Metaphysics of the Incarnation*, 204.
22. Adams, *Christ and Horrors*, 135.

Stepped Characterisation

the other accidentally—changes the semantic rules. Let's revert to the classic objection to qua-propositions:

> 1 The Word *qua Divine* is not created entails that the Word is not created
> And 2 The Word *qua human* is created entails that the Word is created
> Thus: 3 The Word is not created and the Word is created.

This led to a contradiction (3). However, if one brings the two different ways of ownership into the equation, the fatal contradiction does not arise, according to Adams. She argues that the *qua ad simpliciter* inference only holds in the case of a *necessarily* owned nature:

> x *according to his necessary nature* is G entails x is G.

But in the case of an *acquired* individual nature, the implication does not hold:

> x *according to his acquired nature* is G does *not* entail x is G.

This implies that, although (1) is still valid, (2) is no longer valid: it is not true that 'the Word *qua human* is created' entails 'the Word is created.' The *qua ad simpliciter* inference is invalid because the Word accidentally owns the individual human nature: 'it is an alien supposit of the human nature.'[23] Thus the contradictory (3) is avoided.

In the following section, I will elaborate on this proposal because Adams does not further clarify why the *qua ad simpliciter* inference is invalid in the case of an accidentally owned second nature. After all, one could object that accidentality *as such* does not disqualify entities for fulfilling the 'unqualified-characterisation' role. For example, Socrates's accidental property of being snub-nosed characterises him 'simpliciter.'

3.5: PROBING DEEPER: THE METAPHYSICS OF STEPPED CHARACTERISATION

I presupposed a compositionalist metaphysics in which the Word assumes an *individual* human nature and the relation between the Word and the individual human nature is seen as in some way similar to the *substance-accident relation*. Before I embark on my actual argument, I want to briefly argue that this metaphysical apparatus is by no means eccentric. There is a considerable

---

23. Adams, 136.

48 *Chapter 3*

range of metaphysical models that would support ontological concepts like 'an individual nature' and 'a substance-accident relation.' Despite the overwhelming complexity of metaphysics, I will try to set out three minimal metaphysical requirements for such models. Firstly, a two-category analysis of reality: the recognition that there is something like 'this-ness' and 'what-ness' and that the one cannot be reduced to the other. This corresponds on the semantic level with the basic structure of a sentence: subject and predicate. This binary structure reflects something in reality; it isn't merely a language phenomenon. Secondly, properties—or 'property-role fulfillers,' depending on which metaphysics one prefers[24]—are entities that things are said to 'possess,' 'exemplify,' or 'be inhered by.' Finally, the acknowledgement of a distinction between essential and accidental property-role fulfillers. A broad group of *non–ad hoc* classic, medieval, and modern ontologies fits with these minimal requirements. For example, although a trope-bundle theory wouldn't meet the first two requirements, a substrate or nuclear trope theory probably would.[25]

Now my proposal focuses on the fact that the Word accidentally owns an individual human nature. Due to that individuality, the human properties first characterise the human nature and, in the next 'step,' this individual human nature characterises the Word. I call this 'stepped characterisation.' Thus, the Word is characterised indirectly by the human properties: the Word 'borrows'[26] the human properties from the human individual nature. Or, like Cross said: the Word 'piggybacks' them.[27] One thus can speak of a 'proximate' and a 'remote' owner of such properties.[28] To give an example of stepped characterisation of the Word by an accidental human property like 'is suffering':

A. suffering characterises the human individual nature of Christ directly
B. the human individual nature characterises the Word directly
C. instead of directly characterising the Word, suffering characterises the Word in a *stepped* way, namely: step A followed by step B.

Or take for example an essential human property like 'contingency':

D. contingency characterises the human individual nature of Christ directly
E. the human individual nature characterises the Word directly

---

24. Pawl, *In Defense of Conciliar Christology*, 52.
25. I myself adhere to an ontology with kind-natures and individual natures; see further chap. 2.5.
26. Stump, 'Aquinas' Metaphysics of the Incarnation,' 197–218.
27. Cross, 'The Incarnation,' 455–57.
28. Cross, 191–92; for the objection from Property Borrowing, see Pawl, *In Defense of Conciliar Christology*, 64–65.

Stepped Characterisation 49

F. instead of directly characterising the Word, contingency characterises the Word in a *stepped* way, namely: step D followed by step E.

Does this concept of 'stepped characterisation' lead to a coherent solution? Or am I again just 'muddying the waters'? After all, according to Conciliar Christology, all human predicates must characterise the Word. This, however, caused the coherence problem: the Word is both necessary and contingent. So what's the benefit of terminology like 'characterising the Word in a stepped way'? For either the Word is no longer characterised by contingency, or, if it is still characterised by it, we relapse into the old problem: one and the same subject, the Word, is both necessary and contingent. In short: if characterisation, then inconsistency; if consistency, then no characterisation. Or is this logic of characterisation too monolithic? I will try to find an answer to this question by investigating the underlying metaphysics of stepped characterisation in (C) and (F).

Let's start with further clarifying step (B) (and the identical E): the relation between the individual human nature and the Word. Like Scotus, I compared it to the substance-accident relation: as if the human individual nature inheres in the Word like an accident in its substance. But what does it mean for an accident *to inhere*? In the previous chapter (chap. 2.8), we provisionally entered into this subject. Now we have reason to enter more fully into it. Medievals distinguished three shades of meaning. Being an inhering accident ϕ of any substance x which exemplifies ϕ-ness has the following features:[29]

1: ϕ-ness depends on x
2: ϕ-ness informs x
3: ϕ-ness is a truth-maker, such that x is ϕ.

The first feature, the relation of dependence, must be distinguished from causal dependence. It is the kind of metaphysical dependence I described earlier (chap. 2.5). To put it in modal terms: generally spoken, an accident cannot exist without its substance.[30] So as regards this first feature, the substance has priority. With the second feature, however, the priority switches: here an accident is thought to 'actualise' a passive potency of the substance. For instance, whiteness actualises the potency of being colourable in Socrates. So here, the substance receives while the accident has some kind of priority. As I said, this was believed to be inappropriate for God due to his 'impassibility.' Accordingly, Scotus only accepts (1) and (3) as appropriate for the incarnation: the individual human nature depends like an accident on the Word, but

---

29. Cross, *The Metaphysics of the Incarnation*, 34.
30. See Scotus *Ord.* III, d1, p1, q1, §14–17.

50 *Chapter 3*

it does not *inform* it (2). Moreover, there is a certain relation between (1) and (3): φ-ness is a truth-maker for x *because* φ-ness depends on x. Or, in other words, φ-ness characterises x *because* φ-ness depends on x. Therefore, (3) is based on (1).[31]

I will now show how the fact that (3) is based on (1) warrants our analysis of stepped characterisation. Actually, the argument is quite simple: because characterisation (3) is based on the dependence of a property (1), characterisation tracks dependence. Therefore, if the dependence-relation (1) is direct, characterisation (3) must be direct as well. If, however, the dependence-relation (1) is stepped, characterisation (3) must be stepped as well.

I will first differentiate between accidental (A) and essential (D) properties of the human individual nature. Let's start with accidental properties, inhering in their substances (A). Here one can simply apply the specifics of accidental inherence that I just described: a property like 'suffering' depends directly on the individual human nature of Christ and, consequently, that nature is thereby directly characterised by it. In short: *direct dependence yields direct characterisation.*

We are now in a position to assess how the Word is characterised by human accidental properties (C). A human accidental property first depends on the human individual substance. Now in the case of Jesus, this primary substance, this human individual, depended on the Word. Hence, the dependence-relation (1) is stepped. Therefore, characterisation is stepped too, because it is based on a stepped relation of dependence. If one however demands that straightforward, direct characterisation is the only true standard of characterising the Word,[32] this would imply a straightforward, direct mode of dependence, because characterisation is based on the dependence-relation. After all, one wouldn't expect that straightforward characterisation could be based on stepped dependence. However, the straightforward dependence of human properties on the Word seems to exclude the dependence of these

---

31. In the period between Aquinas and Scotus, 'the truth-making function of an accident was reduced to dependence rather than to informing.' Cross, *The Metaphysics of the Incarnation*, 36. In selecting just these two meanings of 'to inhere,' Scotus provides a conceptual analysis that is akin to modern views: the modern concept of accidental properties is also defined modally.

32. I hesitate whether Pawl (2014, 2016) claims this in his innovative approach to the problem of potentially contradictory predicates. In his analysis, Pawl uses an alternative 'conditional' construction of Christological predicates. The default analysis of a Christological predicate would be something like: 's is possible just in case it is possibly causally affectable.' Pawl's alternative construction is conditional: 's is possible just in case *it has a nature* that is possibly causally affectable.' Pawl convincingly shows that this kind of predicates applies straightforwardly, '*simpliciter.*' I do not think, however, that this amounts to a refutation of stepped characterisation as it is proposed here. Rather, these two approaches go side by side, his one on the level of predicates, and mine on the level of ontology. His approach is comparable to Scotus (*RP* 3.11. 1–2, n. 4): "This does not follow: 'this animal is blind; therefore it does not see,' unless the animal has just one nature, to which one visual system belongs. For if the animal had two natures, to which two visual systems belonged, it would follow only that the animal does not see according to that nature according to which it is blind."

human accidental properties on the individual human nature. For isn't that just the meaning of straightforward dependence? How could an accident be straightforwardly dependent on two different things? The dependence on the first would preempt the dependence on the second.[33] Yet if accidental human properties no longer directly depend on the individual human nature but rather on the Word, this would imply the mingling of the natures. Isn't this Ovid: a man acquiring the body of a snake? Therefore, I reject straightforward dependence of accidental human properties on the Word because the mingling of natures is not desirable given the perspective of Conciliar Christology. Hence these human properties must depend in a stepped way on the Word, not straightforwardly. And this justifies the concept of stepped characterisation because characterisation tracks dependence. And because, as I just argued, stepped and direct dependence of human accidental properties on the Word exclude each other, stepped characterisation (C) between a human accidental property and the Word excludes straightforward characterisation between that property and the Word: stepped characterisation (C) and straightforward characterisation are contraries.[34]

But what if φ-ness is an essential human property like 'being contingent' (D) or 'being human'? Do (nonindividual) essential properties behave sufficiently similarly to the accidental ones with respect to the previous argument for stepped characterisation? Here there is a stepped ontological relation as well because a human essential property is first possessed or exemplified by the human individual substance and next this individual substance depends on the Word. Consequently, characterisation is stepped too because it is based on a *stepped* ontological relation. And even a stepped ontological relation in which the two ontological steps are more dissimilar than in the former case of accidental properties. The first step (D) towards the human individual is essential, whereas the next one (E) towards the Divine Word is accidental. Moreover, in the first step, the human individual nature *exemplifies* the human essential property, whereas in the next step the Divine Word *functions merely as the end term of a relation of dependence*. These are very different ontological relations, although they both 'ground' characterisation.

Taking this argument further, let's suppose that 'being contingent' would be straightforwardly possessed (or exemplified) by the Divine Word. That would of course be impossible, due to the fact that the Word necessarily exists. Doesn't that prove Conciliar Christology wrong? Of course not, because Conciliar Christology is not committed to the thought that the divine

---

33. Compare Scotus *Ord.* III, d1, p1, q2, §103–105: 'quod cum dependentia alicuius fuerit totaliter terminata ad aliquid, ipsa non potest—dependentia eiusdem rationis—dependere aliud.'

34. True, stepped characterisation *encompasses* two steps of direct characterisation (A) and (B); but (C) as a stepped relation between a human property and the Word excludes *one* straightforward relation between that human property and the Word.

52 *Chapter 3*

Word *exemplifies* human essential properties and is thus changed into a creature.[35] The human nature with all its essential properties is dependent on the Word, but that does not imply that the Word straightforwardly 'possesses' or 'exemplifies' all the essential human properties.[36] That would again imply a mingling of natures. Therefore, the ontological relation is indeed stepped: essential properties like 'being contingent' or 'being human' are exemplified or possessed by the individual human nature, and this individual human nature in turn *depends* on the Word.[37] Both ontological relations (D and E) constitute the basis of characterisation, but because the ontological relation is stepped, characterisation is stepped too. I conclude that the ontological relation of both accidental and essential properties is stepped; hence, accidental (C) and essential human properties (F) characterise the Word in a stepped way too.

What about individual properties like 'being Jesus'? This is an essential individual property. Or 'Jesus's suffering'—an accidental individual property? This question only arises from specific ontologies acknowledging the existence of this kind of properties, but in the case of favouring such an apparatus, how does this kind of properties behave with respect to the matter at hand? It's easier to clarify this point in the next section where I return to the question of the *qua ad simpliciter* inference.

To sum up: in this section, I tried to show that, in Christological predication, characterisation tracks a stepped ontological relation of dependence. This ontological relation is stepped because of the individuality of the assumed nature. The assumed nature's accidentality *as such* does not disqualify the human properties for 'simpliciter' or straightforwardly characterising the Word; it is rather the individuality and integrity of the assumed human nature that causes the stepped dependence and hence the stepped characterisation.

---

35. I leave a discussion of Kenoticism aside; Pawl, *In Defense of Conciliar Christology*, 104–16.

36. Scotus *Ord.* III, d1, p1, q1, §17. Is it possible to relate restriction policies of, for example, Morris and Cross to Scotus's view that human properties do not inform the Word? Restriction policies assume that contradictory properties must be blocked from being ascribed to the Word. They could be constructed as 'limitation properties': 'These limitation properties will not be understood as elements of human nature at all, but as universal accompaniments of humanity in the case of any created human being.' We are, according to Morris, fully human of course. And so is Christ. But we, unlike Christ, are merely human too, meaning that we do not exemplify any higher ontological kind, such as Divinity. And fully but merely human beings have these kinds of limitation properties: properties common to us, but not essential to the human kind-nature. Christ as a fully human being—but not merely human—does not have these limitations properties, hence no contradiction arises with his Divinity. Aside from the fact that I am not convinced by the 'blockage' strategy, the point I want to make is that Morris's key motive of blocking contradictory properties involves the same scotistic insight that the Divine nature cannot be informed by something. We cannot ascribe 'being contingent' to the Word in the sense of informing. Morris, *The Logic of God Incarnate*, 65.

37. See also Scotus *Ord.* III, d1, p1, q1, §63, where he argues that the infinite can be united to a finite human being because the 'infinitum non habet in se quodcumque ens formaliter, sed virtualiter vel eminenter.' God isn't *informed* by the incarnation, though He already 'virtualiter vel eminenter' contains everything.

3.6: APPLICATION TO THE ANALYSIS OF QUA-PROPOSITIONS

How does this concept of stepped characterisation relate to the issue of qua-propositions? Let's start with Adams's pivotal claim that the *qua ad simpliciter* inference does not hold in the case of the accidental, acquired nature. The objection was that

2 'The Word *qua human* is created' entails 'the Word is created.'

This led to a contradiction. But Adams argued that the inference in (2) is not valid: the Word *qua human* is created does *not* entail that the Word is created. In the preceding section, I provided more insight into why this is true: because of stepped characterisation. In the first part of (2),

the Word *qua human* is created,

and we are dealing with stepped characterisation. The Word *qua human* is created because 'being created' characterises the human individual nature of Jesus and, in the next step, this human individual nature characterises the Word. Hence, stepped characterisation. In the second part of (2),

the Word is created,

and we deal with straightforward characterisation. However, as I argued earlier, stepped and straightforward characterisation should *not* merge into one univocal concept. Moreover, stepped characterisation and straightforward characterisation cannot be both true of a certain relation R; they are contraries, as I argued. But then the inference from stepped characterisation to straightforward characterisation is of course invalid: the troubling *qua ad simpliciter* inference is invalid in the case of an assumed individual human nature.

On the other hand, in the case of the essential nature, the *qua ad simpliciter* inference is valid, because then there is no instance of stepped characterisation. Take

1 The Word *qua Divine* is not created entails that the Word is not created.

A proposition like 'The Word *qua Divine* is not created' is of course grammatically similar to 'the Word *qua human* is created.' But the Divine nature is owned necessarily and directly by the Word, directly in the sense of 'without another individual nature in between.' Therefore, there is no stepped

54 *Chapter 3*

characterisation on the ontological level, although the grammatical level suggests otherwise. Hence, the *qua ad simpliciter* inference is valid in the case of an essential nature. Thus, I have shown how the logic of stepped characterisation solves the previous dilemma 'if characterisation then inconsistency; if consistency, then no characterisation.' Only the *exclusive* usage of straightforward characterisation is capable of generating inconsistency. Such an exclusive usage, however, does not conform to Conciliar Christology because it implies the mingling of natures.

Individual properties require some attention now, for example, the essential individual property 'being Jesus':

> 4 The Word *qua Divine* is not Jesus entails that the Word is not Jesus
>
> And   5 The Word *qua human* is Jesus entails that the Word is Jesus
>
> Thus: 6 The Word is not Jesus and the Word is Jesus.

In the former cases, the strategy was to block the *qua ad simpliciter* inference in one of the propositions, obviously in (4) in this case. However, I propose to solve this differently. The phrase 'The Word *qua Divine* is not Jesus' in (4) is problematic in the first place. Conciliar Christology would most likely reject it and accept the opposite instead: 'The Word *qua Divine* is Jesus.' Jesus as an individual human being straightforwardly characterises the Word as a depending accident, although, for example, 'being human' characterises the Word in a stepped manner. Consequently, in the case of this individual property of 'being Jesus,' the blockage of the *qua ad simpliciter* inference in (4) is not relevant because no contradiction arises in the first place.

Finally, stepped characterisation constitutes a tool that brings into view the aptness of at least the specificative and the reduplicative analysis. Firstly, it explains why the specificative analysis of qua-propositions is not wedded to a purely mereological Christology. True, the specificative analysis *qualifies* the subject term, but is qualification, or specification, to be exclusively understood as *redirection*? Indeed, 'redirection of the subject term' is troublesome in Christology. But qualification or specification of the subject term can also be explained in terms of stepped characterisation: in the case of a human property of Christ, the subject term is 'qualified' or 'specified' in the sense that the Word is characterised in a stepped way. Again, 'semantics presupposes metaphysics!' Next, the reduplicative analysis. As I said, this analysis merely tells us in virtue of which nature one ascribes a property to the Word. But that leaves room for asking another question: *How* is that applicability established?[38] For instance, by straightforward or stepped characterisation? Of course, if one assumes that the mere fact of applicability logically implies just one kind of characterisation, the question of 'how' seems redundant. But I just showed that there are at least two kinds of characterisation. Therefore, indicating in virtue of *which* nature a property is applicable does not yet touch upon the issue of *how* that characterisation is established. So to sum up: while the predicative analysis indicates in virtue of *which* nature a property is applied, the ontologically fine-tuned specificative analysis specifies *how* that property is applied to the subject.

Finally, the vindication of these first two analyses probably makes the third predicative analysis redundant. Trying to bypass the difficulties of the specificative analysis, the predicative analysis locates the indication of the proximate ownership of a predicate *in the predicate term itself.* For reasons already given earlier, I think that this analysis is doomed to remain problematic. Anyway, I don't think that our ontological tool can remedy its shortcomings. However, because our tool of stepped characterisation supports an ontologically fine-tuned specificative analysis and combines well with the reduplicative analysis, the predicative analysis seems not only troublesome but superfluous as well.

I have defended the strategy of qua-propositions against a major logical objection. As far as this particular objection is concerned, Hick's assertion that the content of Conciliar Christology is 'devoid of meaning' is hereby refuted. Finally, with Augustine, I focus afresh on that amazing content, which makes me bow in worship:

> *The Maker of man became Man*
> *that He, Ruler of the stars, might be nourished at the breast;*
> *that He, the Bread, might be hungry.*

---

38. This broad, nonspecified nature of the reduplicative analysis reminds us of the fact that the term also functioned as a blanket term designating the *set* of different analyses of qua-propositions instead of one of its members as it is used here.

Chapter 4

Two Intellects

4.1: AWE AND THEOLOGICAL REFLECTION

Thus far, I developed a scotistic Christological metaphysic of accident and substance, wedded to a Chalcedonian strategy of predication, the 'qua-propositions.' Now if we confess that Christ has a human nature 'without confusion and without change,' He also has a human, rational soul. Therefore, He has the basic operations of a soul, namely a human intellect and will. Consequently, it follows that Christ must have two intellects, one divine and one human. The same holds for the will: one divine and one human. In this chapter, I concentrate predominantly on the issue of his human intellect; the next chapter addresses the topic of his human will. The addition 'predominantly' is not due to a careless drafting of the chapters but reflects the matter itself: Scotus sees the soul as one 'res,' one 'thing,' and though its two powers can be formally distinguished, they cannot be in any way separated.

Approaching this topic, I am once more overcome with awe. Unquestionably, this must be forbidden territory for theological reflection? Let alone if it comes to the way the schoolmen handled these mysteries. Scotus, along with Lombard, stated that Christ's *human* intellect sees everything 'in the Word': past, present, future, and possible. 'Anima Christi actualiter videt omnia in Verbo quae videt Verbum'; his soul sees 'everything in the Word that the Word sees.'[1] Hence, vast vistas emerge for our postmodern mindset! And frankly, this view of Christ's near-omniscient human soul seemed outlandish to me at first. Yet gradually I started to absorb some of its splendours. Let us then try to reverently ponder the relationship between the two centres of consciousness, while taking heed of Bonaventure's admonition I already cited in chapter 1: 'Do not believe that reading is sufficient without unction,

---

1. Duns Scotus, *Ord.* 3, d14, q2, §9, §14, §58; see also Cross, *Duns Scotus*, 123.

57

58 *Chapter 4*

investigation without wonder, observation without joy, understanding without humility.'

4.2: REHEARSING THE SCOTISTIC METAPHYSICS OF THE INCARNATION

As I said, it seems adequate to somehow speak of *two* centres of intellect in Christ, one divine, one human. This aligns well with my metaphysical stance as set out in chapter 2. There I contended that Jesus has both a human individuality and a human kind-nature: his humanity is truly 'without confusion, without change.' The only difference between Jesus and us is that our individual human nature is standing on its own, it is independent. This was clarified by the Scotistic meaning of 'persona': *the independence* of an individual human nature. Jesus's individual human nature does not have this kind of independence, for it is dependent on the Word. Hence, He does not have a human *persona*, although He does have, or rather is, a human person.[2] Consequently, I say that there is one *Persona* in Christ, combined with two distinct centres of intellect, one divine, one human.

4.3: MY HUMAN LIFE

On hearing that there are two different individual centres of consciousness in Christ, we might lose sight of the intimate identification of the Word with the human nature. If there are two different individual intellects in Christ, did the Almighty then still become truly man? Or, more accurately, become *a* man? If there are really two minds, we seem to be heading for Nestorianism: ultimately, the Word and the human individual nature seem to be two numerically *different* subjects. However, becoming man simply *implies* having a human soul along with a human body, that's just the point of becoming man of course. But still, God's intimate identification with the human nature seems threatened once we start thinking of a second human intellect along with the divine one. True, the metaphysical analysis in chapter 2 is basic as regards this question, but is it also possible to express the intimate character of the incarnation without the use of those refined metaphysical concepts? Without the use of such enormous abstractions as 'Persona'? Is it possible to express

---

2. I use 'person' for the modern concept, 'persona' for the medieval concept, see chap. 1; to avoid confusion, I will speak of two centres of consciousness or two intellects in Christ rather than of two persons in Christ, but this is a matter of expediency, not principle.

our desideratum—neither a *mingling* of the natures nor a Nestorian *separation* of them—in ordinary language?[3]

I think this is perhaps the plainest expression: Jesus's life is *His* human life (for reasons of clarity, I capitalise the divine possessive pronouns in this paragraph). Or, seen from the divine side: '*this is My human life.*' Just like we say 'this is my life,' God can say, due to the assumption: 'this is My human life.' And, correspondingly, we from our side then say: 'this is His human life.' In chapter 2, I showed the precise metaphysical building blocks to back up such an expression, so 'this is His human life' is more than a matter of speech. It really is His, in the sense that it belongs to the Word like an accident. And because it accidentally depends on the Word it *characterises* the Word, like I argued in the previous chapter. He owns this assumed nature as His very own. Hence, God knows Jesus's thoughts and feelings as His *own* human thoughts and feelings, while He knows all our thoughts and feelings as ours, not as His. And if Jesus dies, it's His human life that is brutally murdered on the cross. He does not own other human lives like that, for we own our lives ourselves; we are, unlike Him, as human personae metaphysically independent (chap. 2.5).

To sum up: a distinct human intellect *is* required, a human intellect just like ours. Otherwise, He did not become man after all. True, this strains our ordinary conception of personal identity: this second mind suggests that now Jesus cannot be somehow identical with the Creator of heaven and earth. He is, however, because this human life, his human 'career' so to speak, is His. God accidentally *owns* this human life: 'this is My life.' A life in which He gave himself away: 'this is my blood of the covenant, which is poured out for many for the forgiveness of sins' (Mt. 26: 28). Nestorianism is overcome on the level of refined metaphysics, yet the wondrous union can be expressed with ordinary language as well.

4.4: A TENTATIVE METAPHOR: AN INTERIOR MONOLOGUE

Here is a metaphor that captures at least some features of this immense mystery: think of encouraging yourself. Suppose you have a sharp psychological insight into how you used to react in certain situations when you were small, say, how you reacted when seeing a sheepdog in front of you. Functioning at that boyish level, you used to panic in such situations. But now, when seeing a sheepdog on your side of the street, you start to encourage that boyish personality in yourself. There is a to and fro between these two personalities

---

3. See also 'the identity problem' in Crisp, 'Compositional Christology without Nestorianism,' 60.

60 *Chapter 4*

of yours, an interior monologue between the adult and the boy in yourself. Yet these two psychological levels are of course 'owned' by one and the same person. This is like a dim image of the incarnation: two centres of consciousness, belonging to just one individual Persona, having an interior monologue. Think of Jesus's prayer: 'Father, the hour has come; glorify your Son so that the Son may glorify you' (John 17). Of course, the immense difference is that in Christ there are two different *natures* that belong to one Persona, whereas in this metaphor there are just two different levels of psychological functioning engaged in an interior monologue. But still, possibly a helpful metaphor. We return to this metaphor in the next chapter (chap. 5.2).

4.5: TWO INTELLECTS: RECIPROCAL ACCESS?

In Christ, there are two centres of knowledge. These two intellects somehow have contact: the omniscient divine mind 'obviously' knows Jesus's human mind, just as He knows mine and yours. But is this also the other way around? We moderns firmly believe that a human mind can never fathom the divine knowledge. That must hold for Jesus's human knowledge too: his intellect, as some of us believe an emergent property of myriad cerebral synapses, cannot somehow 'see' the divine knowledge. For if He could, that would imply that the human nature must have been changed drastically. By nature, our brain states are just not wired for infinity, no matter how countless the underlying neurons might be.[4] God, on the contrary, knows *every* human mind exhaustively. Hence, He knows Jesus's human mind too, the difference being that He knows Jesus's inner life as his own human inner life, while He knows our mental life as ours, not his. Consequently, we moderns are inclined to say that there is no reciprocal epistemological accessibility. God entirely knows each human thought of Jesus, each corner of his heart, but Jesus as to his humanity does not know the divine mind.

As mentioned, though, the medieval scholars thought otherwise: they all cherished a maximal view of the capacities of Christ's soul. Along with Lombard, it was held that Christ's human intellect sees everything 'in the Word': past, present, future, and possible. This knowledge is due to grace and the ensuing beatific vision. Even so, this maximal view is not to be confused with total reciprocal accessibility. Scotus, for one, here applies the distinction between '*cognoscere*' and '*comprehendere*': though Christ '*cognoscet*' many

---

4. Commenting on the view of the schoolmen, Rahner says: they 'sound almost mythological today when one first hears them; they seem to be contrary to the real and historical nature of Our Lord.' Karl Rahner, *Theological Investigations*, vol. V (London: Darton, Longman & Todd, 1969), 195.

effects 'in the Word,' He does not '*comprehendet*' them.[5] This difference is comparable to 'knowing' and 'understanding' in modern English: we know that exercise is good for us, but perhaps we do not understand why. However, notwithstanding such medieval limits to Christ's human intellect, as regards Christ's human intellect there seems to be a vast crevasse between medieval and modern estimations.

In sum, present-day theologians shape Christ's human intellect in the image of our brokenness and limitations, while for the schoolmen it is the other way around. They shaped the common human intellect in the image of the glory of Christ's soul![6] Obviously, the common human intellect in its restored, eschatological bliss. This medieval stance is characterised by 2 Corinthians 3: 'And all of us, with unveiled faces, seeing the glory of the Lord as though reflected in a mirror, are being transformed into the same image from one degree of glory to another; for this comes from the Lord, the Spirit.' Yet we moderns feel more at home with Hebrew 4:15: 'For we do not have a high priest who is unable to sympathize with our weaknesses, but we have one who in every respect has been tested as we are, yet without sin.' I will now depict Scotus's high view of Christ's human intellect and perhaps it will gain some persuasive content for us as well, not least spurred by John 5: 20: 'The Father loves the Son and shows him all that he himself is doing; and he will show him greater works than these, so that you will be astonished.'

4.6: INTRODUCING SCOTUS'S STEPS

I first provide an overview of the steps Scotus makes. Ahead of the actual analysis of Christ's human intellect, Scotus first argues that a most perfect grace is bestowed on Christ; and secondly, that He, therefore, has a most perfect enjoyment (fruition) of God. Yet enjoyment presupposes a perfect vision of the Word (*Ord.* III, d14, §7). And as a corollary of that perfect vision, Christ's soul sees an infinity of objects relucent in the Word. Thus far, Scotus's inquiry broadly aligns with the common medieval view as voiced by

---

5. *Ord.* 3, d14, q2, §43. See also Bonaventura, *De Scientia Christi* (Ad claras Aquas Quaracchi, 1882), 32–39.

6. Just a few times Scotus brings up the topic of a lasting difference between Christ and us. For instance, when rebutting the argument that seeing an infinity of objects must imply seeing them less distinctly. Because surely, that's our collective experience: seeing more objects simultaneously causes you to see them less distinctly. Here Scotus suggests that this might be due to our fallen state whereas Christ was not subjected to that (d14, §77, §87). But clearly, here the difference is bound to disappear. In another case, Scotus argues that the Word could mirror a more limited set of objects to us than to Christ (d14, §80).

62   *Chapter 4*

'the magister,' Lombard (d13, §18; d14, §14).[7] Next, Scotus tries to explain why such a maximal kind of knowledge still allows for the biblical testimony that Jesus *advanced* in wisdom. For how can an almost omniscient being advance in wisdom? Scotus tries to explain this with an epistemological innovation, his concept of 'intuitive knowledge.'

Before I put flesh on these bones, we must note in passing that all this presupposes another debate, a topic to which I will return in the next chapter: How are all these 'steps' connected? I mean, does being assumed by the Word necessarily *imply* having maximal grace, fruition, beatific vision, and impeccability? Duns Scotus, Bonaventure, and William of Ware denied this because 'God's self-presentation to the powers of a creature seems to be an action quite separate from his hypostatic indwelling in the essence and powers of an assumed nature.'[8] At first glance this may seem odd: Could God assume a human nature *without* repleting it with grace and fruition? Without *presenting himself* to that nature and so leading it to enjoyment? It rather looks that the hypostatic indwelling necessarily implies maximal fruition in the one thus assumed—hence note that, on second thought, our modern low estimation of Jesus's human intellectual capacities is maybe after all *not* so obvious as we thought. Anyway, Scotus denies this, arguing that the gift of grace is simply a separate benevolent act, just like leading someone to fruition. Hence, God could indeed assume a human nature without repleting it with grace. However, it still is the most graceful and perfect thing to do: when God assumes a human nature it is most *congruous* to replete it with grace and fruition.[9]

Hence, Scotus is convinced that Christ had all these great-making properties like maximal grace, fruition, and impeccability, but, like Bonaventure, he held that the incarnation does not necessarily imply them. The incarnation is logically possible without these other kinds of fulfilment. I will now briefly describe all these successive steps.

---

7. See also Simo Knuuttila, 'The Psychology of the Incarnation in John Duns Scotus,' *Philosophy and Theology in the Long Middle Ages*, 1 January 2011, 737–48; Walter Hoeres, *Der Wille als reine Vollkommenheit nach Duns Scotus* (München: Pustet, 1962).

8. Cross, *The Metaphysics of the Incarnation*, 142–43.

9. Cross, *Duns Scotus*, 142–43. Moreover, Scotus brings up still another argument: any divine causal influence in creation stems from the whole Trinity, not from one of the Personae separately. See also Duns Scotus, *Ord.* III, d2. q1. §22, §32–33, §37. He refers to God's 'potentia ordinata'; hence, there is no analytic implication between incarnation and maximum fruition. Still, Scotus has to exclude the possibility of sin: 'Deus naturae unitae personaliter non potest de potentia ordinate non dare summam caritatem, et ulterius summam fruitionem, quae excludit peccatum.'

4.7: THE HIGHEST DEGREE OF GRACE AND FRUITION (*ORD.* III, D13)

Scotus's first question is whether a most perfect grace is bestowed on Christ. What does Scotus mean by 'the highest degree of grace' which is conferred to Christ (d13, §1, §11)? Especially for protestants, this notion of 'a highest degree of grace' perhaps produces confusion, because grace, for them, is not supposed to be a gradual property. 'For Luther, the grace of God is always something external to humanity, and an absolute, rather than a partial, quality. Humans are either totally under grace or totally under wrath.'[10] So first of all, what is grace? In the eyes of the schoolmen, grace is a supernaturally infused habit, a virtue. It is the 'spiritual beauty of the soul'[11] and as such identical with charity, caritas, love. Such a view of grace allows for gradation. Hence this first question 'whether on Christ's soul could have been conferred the highest degree of grace that could have been conferred on a creature.' Carefully heeding some logical pitfalls, Scotus proves that this is possible.[12]

He then continues with the 'de facto' question: whether this highest degree of grace was in fact bestowed on Christ's soul. Here, his reasoning is simple: just having proved that God could do so, it is therefore probable that He did so. And he disarmingly adds:

> I prefer, in commending Christ, to go to excess in praising him than to fail to praise him as is his due—supposing that, because of ignorance, one must fall into one or other extreme.[13]

Subsequently, Scotus affirms the fact of the highest enjoyment or 'fruition' of Christ's human nature as well.[14] This, however, presupposes the beatific vision, to which we now turn.

---

10. Alister E. McGrath, *Iustitia Dei: A History of the Christian Doctrine of Justification* (Cambridge: Cambridge University Press, 1989), 228.

11. Cross, *Duns Scotus*, 108.

12. Highest, 'summum,' can be taken in two ways: negative and positive. Namely, 'not exceeded by something else' or 'exceeding everything else.' But God could assume another soul and give it a similar grace (§28), so only taken in the negative sense is 'highest' applicable: *not exceeded by something else.*

13. *Ord.* III, d13, §53, translation here is Simpson's.

14. Here Scotus makes the distinction between enjoyment formally, so apart from its cause for instance, and the enjoyment in which the human will has an elicitive role. In the first formal mode, so merely as regards what enjoying essentially is, this highest possible enjoyment is possible; yet the second mode evokes a difficulty, because the will in angels is understood to be more perfect than the human will. Hence, if we take the will's elicitive role into account, how could Christ's will possibly have the *highest* enjoyment possible for a created nature? Still, so Scotus reasons, if the human will is assisted by the highest grace, the highest enjoyment is possible, because grace, as second cause, perfects the act of the first cause, the human will (d13, §80–81).

4.8: MOST PERFECT VISION AND SEEING OBJECTS IN THE WORD (*ORD.* III, D14)

Scotus maintains that Jesus has a most perfect vision of the Word, and even 'first and immediately' (primo et immediate), meaning without the requirement of any preceding, intermediate cause. An example of such an intermediate cause is, for instance, the fact that we, in order to see, need a prior natural light. So, parallelly, does Jesus's human intellect need a prior *supernatural* light to see the Word? No, because the Word itself is the perfect light (d14, §4, §26). A created object needs light due to its imperfection, but the 'divine essence is the highest light out of itself and it is intelligible in itself and in itself most perfectly inciting the intellects. Hence, no cooperative light is required' for the divine essence (§26). And likewise, a prior habit is not required (§27). In sum, the vision is in the soul 'through the Word immediately causing the vision' (§29).

That is to say, as far as a merely passive reception is concerned (§29); when an active, elicitive role of the intellect is intended, a graceful habit is required for the *perfection* of this eliciting role, although a habit is not required for merely eliciting a vision as such (§30).[15] Yet the thought of 'eliciting the vision' should not mislead us: the first cause of the vision is of course God. If God wants to benevolently reveal himself, He will be seen. 'If He wants to be seen, He is seen, if not, then not' (d14, §19, §29).

Yet there is more to this topic because the medieval philosophers were convinced that the beatific vision includes the vision of other objects 'relucent in the Word.' This is the subject of the second question of the fourteenth distinction where Scotus 'investigates whether it is possible that the intellect of Christ's soul sees in the Word everything that the Word sees' (§9, §40). Perhaps hard to get our heads around. But if there is a 'deiform glory'— Bonaventure—through which we become completely receptive for the Word, we are made receptive for all objects relucent in the Word as well, 'and this because the Word is an object manifest to it, and a willing mirror representing all things' (§76). Scotus's reasoning is thorough, engaging topics like the actual or habitual character of this knowledge and the question of whether the human intellect elicits it. He starts his argument again with the natural receptive character of the intellect:

---

15. Here I leave aside that Scotus points out that God, without a preceding habit, could still provide a vision in a perfect way, an elicitive role of the intellect included, namely 'de potentia absoluta.' For the relation between the preceding habit and the maximal vision is itself ordained by God and hence not necessary in itself (as being established by 'potentia ordinata'). And likewise with the relation between grace and fruition in distinction 13: it's an ordained relation. See Cross, *Duns Scotus*, 92–93.

Two Intellects 65

any intellect is receptive to knowledge of whatever object, because it is [receptive] to all of being, and hence it has a natural desire for whatever is intelligible. And if it were to know whatever entity, it would be naturally perfected in it. And just as I say this of knowledge, I say this of the vision in the Word, because that is the most perfect obtainable knowledge of objects. Any intellect is, therefore, receptive to whatever vision in the Word . . . (§59)

At the end of §59, Scotus states that seeing objects in the Word one by one must imply the possibility of seeing them *conjunctively* in a single moment as well.

Any intellect is, therefore, receptive to whatever vision in the Word, and saying this I mean one by one. Hence conjunctively also: any intellect is at a single moment receptive to many visions in the Word with respect to all objects. (§59)

Why this possibility of seeing them *conjunctively* in a single moment? Scotus brings up the hard kernel of *logical inconsistency* to bear on this claim:

For if two can be simultaneously in something because they do not contradict each other, then an infinity of those could be simultaneously in it too, because as regards an infinity there is no other ground for impossibility or incompossibilty than as regards two . . . (§60)

Hence, what restricts the amount of knowledge is not the limited capacity of the intellect, Scotus argues, but the demand for logical compossibility of the envisioned objects. I fail to see why this is compelling, for why would logical inconsistency of combined objects be the *only* limiting factor?

Scotus goes on to discuss several objections to this view of the possibility of simultaneous knowledge of an infinity of objects in the Word. These doubts concern, among others, the issue of the active, *elicitive character* of the human intellect (§71–72). This prompts him to elaborate on the Bonaventurian solution which only asserted the existence of *habitual* knowledge of all things relucent in the Word (§76). He thus tempers his earlier assertions of seeing an infinity of objects in the Word simultaneously (§78–79).[16] In all these elaborate reflections, Scotus prioritises the activity of the Word as the 'causa activa principalis' (§89) that shows everything willingly; meanwhile, he does seem to stick to the possibility of a secondary elicitive

---

16. Interpreted in a new way (§76), Bonaventure's solution ('opinio secunda') becomes more akin to his own however much doubted view (§58–75), which strongly prioritises the activity of the Word instead of the (habitual) activity of the soul. However, many questions remain for me as to the exact interpretation of §76.

66   *Chapter 4*

action of the intellect—again, each human intellect.[17] But he seems to definitely accept the limited capacity of seeing things one for one. Embroidering Avicenna's dictum that 'there is in the wisdom of the Creator no hiddenness save according to what can be received,'[18] he says:

> although the Word as willingly displaying all things is willingly present to this soul, it nevertheless cannot receive all at once, but rather whatever single entity one by one. Thus, it can see one thing after another as regards any of the numerically infinite things [the soul] turns itself to. (§79)

The view that the intellect retains an elicitive role is, it seems to me, perfectly congruous with the task of selecting all objects one by one out of the myriad of all the relucent objects in the Word: think of picking out relucent stars, one by one, from the starry heaven.

Let me try to cautiously summarize Scotus's view as regards the beatific vision of Christ, no doubt susceptible to improvement: (1) Christ has the beatific vision immediately, that is, without any intermediate factors. (2) The intellect's vision of the Word is due to the Word as a first cause that willingly presents itself to the soul's intellect which receives the vision due to its natural receptive character. (3) As part of that vision, the intellect sees everything relucent in the Word and is able, due to its eliciting role as a secondary cause, to pick out objects one by one to specifically gaze upon. (4) The elicitive activity in the soul, perfected by grace, perfects the vision. (5) Scotus firmly upholds that Christ's human knowledge of the divine Word is not comprehensive (§70). (6) Our beatific vision, though inferior to his (§80), will one day be comparable.

4.9: INTUITIVE VERSUS ABSTRACTIVE KNOWLEDGE

The prayerful life of the schoolmen was saturated with scripture. Hence, confronted with this blissful picture of Christ's human intellectual capacities, the question arose how this can be squared with Luke 2: 52: 'Jesus advanced in age and wisdom before God and men' (d14, q3, §91). If the knowledge of Christ borders on omniscience, this inevitably jeopardizes the scope for advancement. So where to find the leeway for advancement? Here, Scotus applies the distinction between abstractive and intuitive knowledge, the latter

---

17. He even defends (§85–88) that this elicitive action could be infinite, though only extensively infinite, not intensively. Extensive infinity is about quantity, intensive infinity comprises qualities as well.

18. Translation Simpson's.

Two Intellects 67

being a famous epistemological innovation of his.[19] The line of thought is that, despite his beatific vision, Jesus could advance in *intuitive* knowledge.

Intuitive knowledge is defined by Scotus as a special aspect of knowledge, namely knowing that the object actually exists.[20] Abstractive knowledge, whether of singulars or quiddities, does not take that aspect into account, yet intuitive knowledge is characterised exactly by conveying to us the knowledge of the existence—or nonexistence—of the object. This kind of knowledge comes in two forms, perfect and imperfect.

The perfect kind concerns present knowledge or experiences: I see my computer at this moment and know it exists. Another vital example of perfect intuitive knowledge is the experience of God's glory for the saints—as a matter of fact, this seems to have been the crucial reason for conceiving intuitive knowledge in the first place. As Vos argued: 'The theological point of this approach is that Christians do not expect the knowledge of the blessed to be of the *abstractive* type.'[21]

Next, the imperfect intuitive knowledge, which concerns the past and the future (§111). This kind of intuitive knowledge is especially at home in the theory of memory: we would not be able to know whether things from the past existed if there was no such thing as intuitive knowledge because abstract knowledge does not pick up that aspect, according to Scotus.

Scotus applies this intuitive knowledge to the present challenge concerning the advancement of Christ's human knowledge. He argues that intuitive knowledge, due to its very nature, is capable of successive growth, also in the case of Jesus. For this kind of knowledge is *eo ipso* connected with experiencing the *existence* of the known object. Scotus offers this example:

> Then, 'Peter's sitting down' would not be apt to be known unless Peter's sitting down were in itself now present. Thus, since many objects as regards their actual existence, neither were nor could have been present to Christ's intellect, it will not be able to have intuitive knowledge of them. (§112)

So because 'knowing that they exist now' or 'remembering that they existed back then' is an integral part of intuitive knowledge, it is possible to grow

---

19. A. Vos, *The Philosophy of John Duns Scotus* (Edinburgh: Edinburgh University Press, 2006), chap. 8; John Marenbon, *Later Medieval Philosophy (1150–1350): An Introduction* (London; New York: Routledge & K. Paul, 1987); Robert Pasnau, 'Cognition,' in *The Cambridge Companion to Duns Scotus*, ed. Thomas Williams, Cambridge Companions to Philosophy (Cambridge, UK; New York: Cambridge University Press, 2003), 285–311.

20. There is an intense scholarly debate on this topic, see Pasnau, 'Cognition,' 296–300.

21. Vos, *The Philosophy of John Duns Scotus*, 325; see also Julius R. Weinberg, *A Short History of Medieval Philosophy* (Princeton: Princeton University Press, 1964), 214: 'Aristotle has argued that all human cognition is derived in some way from the sensation of singular things of the physical world. The objects of human cognition, thus conceived, are the essences or quiddities of physical things. These are derived by abstraction from the data of sensation.'

68   *Chapter 4*

in knowledge because the events gradually come to pass. If events are not present, 'they are not apt to be intuitively known.' If they subsequently happen, then they acquire the 'aptness to be known intuitively.' Thus, Scotus hopes to reconcile two seemingly disparate epistemological goals: both a maximal infused knowledge of Christ's human mind and at the same time its *advancement*. Hence, as regards this intuitive knowledge, 'it is necessary to say that He advanced just like other souls, and in some way gets to know other objects' (§114).

Though I think that this view of intuitive knowledge is coherent[22] and even maybe epistemologically right on the mark seen from the perspective of, for instance, Reformed Epistemology,[23] an obvious objection could be that it is barely made clear why such an enlargement of intuitive knowledge also touches an advance in *wisdom*.

4.10: THE NEW TESTAMENT

We now turn briefly to the New Testament, for how does Scotus's view relate to the scriptural evidence? In the Gospels, we encounter a child growing in knowledge of his heavenly Father: 'all who heard him were amazed at his understanding and his answers' (Luke 2). And He becomes a man full of the Spirit, full of grace and wisdom, replete with a special awareness of unity with his heavenly Father and, John 5: 20, 'the Father loves the Son and shows him all that he himself is doing.' Yet He seems to explicitly avow that He is ignorant about certain facts: 'But concerning that day and hour no one knows, not even the angels of heaven, nor the Son, but the Father only' (Mt. 24: 36). This has always been one of the most perplexing texts, causing all church fathers to vainly wrestle with it. Scribes (for instance א[1], a corrector of the Codex Sinaiticus) even eliminated the words 'nor the Son' from the Greek text; church fathers, like Jerome, just denied it: 'by what reasoning can He who knows the whole be shewn to be ignorant of a part?'[24] A perhaps more convincing way could be to consider that 'Son' here is not intended in its Trinitarian, transcendental sense, but in its original Jewish sense (chap. 5.2). 'In these traditions divine sonship language was applied to the divinely chosen king, the devout, righteous individual . . . ; in these cases divine sonship

---

22. Pasnau is critical, see Pasnau, 'Cognition,' 296–300.

23. See, for instance, Nicholas Wolterstorff, *Thomas Reid and the Story of Epistemology*, first paperback edition, Modern European Philosophy (Cambridge: Cambridge University Press, 2004).

24. Thomas Aquinas, *Catena Aurea: Commentary on the Four Gospels, Collected out of the Works of the Fathers: St. Matthew*, ed. J. H. Newman, Vol. 1 (Oxford: John Henry Parker, 1841), 832.

Two Intellects 69

connoted *special favour and relationship with God.*'[25] Of course, in the New Testament, through Jesus's ministry, the term 'Son of God' is redefined, but its original layer is thereby not effaced. Maybe it is still palpable, especially in this passage? If so, the ignorance actually refers to Christ's human intellect. And Scotus's view of the priority of the revealing Word could be used to account for the ignorance, to wit, that God does not reveal *all* the facts relucent in the Word.

Does this imply that He even could have been mistaken? Well, some New Testament scholars argued that Jesus actually *was* mistaken. The most famous example is perhaps Albert Schweitzer commenting on Matthew 24: 34: 'I can promise you that some of the people of this generation will still be alive when all this happens.' Notably, it was Schweitzer who concluded that Jesus was wrong on this point. But Schweitzer presumed that Jesus was speaking about his second coming. It is, however, much more probable that Jesus spoke about a future Roman attack on the city. It is true that his words also evoke the awareness of a final coming, but the first hermeneutical stratum concerns the destruction of the city with its temple in 70 AD.[26] And surely, some of the people of that generation were still alive then.

As to the exact nature of his self-knowledge, Tom Wright stresses that Jesus believed that He was to enact and embody YHWH's return to Zion (see also chapter 8). Let me quote Wright more extensively:

> He would take upon himself the role of messianic shepherd, knowing that YHWH had claimed this role as his own. He would perform the saving task which YHWH had said he alone could achieve. He would do what no messenger, no angel, but only 'the arm of YHWH,' the presence of Israel's god, could accomplish. As part of his human vocation, grasped in faith, sustained in prayer, tested in confrontation, agonized over in further prayer and doubt, and implemented in action, he believed he had to do and be, for Israel and the world, that which according to scripture only YHWH himself could do and be.[27]

In this breathtaking passage, Wright focuses on Jesus's self-knowledge. He contends that Jesus did not know that He was God 'in the same way that one knows that one is male or female.' Nor did He know that He was, say, the second *Persona* of the Trinity. His self-knowledge was 'of a more risky, but perhaps more significant, sort: like knowing one is loved. One cannot prove

---

25. Think of 2 Sam. 7: 14, see Hurtado, *Lord Jesus Christ*, 22; see also N. T. Wright, 'Jesus' Self-Understanding,' in *The Incarnation: An Interdisciplinary Symposium on the Incarnation of the Son of God*, ed. Stephen T. Davis, Daniel Kendall, and Gerald O'Collins (Oxford; New York: Oxford University Press, 2002), 52–53.

26. For an extended defence of this, see N. T. Wright, *Jesus and the Victory of God*, Christian Origins and the Question of God 2 (London: Fortress Press, 1996), chaps. 10, 15.

27. Wright, 653; Wright, 'Jesus' Self-Understanding.'

70   *Chapter 4*

it except by living it.' In that sense, Jesus would *consciously* 'embody in him-self the returning and redeeming action of the covenant God.'

Wright thus proposes a more existential kind of knowledge—in our exis-tentialist era. However, I am not convinced. Why would 'knowing one is loved' exclude a more soaring, contemplative vision of true unity? A unity which we call, no doubt wanting in clarity, 'incarnation' and 'hypostatic union.' Would not He comprehend that union far clearer than we, given that 'the only one who truly knows the Father is the Son' (Mt. 11: 27)? Or are we led to believe that Jesus, at least on a propositional level, knew less than we, his disciples? Or that He needed the resurrection to arrive at certain insights, just as we needed it?

To further corroborate the medieval view that Jesus's knowledge was not exclusively existential, I want to bring up some further scriptural evi-dence. One could think of the surprising conversation about Abraham (John 8: 54–59):

> Jesus answered, "If I glorify myself, my glory is nothing. It is my Father who glorifies me, he of whom you say, 'He is our God,' though you do not know him. But I know him; if I would say that I do not know him, I would be a liar like you. But I do know him and I keep his word. Your ancestor Abraham rejoiced that he would see my day; he saw it and was glad." Then the Jews said to him, 'You are not yet fifty years old, and have you seen Abraham?' Jesus said to them, 'Very truly, I tell you, before Abraham was, I am.' So they picked up stones to throw at him, but Jesus hid himself and went out of the temple.

The pericope is so original and unique that it conveys a very authentic impression: here the 'ipsissima vox Dei' probably resonates.[28] Jesus says that He knows the Father—he would be a liar otherwise. And He seems to iden-tify himself with God by saying: 'before Abraham was, I am.' The suggested identification with the Lord is of course stressed in the Greek by the Lord's Name ἐγὼ εἰμί. And exactly these repeated hints of identification[29] are the reason why his listeners pick up stones. In this story, there is no suggestion of a strictly existential kind of self-knowledge. On the contrary, his words rather evoke a soaring intellect overflooded with divine insight: 'Very truly, I tell you, before Abraham was, I am.'

And there is also support for the medieval view of his seeing an infinity of objects relucent in the Word:

---

28. See J. R. Michaels, *The Gospel of John* (Grand Rapids, MI; Cambridge, UK: William B. Eerdmans Publishing Company, 2010), 537.

29. Bauckham, *Jesus and the God of Israel*, 18. He speaks of 'divine identity Christology.'

Two Intellects 71

Nathanael said to him, 'How do you know me?' Jesus answered him, 'Before Philip called you, when you were under the fig tree, I saw you.' (John 1: 48)

And who would not think of Jesus's supernatural knowledge in the story of the Samaritan woman:

You have said it well, 'I have no husband,' for you have had five husbands, and the one you have now is not your husband. What you have just said is true. (John 4:17)[30]

Another important text that pertains to our present topic is the story of the transfiguration on the mount (Mt. 17). Obviously, the transfiguration was not a surprise for Jesus, though it indubitably was for his disciples. Evidently, Jesus here momentarily discloses the rapture of his glory, but it is difficult to believe that He himself was not aware of it perpetually.

These are just a few examples of why I think that we should at least be very careful with depicting Jesus's self-knowledge as exclusively existential. The medieval tradition, as exemplified by for instance Duns Scotus, offers us a different hermeneutic lens, a thought-provoking reminder in our post-Kantian, existential era. Let me recall what Scotus said: 'I prefer, in commending Christ, to go to excess in praising him than to fail to praise him as is his due—supposing that, because of ignorance, one must fall into one or other extreme.'

4.11: CONCLUDING REMARKS

In conclusion, this medieval view enables us to account for a whole range of Gospel events like 'I saw you under the fig tree' which could otherwise easily be demythologised. On the other hand, it also seems to make room for a limitation of Christ's knowledge because (1) the beatific vision is an extra gift, not implied in the hypostatic union; (2) his knowledge is not comprehensive; (3) the initiative is on the part of God actively revealing himself in the Word; (4) the acquaintance with objects relucent in the Word is 'one by one.' This pliability of the Scotistic view perhaps promotes open-mindedness: the ability to contemplate scripture with a minimum of dogmatic bias, whether old or new. Surely knowing that, in the end, 'By love He may be gotten and holden, but by thought, never'—from the *Cloud of Unknowing*.

---

30. Michaels, *The Gospel of John*, 246.

Chapter 5

Two Wills

5.1: THE DIVINE AND THE HUMAN WILL IN CHRIST

Christ's soul has two fundamental operations: a human intellect and a will. I now continue with the will. Let's recall that the intellect and the will are actually one 'res,' one 'thing' (chap. 4.1). For Scotus, the *one* soul 'has two different ways of acting and two corresponding causal powers.'[1] Hence, the soul remains *one* capacity which rationally wills freely; free will is itself an intelligent capacity. He quotes Augustine in this respect: 'Hence, any free rational nature is in such a way the cause of an act of will, that free will encompasses these two potencies, namely the intellect and the will.'[2] And like I argued as regards the Trinity (chap. 1.7), it is distinctive for the intellect that it is a natural inclination, a 'one-way capacity,' while the will is a 'two-way capacity.'

According to conciliar Christology, there are two wills in Christ, one divine, one human. The Third Council of Constantinople said the following about that relation:

> We proclaim equally two natural volitions or wills in him and two natural principles of action which undergo no division, no change, no partition, no confusion, in accordance with the teaching of the holy fathers. And the two natural wills not in opposition, as the impious heretics said, far from it, but his human will following, and not resisting or struggling, rather in fact subject to his divine and all-powerful will.[3]

---

1. Scotus uses his 'distinctio formalis a parte rei'; see Cross, *Duns Scotus*, 83–84.

2. *Lect.* III, d17, §8–12. Idem *Lect.* II, d25, §78.

3. Timothy Pawl and Kevin Timpe, 'Freedom and the Incarnation,' *Philosophy Compass* 11, no. 11 (2016): 743–56, https://doi.org/10.1111/phc3.12362; Norman P. Tanner, ed., *Decrees of the Ecumenical Councils* (London: Washington, DC: Sheed & Ward; Georgetown University Press, 1990), 128.

74   *Chapter 5*

Hence, Christ's human will perfectly obeys and follows the divine will. And these obedient human acts are predicated of the Word, according to the Council: 'the natural will of his flesh is said to and does belong to the Word of God.' But how can we speak of a human and a divine will in just one ultimate *Persona*, the Word? In chapter 3, I endorsed and further expounded the Patristic approach of qua-propositions. Exploiting this strategy, we say that Christ wills x by virtue of his divine nature and He obediently wills x too by virtue of his human nature. And this latter way, willing x with his human will, is *predicated* of the Word. In chapter 3, I further clarified this kind of predication as 'stepped characterisation.'

5.2: CAUSAL AND PREDICATIVE ASPECTS OF AGENCY

Cross elucidated this topic along Scotistic lines: 'we need to make a distinction between what we might call the *causal* and the *predicative* aspects of agency.' Jesus's human acts can be *predicated* of the Word, but they *causally* depend on the will of the human nature.[4] This distinction between the *causal* and the *predicative* aspects of Christ's agency is crucial. Scotus calls the predicative aspects 'denominative':

> And when they say that the Word performed the activities of the [human] nature, I say that this is true, just as the Word is called 'man.' For due to the assumed nature, everything that pertains to that nature is said of the Word (just as white and black or a quantity). However, the Word does not have a special eliciting role as regards the act of willing, that is, not more than the Father or the Holy Spirit has. Hence, the Word does not elicit an act of willing of the created will of Christ in an increased or more special way than if the nature were not assumed. But because it subsists in that nature, it is said *denominatively* that it elicits the act and wants that act. (*Lect.* III, d17, §15)[5]

So the human acts are only caused by the Word to the extent that they are caused by the Word in unison with the other Personae, because the works of the Triune God 'ad extra' are undivided (chap. 1.9). Put differently, the Word has no special *causal* role as regards the human deeds, distinct from the shared, undivided action of the Trinity. Yet the Word does have a special role as regards predication: the human acts are '*denominatively*' predicated of the Word by virtue of stepped characterisation. Hence, the human nature elicits

---

4. Cross, *The Metaphysics of the Incarnation*, 219.

5. Cross cites Scotus, *RP* III. 17. 1–2, n. 4: 'How therefore is the Word said to will? I say that, just as the Son of God is coloured, so He is said to will because his soul is said to will, and because the nature subsists in the Word, the Word is therefore denominated in this way.' See Cross, *The Metaphysics of the Incarnation*, 222.

Two Wills 75

its actions through its own intrinsic causal powers, although it is continuously sustained by the creative action of the Triune God, just like anyone of us.[6] This safeguards proper human freedom for Christ: even when the human nature is hypostatically joined to the Word, the scope for its freedom does not essentially alter, just as Chalcedon requires: 'two natures without confusion, without change.'

We are now in a position to once more ponder the metaphor of the interior monologue (chap. 4.4). In the high priestly prayer, Jesus addresses his Father: 'Father, the hour has come; glorify your Son so that the Son may glorify you' (John 17). Here we are perhaps led to believe that there is a certain kind of Trinitarian dialogue, a dialogue between the two Personae; an interpretation bolstering social trinitarianism. Yet exegetically, the term 'the Son' is ambiguous—aggravated by the lack of capitalisation in the original Greek. 'The Son' could mean a transcendental proto-Trinitarian sonship, but in the original Jewish context it denoted a divinely chosen human messiah-king (chap. 4.10). In this latter instance, 'Father' refers not to the first Persona, but to 'God the Father,' to Adonai, יהוה. This pervasive New Testament semantic duality can be elucidated by the distinction between the causal and denominative aspects of agency. Firstly, the priestly prayer is a dialogue between God and the assumed human nature because the act of praying depends *causally* on the human nature. Yet secondly, that prayer of the assumed human nature is at the same time denominatively ascribed to the Word: the priestly prayer is still God's *own* prayer! As I said, his 'interior monologue' (chap. 4.4). For all the acts of the human nature *characterise* the Son, the Word. Therefore, causally seen, the individual human nature prays, denominatively seen, the Son in the proto-Trinitarian sense prays. Hence, the two analytic aspects of agency neatly fit the semantic ambiguity I just mentioned: 'Son' as a proto-Trinitarian term or 'son' as the divinely chosen messiah-king. These two aspects must be distinguished. Yet we should not *conflate* them by somehow imagining that the Son *does* or *causes* the praying (again, except that the Son or Word shares in God's Triune activity that grounds the human existence and acts). This conflation leads to social trinitarianism (see chap. 1.3 for reasons that led me to reject social trinitarianism) and could also tend to supplant the acts of the human nature, for instance as regards providing satisfaction. In the analysis of the atonement, I will return to this insight that the human nature is causally active whereas its acts characterise the Word (chap. 7.3).

In sum: although the acts of the human nature depend causally on the human nature, they still can be predicated of the Word, by stepped characterisation. Hence, the divine Word, by virtue of the human nature, washed Peter's

---

6. There is no *ontological* independence in creation: everything is created from moment to moment, just like the moments themselves.

76   *Chapter 5*

feet. That is, *denominatively* spoken. Causally spoken though, the human will of the Messiah chooses to wash Peter's feet and herein perfectly obeys the 'divine and all-powerful will' of God the Father.

5.3: THE FREEDOM OF THE HUMAN WILL

Before turning to Jesus's free will, I outline a general view of human freedom. The philosophical literature on this subject being immense, I try to limit myself to the minimum responsible degree. In what follows, I assume a Scotistic free will approach, without extensively arguing for it.[7]

According to Scotus, the human free will encompasses two basic powers: a natural inclination and freedom, the 'voluntas naturalis' and the 'voluntas libera.'[8] Each of these is a partial cause of an act of the will. Through the natural inclination, we seek whatever perfects our nature. This sense is reflected in the Latin 'velle': to want, wish, or desire something. Anselm refers to this inclination towards self-perfection or self-actualization as an 'affection for the advantageous,' the 'affectio commodi.'[9] According to Scotus, such a natural inclination is a 'one-way capacity.'[10] If it acts, it always acts: 'semper uniformiter agens,' always causing uniformly (*Lect.* II, d25, §74).

The other aspect of the will is the 'voluntas libera': alongside the existing natural inclination, the will is also free. We are, according to Scotus, 'dominus actuum suorum,' master of our own acts. This is about being in control over our own choices, for the will is a self-determining power. Hence, although the 'voluntas naturalis' motivates the will as a partial cause, it cannot fully determine its movement. Scotus sees the 'voluntas libera' as a 'two-way capacity,' in contradistinction to the natural inclinations proper to the intellect and the 'voluntas naturalis': it can will or not will.[11] Here is how Scotus describes the relationship between the 'voluntas libera' and the 'voluntas naturalis':

> Thus, it becomes clear in which way the will is free. It can be said of me that I 'freely see' because I can freely use my visual capacity of seeing. Likewise in the present issue: however much a cause is natural and always causes uniformly (as long as it is up to her), it nevertheless neither determines nor necessitates the will. Instead, the will, by virtue of its freedom, can concur with the [natural cause] in order to will or not will; it thus can freely use [the natural cause].

---

7. See therefore, for example, Labooy, 'Antwoord aan Jeroen de Ridder en René van Woudenberg,' 557–80.

8. *Lect.* III, d17, §8–9. Cross, *Duns Scotus*, 83–89.

9. Allan Bernard Wolter and William A. Frank, trans., *Duns Scotus on the Will and Morality* (Washington, D.C.: Catholic University of America Press, 1997), 39.

10. Wolter and Frank, 139.

11. *Lect.* II, d25, §73–74.

Therefore, it is said that it is in our power to freely will or not will. (*Lect.* II, d25, §74)

Hence, just like we can decide to use or not to use our visual capacity—we can decide to close our eyes for instance—we can freely decide to use our natural inclinations, the 'voluntas naturalis.' Because of this, Scotus understands the 'voluntas libera' as the principal cause and the 'voluntas naturalis' as the secondary cause of these two partial causes (§73).

Scotus uses this distinction between the 'voluntas libera' and the 'voluntas naturalis' to grossly map out the vast philosophical terrain as regards human freedom. He presents his own solution as a midway between two opposite poles, that of Thomas Aquinas and that of Henry of Ghent. He rejects Thomas's view in which, according to Scotus, the will as an intelligent capacity is determined by its natural 'one-way' intellective inclination. Here, perfectly knowing the object determines the act. He equally declines the opposite view of Henry in which the will, the 'voluntas libera,' truncates the role of the intellective inclination towards the object. For in causing the act, the object merely functions as 'removing the impediment to will' or as a 'necessary condition for acting.' And that 'would make the will blind' (§78). Let me illustrate this: imagine a blind man wanting to touch the face of his beloved. Her face being present is a necessary condition for that act. However, his will is not *attracted by the beauty* of her face. Likewise, according to Henry, the will is not attracted by the object, the latter merely serving as a necessary condition for acting.[12] Within this landscape, it seems reasonable to depict Scotus's view of the human mind as a via media: not merely light, nor merely blind will, but enlightened free willing.

The tension between the 'voluntas libera' and the 'voluntas naturalis' also characterises the divide in the contemporary philosophical debate, that is, the rift between a *libertarian* and a *compatibilist* analysis of freedom. For those less familiar with the terminology: compatibilism is the view that genuine human freedom is compatible with determinism being true. Present-day libertarianism sees the 'voluntas libera' as the principal cause of an act, present-day neurobiological compatibilism asserts that the 'voluntas libera' is an illusion; according to them, the 'voluntas naturalis' determines the human act completely and 'free will' is merely the *experience* of acting spontaneously.

---

12. *Lect.* II, d25, resp. §22–27; §54–68; a summary in §69, see also §78. For Aquinas compare Kevin Timpe, *Free Will in Philosophical Theology*, Bloomsbury Studies in Philosophy of Religion (New York; London: Bloomsbury Academic, 2014), 91.

78   *Chapter 5*

Until now, one could perhaps get the impression that the human free will is entitled to assign a moral value to whatever it might choose.[13] Yet alongside the just described 'voluntas libera,' Scotus, following Anselm, distinguished another aspect of liberty, namely 'a liberty that frees us from the need to seek self-perfection as our primary goal or as a supreme value.' It 'consists in free will's congenital inclination towards the good in accord with its intrinsic worth or value rather than in terms of how it may perfect self or nature.'[14] Anselm called this the affection for *justice*. Hence, the affection for the *advantageous* is directed to the prospering of the self—also in its affection for God—the affection for *justice* is directed to the highest good for its own sake. By pursuing the latter, we will find true freedom.[15] For as Augustine said: 'You have made us for yourself, O Lord, and our heart is restless until it rests in you.' I will return to this subject in relation to merit (chap. 7.2).

5.4: DIVINE WILL AND FREEDOM OF THE WAYFARER

What is the general relationship between the divine and the human will? In the second book of the *Lectura* (d34-37), Scotus examines the fallen human will in its relation to the divine will. Let me start there. There are, he argues, two basic alternatives: a human act is either *mediately* or *immediately* caused by the divine will. In the former case, a human act is primarily caused by the human will, while God causes that act only in so far as He, as the Creator, sustains the existence of that human will.[16] For Scotus, this mediate approach is attractive to the extent that it straightforwardly solves the problem of evil: when the divine will only sustains the existence of the human will, evil is not caused by God but by the human will. Here, the contours of the contemporary Free Will-Defence (FWD), as propagated by for instance Alvin Plantinga, are easily recognizable.[17] Yet Scotus raises several objections: firstly, because he holds that God knows the future due to the fact that He knows what He is going to do, it now seems that divine omniscience is in jeopardy because God cannot have foreknowledge of human acts which are not in his power (*Lect.* II, d34-37, §129). Secondly, this seems to threaten his almightiness (§130).

---

13. Hoeres describes the (sinful) possibility of the will releasing itself from its intellectual grid 'womit der Wille dann zu einer Fähigkeit leeren Zielentwerfens überhaupt wird.' Hoeres, *Der Wille als reine Vollkommenheit nach Duns Scotus*, 121.

14. Wolter and Frank, *Duns Scotus on the Will and Morality*, 39–40.

15. Timpe, *Free Will in Philosophical Theology*, chap. 2.

16. *Lect.* III, d34-37, §119, p. 356.

17. Plantinga, *The Nature of Necessity*.

Two Wills 79

Scotus, therefore, examines the second route, the view that God sustains the human act in a much more encompassing way, yet without becoming the immediate cause of sin (§134–135). So again, the FWD is not in peril (§120). Principally, the difference with the former solution is that now the divine will, far from merely sustaining the existence of the human will, causes the human act to be righteous through the gift of grace—as we saw, a virtue (chap. 4.7). But does not that result in making God the auctor of sin, because this seems to entail that God causes human beings to sin by withholding this necessary gift of grace (§139-§144)?

Scotus's answer basically consists of the claim that when two (essentially ordered[18]) causes operate together, the superior cause does not need to usurp the causal activity of the second less perfect cause (*Lect.* II, d34-37, §147–154). Both causes are needed, without the superior cause preempting the operation of the inferior one. Put differently: God's cooperative grace is necessary but not sufficient for a righteous human act.[19] For God grants righteousness in the act, if the other cause, the human will, acts in the way it ought to, 'si voluntas recte coageret,' 'if the human will would co-act righteously.' Scotus expresses this also by using the distinction between the divine *preceding* will and the divine *consequent* will. With his preceding will ('voluntate antecedente'), God would provide all necessary circumstances and natural and spiritual gifts needed for acting graciously. Scotus offers the comparison of a king, who provides everything indispensable for the peaceful life of his subjects. Yet the human will is not totally determined by this divine preceding will. Some subjects could refuse to use these gifts. Now the divine consequent will comes in: it is what God *in fact* realises. For if the human will refuses to co-act righteously, this is integrated into the divine consequent will, Scotus argues. So 'whatever God gives with his preceding will, He will give also by his consequent will, unless something (in the human will) is causing an impediment.'[20] For our purposes, we have sufficiently explored the relationship between the divine will and that of the wayfarer. I now turn to the special case of the incarnation.

---

18. Causes are essentially ordered if the enduring operation of the first cause is needed for the second to act, like an arm and a hammer. Accidentally ordered causes can operate without the continued operation of the primary cause, like the relation between father and son (*Lect.* II, d34-37, §126).

19. With Timpe, I adhere to the second variant of Non-Determining Grace (NG2); Timpe, *Free Will in Philosophical Theology*, chap. 4.

20. Compare Timpe, quoting Stump: 'Suppose that God offers to every person the grace that produces the will of faith, but that it is open to a person to refuse that grace.' Timpe, 58; for additional modal subtleties, see Cross, *Duns Scotus*, chap. 7.

5.5: FREEDOM OF THE HUMAN WILL OF CHRIST

Conciliar Christology demands that Christ's will is the same as ours as regards its essential properties. Consequently, it must have the essential properties described in the preceding paragraph: that the superior cause does not preempt the operation of the inferior one, the human free will. Hence, an instrumental view of Christ's human will is problematic, given conciliar Christology (chap. 2.11). Think of God using Jesus's human will just as a person uses an axe: along this view, God's will does preempt the human will. For He uses the human will to perform human acts 'in much the same way as the action of an axe chopping a piece of wood just *is* the action of the person wielding the axe.'[21] Scotus, however, argues for a normal degree of leeway for the assumed will. To solidify this view, he appeals to the maxim 'opera ad extra individa sunt' (chap. 1.9, 2.11). This passage, even clearer than the former one (previous *Lect.* III, d17, §15), brings home the idea:

> The Word does not have a kind of causality as regards the nature united with itself that the other Personae lack, only its being the end-term [of the dependence of the human nature][22] is different. Therefore, all actions in Christ which are elicited by the natural potency of Christ are elicited equally by the three 'Personae.' Hence, the created, human will of Christ is not more deprived through the fact that the Word somehow elicits than through the fact that the Father and the Holy Spirit elicit. And, consequently, the union to the Word does not more deprive the will of its created freedom as regards eliciting its own acts than my will or yours. (*Lect.* III, d17, §13)

In other words, being assumed in itself does not affect the scope of freedom for the human will, at least not as regards its essential properties. Yet some topics seem difficult to match with this doctrine of Christ's human freedom, like his foreknowledge, his inability to sin and the perpetuity of his blessed state. To these three partly overlapping difficulties we now turn. First, Christ's foreknowledge, to which the Councils adhere.

---

21. There are several philosophers, ancient and modern, who support an instrumental view of the human will in Christ, for example, in a way, Thomas Aquinas, according to Cross, *The Metaphysics of the Incarnation*, 122–23; and Brian Leftow, 'The Humanity of God,' 20–44. Although I adhere to his basic view of a compositional Christology (definition 8), I am critical of his use of instrumentality; see especially 36: there he asserts that 'Double' is a model for the relation between GS and B+S. This violates the Chalcedonian demand that the human nature must be unaltered.

22. As we said earlier, because the Word is the end-term of the dependence relation of the human nature, the human acts can be predicated of the Word by stepped characterisation.

5.6: CHRIST'S FREEDOM VIS-À-VIS HIS FOREKNOWLEDGE

In his 'The Freedom of Christ and the Problem of Deliberation,' Pawl delves into this dilemma of Christ's foreknowledge. For how can one be genuinely free if one infallibly sees in the Word what one is going to do in the future? Is it possible to 'deliberate' in a robust enough sense, if you already know what your action will be, because the human intellect sees these facts lighting up in the Word? And if you cannot deliberate about a future action, then one 'lacks one sort of freedom vital for human flourishing.' However, those affirming Conciliar Christology also want to uphold the freedom of Christ's human will. How to avoid this unwelcome result? Pawl construes the Problem of Deliberation with these three key premises:

I. [CPD] Certainty Precludes Deliberation
    For any human agent, S, any action, A, and any future time, t: if S is certain that she will not do A at t, then S cannot include A as a deliberative option for what to do at t.
II. [DRO] Deliberation Requires Options
    For any human agent, S, any action, A, and any future time, t: if S does not believe that S has two or more deliberative options for what to do at t, then S cannot deliberate about what to do at t.
III. [FRD] Freedom Requires Deliberation
    For any human agent, S, any action, A, and any future time, t: if S cannot deliberate about what to do at t, then S lacks one sort of freedom vital for human flourishing at t.

If these premises are valid, they entail that someone endowed with foreknowledge is hampered in his freedom, because foreknowledge excludes deliberative options. Pawl discusses several ways to ward off this outcome. Though casting some doubt on premiss I, he eventually favours refuting premiss III, that Freedom Requires Deliberation. Because:

> Figuring out what course of action to pursue—that is, deliberating—is important for those who are unsure about what to do in some circumstances. And since all of us mere humans are unsure about what to do with some regularity while on earth, deliberating is important to us. But it isn't important to us qua having a human nature. It is important to us qua ignorant of the true good.[23]

---

23. Timothy Pawl, 'The Freedom of Christ and the Problem of Deliberation,' *International Journal for Philosophy of Religion* 75, no. 3 (June 2014): 245, https://doi.org/10.1007/s11153-014-9447-4.

82 *Chapter 5*

Christ, however, so Pawl continues, 'unlike mere humans, need not deliberate as a means to discovering the course of action to pursue.' I agree with this refutation of premiss III. Deliberation is clearly not a perfection. However, I want to undercut premiss I as well, by exploring the overlap between the Problem of Deliberation and the more general problem of the concordance of divine foreknowledge and future contingents. For if we assume that Christ indeed did not deliberate, one could nonetheless object that his freedom is eliminated by his foreknowledge. For He, by seeing all future facts relucent in the Word, infallibly knows what He will do in future situations. This looks like a Christological apparition of the perennial problem of the concordance of human freedom and infallible divine foreknowledge.

The solution I propose hinges on the Scotistic modal theory of synchronic contingency. I first need to add some technical terminology. I already argued that human freedom implies a capacity to choose between alternatives, in modern terms: the 'principle of alternative possibilities' (PAP). This principle, often perceived as the hallmark of libertarianism, needs refinement. I add a modal insight, without arguing for it extensively here.[24] Usually, PAP is analysed *diachronically*. The alternative possibilities, then, hold for succeeding moments: if John does p at t,[1] PAP demands that he is able to perform $-p$ at a *future* moment t.[2] According to Scotus, however, this leads to determinism because it implies that for each moment t^x there is only one possibility on the ontological level. The alternative possibility only holds for a *succeeding* moment, a moment that is itself, again, the only ontological possibility of that moment. Scotus famously revolutionised modal logic[25] by pointing out that contingency is only real if it is interpreted *synchronically*: p is contingent if:

p at t^1 and possible that $-p$ at t^1.

This modal insight is also required for PAP: an alternative possibility for action is real only if it is a *synchronic* alternative possibility. I now apply this modal insight.

God knows all contingent facts of the past and future, and He knows them in their synchronic contingent character as well. For if He did not know that p was contingent, He would not be omniscient. Hence, as regards contingent facts, He knows that *p at t^1 and possible that $-p$ at t^1*. Yet the fact that God even necessarily knows this—for God cannot be ignorant of anything—does

---

24. See further G. H. Labooy, 'Freedom and Neurobiology, a Scotistic Account,' *Zygon* 39, no. 4 (2004): 919–32; G. H. Labooy, *Freedom and Dispositions: Two Main Concepts in Theology and Biological Psychiatry: A Systematic Analysis*, Contributions to Philosophical Theology, Vol. 8 (Frankfurt am Main; New York: Peter Lang, 2002).

25. John Duns Scotus, *Contingency and Freedom: Lectura I 39*, ed. A. Vos, The New Synthese Historical Library, Vol. 42 (Dordrecht; Boston: Kluwer Academic Publishers, 1994).

Two Wills

83

not bestow necessity on contingent facts. If other facts would have been the case, God would have necessarily known those different facts as having been actually the case. Thus, God's epistemological relation with contingent facts of both past and future is clarified by distinguishing these two propositions:

a. Necessarily (God knows that p then p)
b. God necessarily knows that p therefore necessarily p

Decisive is that (a) does not entail (b). Only (a) is a true account of God's epistemological relation with created reality. At stake here is the medieval distinction between the necessity of the implication (a) and the necessity of what is implicated (b). So God's necessary knowledge of future contingents does not confer necessity to these future contingents.[26] He knows them necessarily, but if some other future fact would have been realised, then God would have necessarily known that fact.

Returning to Christology: according to the schoolmen, Jesus, by seeing everything in the Word, has foreknowledge. And among the innumerable contingent future facts, He there sees also his own future acts, like 'running the moneychangers out at t1.' Now Pawl reasoned that, given this foreknowledge:

> then Christ was certain at t0 that he would do nothing but run the moneychangers out at t1. Due to that certainty, he was unable to consider any other actions as deliberative options for action at t1.[27]

So the Certainty of cleansing the temple Precludes other Deliberative options! (CPD, premiss I). According to the aforementioned modal analysis, however, his certain foreknowledge does not preclude the contingency of him casting the moneychangers out at t1. So if He is not going to do that at t1, then Christ would have foreseen that in the Word at t0. For Christ foresees his own contingent future acts because the divine foreknowledge, accessible for him in the Word, *integrates* his free future choices, like for instance the cleansing of the temple. But that certain foreknowledge does *not* exclude future synchronic deliberative options (as CPD claims). Because Jesus, at t0, foresees a contingent fact as caused by his human choice at t1. But that fact at t1 is one among many other synchronic options. Hence, the requirement that Deliberation Requires Options (premiss II) is satisfied and CPD (premiss I) is not valid.

---

26. See also E. Dekker, *Middle Knowledge*, Studies in Philosophical Theology 20 (Leuven: Peeters, 2000); James K. Beilby, Paul R. Eddy, and Gregory A. Boyd, eds., *Divine Foreknowledge: Four Views* (Downers Grove, IL: InterVarsity Press, 2001).

27. Pawl, 'The Freedom of Christ and the Problem of Deliberation,' 242.

84   *Chapter 5*

Along this modal analysis, moreover, it is no longer evident why those future free choices could not be the result of prior deliberation. I do not argue that Jesus deliberated along his human knowledge; maybe He did not because deliberation is not a perfection. But I am just testing the validity of the premisses. I conclude that premiss I is invalid, just as premiss III (with Paul); premiss II is valid and, moreover, satisfied in this case of Jesus's foreknowledge.

5.7: COULD CHRIST'S HUMAN NATURE SIN?

In medieval thought, the canonical view was that Christ not only did not sin but also could not sin: the 'impeccabilitas Christi.' Scotus provides a summary of Anselm's proof: 'if such a nature would not necessarily enjoy the beatific vision (frui), then it could sin, and thus God would be said to sin.'[28] We moderns, however, are inclined to ask: What was the point of the temptation in the desert, if Jesus could not sin? Does not this turn the story into a sham? It is easy to be tempted like that![29] In total, modern sensibilities, parallel to modern estimations of his limited knowledge (chap. 4.5), tend to suggest that the 'impeccabilitas' makes the gulf between Jesus and us too broad. Yet the schoolmen were by no means impervious to this kind of critique. Scotus puts it like this: Does not the inability to sin somehow remove the ability to merit?[30]

With these reservations in mind, we turn to Scotus's view of Christ's impeccability. As said before (chap. 4.6), he maintains that the union with the Word did not necessarily imply the gift of maximal grace. And only that gift bestows impeccability. Hence, not taking that additional gift of grace into account, the assumed nature in itself could sin. It is only thanks to the gift of maximal grace that Jesus is impeccable.[31]

Secondly, being blessed and thus impeccable does not remove free will. In the next paragraph, we will elaborate on the exact kind of freedom of the blessed. But for this moment, Scotus upholds both the freedom of Christ and his impeccability. He enjoys infallible yet free love.

---

28. *Ord.* III, d2, §4.

29. See Richard Swinburne, 'The Coherence of the Chalcedonian Definition of the Incarnation,' in *The Metaphysics of the Incarnation*, ed. Anna Marmodoro and Jonathan Hill (Oxford: Oxford University Press, 2011), 163. In what follows, Swinburne makes a very interesting distinction between being tempted to do a wrong act and being tempted not to do a supererogatory act. However, I remain doubtful: for in this special case, it was the will of the Father that Jesus performed a supererogatory act. And then this valuable distinction is no longer helpful in this particular case, for then not doing the required act is wrong. In other words: the kernel is human obedience.

30. *Lect.* III, d18. §2–3.

31. *Ord.* III, d12, §13. *Lect.* III, d12, §7–11.

Two Wills 85

Thirdly, concerning merit: Scotus seems to admit that impeccability would affect one's capability of acquiring merit. For he states that it is due to divine dispensation that impeccability squares with the potency to merit.[32] This seems like using the voluntaristic 'magic wand,' but I think it must be interpreted in the light of Scotus's view of merit: as we will see in due course (chap. 7.2), the 'root of all merit' consists in the affection for justice of the will, especially if it compels one to endure a situation 'contrary to the affection for the advantageous' (*Lect.* III, d18). Hence, the impeccable saints in heaven are unable to merit because of 'lack' of adversity. Only once, by special divine dispensation, a blessed, impeccable person was nevertheless a wayfarer capable of 'enduring a situation contrary to the affection for the advantageous.' So I suggest that what is meant by 'due to divine dispensation' is in fact the incarnation and the subsequent story of the Gospel. Scotus's recourse to a special dispensation is not the easy-going panacea of voluntarism.

Given this kind of layered impeccability, what about the objection of the temptation in the desert? Modernity is very sensitive to the demand that Jesus must be psychologically similar to us: we tend to imagine that it is vital for the authenticity of our redemption that He struggled with a seducible psychological makeup just like we, save that He did not trespass. And exactly this victorious struggle with his own seducible state is supposed to restore merit. However, did Jesus struggle with his own sin or with ours? Quoting Scotus: 'He was not grieved by his own sin, because He had not any, but by those of others.'[33] The human ability to sin becomes a sin the moment we are experiencing seduction, regardless of whether we give in to the temptation or not. Like Scotus says: we sin if we want to sin.[34] Perhaps we may say that, structurally prior to the moment of making a choice, Christ's intellect cannot present a sinful volition as a *viable* option nor as an *attractive* one, but only as what it is, a sinful and therefore *repugnant* option. Consequently, our intuition that really meritoriously not-sinning demands a seducible psyche sooner reflects our own sinful state than a credible Christological maxim. Impeccability implies inseducability. Not that the Son of God did not struggle. On the contrary, his last week was even full of agony. But in his fear and agony, caused by all the hatred and excruciating torture, He bore the pain of our sins, not of his.[35]

---

32. *Ord.* III, d12, §8: hoc (the impeccabilitas) *dispensative* staret potestas merendi. It is God's special dispensation in order to redeem mankind. See also *Lect.* III, d18, referred to in the chapter on atonement.

33. *Ord.* III, d15, §77.

34. *Lect.* III, d12, §15: 'immo peccat, si vult peccare.'

35. Compare *Ord.* III, d15: 'De dolere et tristitia in anima Christi.'

86   *Chapter 5*

This is also bolstered by exegesis: nowhere in the story of the temptation in the desert are we told that He struggled with the devil. We only hear that He was *very hungry* (Mt. 4). The *devil* wanted to struggle with him, this seducer, but it came to Jesus from without, not from within. 'The delight of sin never gnawed His soul, and therefore all that temptation of the Devil was without not within Him.'[36] He, the new and decisive embodiment of much-tempted Israel, prevailed just because He did not need to struggle with his *own* seducible state. Being perfectly fulfilled with grace, Jesus just answered: "Go away Satan! The Scriptures say: 'Worship the Lord your God and serve only him'" (Mt. 4).

5.8: INFALLIBLE LOVE OF THE BLESSED— INTRINSICALLY PERPETUATED

Having scratched the topic maybe a dozen times, we now deal with the difficulty of the freedom of the blessed head-on. This bears on Christology, because Jesus was maximally blessed, as the schoolmen contended. Scotus deals with this dilemma in the *Ordinatio* (IV, d49). When explaining the perpetuity of the love of the blessed, he distinguishes four views. Rejecting the first three, he acknowledges only the fourth:

> I say, therefore, that the cause of this perpetuity is neither a formal property of beatitude, as if thereby the beatitude be formally necessary; nor is its cause the nature of these powers, as if its operation were necessarily perpetual towards the object; nor is it a habit in the powers, necessarily determining the powers to operate perpetually; instead, its cause is solely the divine will, which in such manner intensively perfects such a nature, that it conserves it in such perpetual perfection. (*Ord.* IV, d49, §348)

To put it succinctly, these are the four examined causes of the perpetuity of beatitude:

A. perpetuity is a formal, necessary aspect of beatitude
B. perpetuity is necessarily caused by essential powers in the soul
C. perpetuity is necessarily caused by accidental powers (habits) in the soul
D. the divine will perfects the nature so that it conserves it in perpetual perfection

In this section, we concentrate on the first three rejected alternatives, all characterised by an *intrinsic* cause of perpetuity, intrinsic, that is, intrinsic to the

---

36. Gergory I, Catena Aurea.

Two Wills

soul. The first view draws a comparison with the heavens which in Greek philosophy were said to be formally incorruptible: in a similar vein, it is argued that beatitude is incorruptible too (§321–325). Scotus discards this claim in one fell swoop: 'except God, nothing has formally necessary existence, only contingent existence' (§331). The next view (B) is defended by, for example, Thomas: 'ex voluntate necessario fruente objecto viso.' So the angelic doctor ascertains that beatitude is out of itself essentially perpetual because, causally, the will is necessarily directed towards the ultimate goal if only that goal is clearly seen and therefore perfectly enjoyed.[37] Scotus declines this view because 'necessarily enjoying' is contrary to the essence of the will. For as I just showed, the will is a 'voluntas libera' (§341). Next, (C) is refuted on the ground that the basic potency of the free will uses the habit, not the other way around (§344). Hence, the same objection against (B), namely the freedom of the will, can be levelled against (C).

Recently, Kevin Timpe offered a sophisticated example of (C), calling it 'perfected freedom.' It is an account in terms of virtue libertarianism. Put briefly, Timpe argues that, due to freely received revivifying grace, human beings are finally brought to a state of perfect freedom in which they are no longer able to perform malicious acts. This inability does not preclude freedom while freedom is defined in terms of *reasons-constraint* on free choice.

Reasons-constraint on free choice: If at time *t*, A has neither any motivational intellectual reasons for X-ing nor any motivational affective reasons for X-ing, then A is incapable, at *t*, of freely choosing to X.[38]

Hence, intellectual and affective reasons, shaped by our virtues, constrain the field of available actions—mark the huge difference with the view of Henry of Ghent discussed earlier, who eliminated the motivational impact of reasons. And these perfected virtues are, in their turn, shaped by grace and our assent to it.[39] They together make it impossible to sin. Timpe calls this 'accidental impossibility'; it is an accidental property for wayfarers. And he specifies this accidental impossibility as *psychological* impossibility.[40] By psychological impossibility, 'I mean something of the following form: it is impossible that, given all the psychological facts about person A at time *t*, A freely chooses to do action X at *t*.' And this impossibility of sinning 'should

---

37. Thomas: 'beatitudinem essentialiter esse per se et ex se perpetuam, et formaliter necessariam; causaliter vero a voluntate, quae necessitatur ad finem ultimum clare visum.' See also Scotus, *Ord.* IV, d49, p370.

38. Timpe, *Free Will in Philosophical Theology*, 23 (elaborating on the work of Van Inwagen).

39. Or, as Timpe puts that aspect of 'assent' precisely: 'the conjunction of God's grace and the individual's refraining from resisting will be jointly sufficient for the individual's coming to saving faith.' Timpe, 64.

40. Timpe, 74–75.

88   *Chapter 5*

be understood in a strong sense: necessarily, given her lack of reasons for X-ing, A will not freely choose X.' So if A is endowed with psychological impossibility to sin:

It is impossible, given A's moral character at t, for A to choose freely X at t.[41]

Now the key question is whether this psychological impossibility is still driven by free will, or is the will, in this perfect state, somehow transformed into a 'one-way' appetite? Scotus would probably argue that this view implies that the ability to freely *use* the natural causes is subverted due to the renewed moral character. As I see it, that is not what Timpe is arguing, for he declines straightforward causal determination: for 'it is possible to have free will even if one's character entails that certain options that are causally open to you are ones for which you see no good reason, and thus are not capable of choosing.'[42] However, arguably, saying that X is 'causally open' but at the same time 'not capable of being chosen' could contain a covert contradiction. This could perhaps be clarified still further.[43]

5.9: INFALLIBLE LOVE OF THE BLESSED— EXTRINSICALLY PERPETUATED

Over against these intrinsic powers, Scotus argued that the cause of perpetuity is 'solely the divine will, which in such manner intensively perfects such a nature, that it conserves it in such perpetual perfection' (§348). Expounding this fourth view (D), Scotus exploits the distinction between, on the one hand, the soul's proximate, intrinsic cause and, on the other hand, a remote extrinsic cause, that is, the divine will. Asking in what sense archangel Michael is impeccable, Scotus commences:

[This]can be understood in two senses: either by something intrinsic to him which excludes such a power, or, secondly, by an extrinsic cause, which bans a proximate power of him. For example, if one has vision, one would have an

---

41. Timpe, 75.

42. Timpe, 75. The context is damned freedom here, but for present purposes that doesn't make any difference.

43. In a former study, following Dekker and Veldhuis, I used a distinction between formal and material freedom to further analyse this. This distinction hinges on the distinction between volitions and the capacity to effectuate a volition. Formal freedom is the ability, essential to humans, synchronically to will or not to will or to will the opposite of a certain state of affairs p, regardless of whether p (or –p) can be effectuated. And material freedom is the property, accidental to humans, that they can effectuate a certain state of affairs p. By applying this distinction, we can further clarify what it means to be 'causally open' while at the same time 'not capable of being chosen.' We propose: it is materially impossible to choose, yet formally open. See Labooy, *Freedom and Dispositions*, 185.

intrinsic potency of seeing whatever corporeal object, but still, due to some extrinsic cause, sight could be made perpetually impossible for the proximate power, for instance when that [remote] potency causes a perpetual visual distance towards that corporeal object, just like when there is a perpetual obstacle between the empyreal heaven and the eye of the damned. That eye could not see the empyreal heaven, speaking of the proximate power, and this due to an extrinsic cause perpetually hindering the [proximate] potency. (§350)

The example is clear: in this case of the damned, there is not any *intrinsic* cause for their inability to see the heavens. Their proximate vision is not obstructed. Similarly, apart from the fact that the remote cause blocks it, Michael is still able to sin. Therefore, his freedom is not in jeopardy, according to Scotus. However, is not this jumping out of the frying pan into the fire? Because still, the essential freedom of the will is blocked, albeit not by an intrinsic but by an extrinsic force (§357–59, §366). To ward off this objection of determinism, the *doctor subtilis* invokes the idea that human freedom is *qualitate qua* restricted. For it is related to a specific domain, an appropriate level. True, the will is called to be the 'master of its own acts,' but this pertains only to its own realm, 'in suo ordine.'[44] What belongs to our dominion? Think of controlling your body, freely using your neurobiological brain states to that end, loving your neighbour, and obeying the laws of your country. If these acts were hampered by factors which ought to be controlled by the will, that would entail that the will is no longer free. However, when a superior cause determines the will, its freedom is not at stake, because being able to influence a will of a higher order is simply not 'in suo ordine.' Hence, it is not against the nature of the will that it is determined by a superior cause such as the divine will (§360).[45] So the beatified human will is as regards itself still capable of sinning. Nevertheless, a blessed person

is not able with proximate possibility to sin, because proximate possibility is impeded or prevented (not suspended) on account of the action of a superior cause preventing him and continually acting for the opposite, namely for the beatific act. (§365[46])

And then (§367) this same point is made while contrasting it with (C): there the will is not impeded by the divine will but by a power 'in suo ordine,'

---

44. Douglas C. Langston, 'Did Scotus Embrace Anselm's Notion of Freedom?,' *Medieval Philosophy and Theology* 5 (1996): 145–59.

45. Non est autem contra natura eius determinari a causa superiore, quia cum hoc stat quod sit causa in suo ordine. §361.

46. Translation Simpson's; I leave the theme of absolute versus ordained power out of consideration here.

90 *Chapter 5*

namely, a habit. And that, according to Scotus, would make the will unfree because the 'free will uses the habit, not the other way around.'[47]

Confronted with this extrinsic view, Peter Simpson understandably alludes to the famous 'Frankfurt-style counterexamples' in the modern philosophy of mind.[48] Is God to be equated with the nefarious neurosurgeon staged in those thought experiments? This hypothetical neurosurgeon manipulates your brain states each time you are about to vote for the presidential candidate he dislikes, and if you want to vote for the one he prefers, he does not interfere. Scotus would probably answer that the power to vote is and for ever should be in your own control, 'in suo ordine.' Therefore, there is a decisive difference with the case at hand, which is not 'in suo ordine.'

Hence, (D) is characterised by the impeding extrinsic divine influence, as opposed to the priority of the human will in (B) and (C). There, the will, through its own power, though induced by grace, perpetually and infallibly directs itself towards the divine object. For reasons given, Scotus rejects that (see also §274). He locates the cause of the perpetual enjoyment in the presence of the object. The perpetuity of the enjoyment

> is due to the object and the presence of it, yet not out of whatever eliciting potency [in the human will].[49] (§304, first part)

Yet Scotus adds that the habit must still exert its proper role because any enjoyment which lacks charity remains suboptimal. So while not establishing the perpetuity of the enjoyment, the habit in the soul still *embellishes* it:

> For it would have more [enjoyment] if there was charity, through which in some way the act is intensified < >. (§304, final part)

So (C) is partly rehabilitated, though it bears less weight now. It is no longer the cause of beatitude, nor of its perpetuity. Yet it does make the enjoyment more beautiful. But (B) cannot be vindicated likewise because it does not square with freedom, according to Scotus. The parallelism with the former topic of the beatific vision is striking: the same priority of the receptiveness of the soul, the same secondary role of the powers of the soul as embellishing or eliciting.

I would hesitantly summarise that we retain not one but two promising ways forward as regards this perpetuity problem, namely (C) and (D)—provided that (C) can be clarified consistently and, as regards (D), provided that

---

47. The issue of the laudability of the blessed runs parallel: because the freedom of the will is not impeded in its own order, all its actions remain laudable (§369).

48. See the note in his translation of §351.

49. My understanding.

Two Wills 91

one accepts the conceptual tool of freedom 'in suo ordine.' Incidentally, this last distinction made its way into Reformed scholasticism.[50] This distinction could perhaps also be used to repair an instrumentality view of the incarnation (see chap. 2.11). Finally, what is an adequate account of the freedom of the blessed in heaven is one for Christ as well: I see no additional caveats if applicated to our Lord and Saviour.

5.10: INITIATIVE OF THE HUMAN WILL IN CHRIST

I am drawing this discussion to a close. One final topic: initiative and creativeness. The Council of Constantinople seems to say that Christ has no initiative. For the two natural wills are not in opposition:

> but his human will following, and not resisting or struggling, rather in fact subject to his divine and all-powerful will. For the will of the flesh had to be moved, and yet to be subjected to the divine will, according to the most wise Athanasius.[51]

Hence, does not this exclude all initiatives of the human will? Following Timpe, I would argue that Jesus has initiative. He cannot sin, but He can choose between different good options. For example, choosing to go for a walk or choosing to eat a pomegranate instead of grapes. Because in ordinary circumstances all these actions are good, He surely is not 'resisting or struggling.' On the contrary, his human will is 'rather in fact subject to his divine and all-powerful will.' Therefore, we argue that the Council's doxological genre leaves ample room for this level of freedom. The pure goodness in these acts stems from grace, their specific targets though might be due to human initiative, followed by God's consequent will. Christ's human will obeys the divine will in every respect and in each act; He purely honours the Father in everything, but that does not exclude freedom in the sense now under consideration.[52] He may even use deliberation on this level—though not, I think, on the level of good versus bad. He thus may honour the Father, also in his initiative and his human creativity. As a corollary of this: on the new heaven and earth, there could be art. But art truly reborn, that is, glorifying the supreme Artisan.

---

50. W. J. van Asselt, J. M. Bac, and D. te Velde, *Reformed Thought on Freedom: The Concept of Free Choice in Early Modern Reformed Theology*, Texts and Studies in Reformation and Post-Reformation Thought (Grand Rapids, MI: Baker Academic, 2010).

51. Pawl and Timpe, 'Freedom and the Incarnation,' 746.

52. As regards Plantinga's objection as to morally significant freedom, we concur with Timpe; see Timpe, *Free Will in Philosophical Theology*, 92–94.

Chapter 6

Supralapsarian Christology

6.1: THE PREDESTINATION OF CHRIST TO HIGHEST GLORY

The present chapter addresses the view that the incarnation is not contingent upon the fall.[1] Even if Adam did not sin, the Word would have assumed a human nature. Boldly stated: a world without fall is not one without Christmas. Yet Scotus does not prioritise this 'if Adam did not sin' or 'counterfactual' approach; for his is a clear-headed view of our own tangible reality wherein God appropriately chooses the highest ends first.[2] And that is because God's will is rightly ordered: first things first, ends before means. And, as stated before, prior to anything else, He wants others to share in his glory. He therefore ordains the predestination of Christ to the highest glory (chap. 1.10). Hence, Christ's predestination to the highest glory is chosen *explanatory prior*[3] to the fall; this is called a 'supralapsarian' (prior to the fall) cause of the incarnation. In this divine scenario, the primary reason for

---

1. van Driel, 'God and God's Beloved,' 995–1006; Justus Hamilton Hunter, *If Adam Had Not Sinned: The Reason for the Incarnation from Anselm to Scotus* (Washington, DC: The Catholic University of America Press, 2020); Schumacher, *Early Franciscan Theology*; Edwin Chr. van Driel, *Incarnation Anyway: Arguments for Supralapsarian Christology* (Oxford; New York: Oxford University Press, 2008); Nico den Bok and G. H. Labooy, eds., *Wat God bewoog mens te worden: gedachten over de incarnatie* (Zoetermeer: Boekencentrum, 2003); Henri Veldhuis, 'Zur hermeneutischen Bedeutung der supralapsarischen Christologie des Johannes Duns Scotus,' in *Menschwerdung Gottes—Hoffnung des Menschen*, ed. Herbert Schneider, Veröffentlichungen der Johannes-Duns-Skotus-Akademie für Franziskanische Geistesgeschichte und Spiritualität Mönchengladbach 12 (Kevelaer: Butzon und Bercker, 2000), 81–110; Dominic Unger, 'Franciscan Christology: Absolute and Universal Primacy of Christ,' *Franciscan Studies* 2 (1942): 428–75.

2. Veldhuis, 'Zur hermeneutischen Bedeutung der supralapsarischen Christologie des Johannes Duns Scotus,' 96–98; van Driel, *Incarnation Anyway*, 164–65.

3. Note that the sense of 'prior' presently at issue concerns the priority or posteriority of *aims* within, so to speak, the one 'now' of God's eternity. It is not about temporal priority. I will speak of an aim being chosen 'structurally prior' or 'explanatory prior' than the means to that aim.

94   *Chapter 6*

the assumption of the human nature is no longer the need for redemption because of Adam's fall. If, conversely, the fall and the need for redemption are explanatory prior to the incarnation, we speak of an 'infralapsarian' Christology. In that case, the redemption is the aim and incarnation the means. But Scotus argues that it is 'most absurd' to hold that sin was the cause of the highest grace that God bestows upon the human nature in Christ (*Ord.* III, d7, q3, §66). Is sin really that fecund? In this chapter, I will briefly describe some key points from the history of the supralapsarian debate before Scotus; next, against that background, Scotus's innovative version of it; and, finally, some hermeneutical implications.

6.2: PLATONISM TRANSFORMED

Firstly, I will briefly consider an influential philosophical forebear of supralapsarianism.[4] This will prove conducive to a deeper understanding of Scotus's landmark position in this debate. Like I said, prior to anything else, God wants others to share in his glory. A comparable motive propelled ancient philosophy: the classical Greek thought of the 'plenitude of being.'[5] According to the platonic tradition, the Absolute or highest principle must *necessarily* produce lower categories of being. For how can the highest being, which is at once the highest good, be envious and keep being only to itself? Hence, 'the good is diffusive of its being,' according to Dionysius. Therefore, it is absolutely impossible that lower ontological possibilities remain unexemplified: the highest principle must necessarily emanate in the material cosmic order and every genuine possibility must be exemplified. This 'plenitude of being' was called the '*Great Chain of Being*,' the 'scala naturae.'

A comparable yet radically transformed motive of the 'diffusion of the good' is operative in Scotus's supralapsarianism and the related Trinitarian thought. Social trinitarianism, as I argued, locates the demand for generosity on the *essential* Trinitarian realm. The divine love must be shared with persons *within* the Godhead. Duns Scotus, I maintained, honours the motive of the generosity of love but situates it on the level of the *economic* Trinity (chap. 1.10). God wants *created beings* to share in his glory, and that constitutes the primary reason for the incarnation. Thus, the ancient necessitarian motive of the principle of plenitude is fully personified: God *freely* chooses to share his love with contingent creatures. In Greek thought the language of 'being good' and 'not being envious' remained metaphorical in the end due to the absence of a truly personal view of the divine; with the schoolmen,

---

4. Here I am indebted to the eminent contribution of Bok, 'Eén ding is noodzakelijk,' 225–81.
5. See how the principle of plenitude is still active in, for example, Scotus *Lect.* III, d20, n40.

'not being envious' is no longer just a metaphor. As a corollary, necessary emanation turns into creation, just as participating at a lower level in divine being turns into created beings participating in the love for God. In this chapter, I will show how these two comprehensive paradigms grind against each other like tectonic plates, until Scotus's approach brings more clarity. Incidentally, the ancient Greek model is much alive in certain strands of modern Trinitarian theology.[6]

6.3: A GLIMPSE OF THE THIRTEENTH-CENTURY SUPRALAPSARIAN DEBATE

In *If Adam Had Not Sinned: The Reason for the Incarnation from Anselm to Scotus*, Justus Hunter focusses on the thirteenth-century supralapsarian debates with special consideration for logic and the modal status of the deductions. This makes his contribution especially valuable for this brief historical survey. Hunter describes how Anselm's *Cur Deus homo* was very influential in the thirteenth century. Not that Anselm addresses the counter-factual question 'what if Adam did not sin'; rather, his influence must be sought in his 'method for reasoning about divine operations *ad extra* in *Cur Deus Homo.*'[7] There, Anselm set out to deductively prove that the incarnation is necessary in order to redeem fallen humanity—the infralapsarian view. For according to Anselm, God, being true to his own nature, is *obliged* to act in the most perfect way *ad extra*.[8] Thus, Anselm's allegedly deductive arguments radically restrict the scope for divine freedom in dealing with created reality. In the following chapter on atonement, we will see how Scotus opposes exactly this necessitarian strand in Anselm's thought. But this Anselmian modal tendency set the stage for the thirteenth-century debates. Hunter distinguishes three moments in these disputes, in which the first moment emulates the Anselmian modal pattern in which God is *obliged* to act:

> In the first moment—represented by Robert Grosseteste, Alexander of Hales, and the *Summa Halensis*—theologians supplied deductive arguments for the conclusion that the Son would become incarnate in any possible world.[9]

I will give some examples. Grosseteste provided a few dozen arguments in which Hunter distinguished two main categories: the *divine attributes*

---

6. 'A God along the lines of a Platonic or Hegelian Absolute is no uncommon phenomenon in present-day theology.' Maarten Wisse, *Trinitarian Theology beyond Participation: Augustine's De Trinitate and Contemporary Theology* (London; New York: Bloomsbury T. & T. Clark, 2013), 40.

7. Hunter, *If Adam Had Not Sinned*, xvi.

8. Hunter, chap. 2.

9. Hunter, xiv–xv, see also 214–20.

96 *Chapter 6*

strategy and the *created effects strategy*.[10] Along the divine attributes strategy it is reasoned that for instance the perfect goodness of God secures that the incarnation must be actualised in all possible worlds, 'lest God would be less than supremely good.'[11] Or, arguing from the divine attribute of generosity, Grosseteste revitalises the *principle of plenitude*: 'God is supremely generous, and therefore supremely lacking in envy.' Hence, He 'creates every kind of creature that can exist.'[12] But, according to Grosseteste, we see that God actualised even the most insignificant of possible things, such as insects or reptiles. Therefore, 'If (God) does not omit the nature of the insect lest creation be imperfect and less beautiful, would He omit Christ, the greatest beauty of the universe?'[13] Other arguments from the principle of plenitude are inspired by the Trinity: there is a being with three Personae and one substance, namely God; accordingly, there must be an entity with one Persona and three substances, namely Christ, spanning the divine substance and two human substances, soul and body.[14]

Into the second category fall all kinds of arguments where God assumes the human nature on behalf of the perfection, unity, or fullness of the universe and its creatures. Thus, Grosseteste argues that the interior and exterior senses of humanity each have their own distinct objects, which, in beatitude, bring about the perfection of those senses. Now if the human nature was not assumed, only the interior sense would be beatified in the contemplation of God. The existence of the God-man, also in worlds without fall, is therefore a necessary condition for the complete fulfilment of our exterior sense: in beatitude, we will contemplate the Son with our own *bodily* eyes as well.[15] Or on behalf of the unity of the universe it is argued that the human being alone is 'the obvious creature with which the Son would become united for the sake of uniting himself to every particular being.'[16] And therefore He was not made an angel, because an angel does not straddle both spirit and matter. Instead, God became man, for 'all natures are united in the human.'[17]

In sum, narrowing the leeway for God's acts, Anselm deductively argued for the infralapsarian cause. I illustrated how Grosseteste followed suit: fighting Anselm with his own weapons, he deductively argued for the supralapsarian cause. It evoked this critical reaction:

---

10. Hunter, chap. 3; compare also Schumacher, *Early Franciscan Theology*, 234–41.

11. Hunter, *If Adam Had Not Sinned*, 82.

12. Hunter, 83; see also van Driel, 'God and God's Beloved,' 996.

13. Hunter, *If Adam Had Not Sinned*, 83–84.

14. Schumacher, *Early Franciscan Theology*, 235–36.

15. Hunter, *If Adam Had Not Sinned*, 94–95.

16. Schumacher, *Early Franciscan Theology*, 234; Adams, *Christ and Horrors*, 178–81.

17. Schumacher, *Early Franciscan Theology*, 231–37. No wonder that 'Aquinas and Bonaventure worried that if God becomes Incarnate to perfect the universe, then Christ would be seen as a means to that end.' Adams, *Christ and Horrors*, 179–80.

Supralapsarian Christology

> Theologians of the second moment—represented by Guerric of Saint-Quentin, Odo Rigaldi, and Albert the Great—rejected the deductive arguments of the first moment in order to secure God's freedom over creation.[18]

Guerric's main argument is the transcendence of God; for his power is not bound to anything. It simply 'cannot be the case that God is required to become incarnate for the sake of the beauty or completion of the universe. Otherwise, as Guerric puts it, the Creator would be in servitude to the creature.'[19] Key in this development is a more confident application of the distinction between divine capacity and will. 'There must be some distinction between what God *can do* and what God *does*. Power, or capacity, exceeds volition.'[20] Next came a 'summative' phase in the debate, according to Hunter:

> Theologians of the third moment—such as Thomas Aquinas and Bonaventure of Bagnoregio—likewise preserve divine freedom, but also appropriate the arguments of the first moment as arguments from congruity or fittingness (*convenientia*). These third-moment theologians effectively resolve the set of questions raised in the first two moments. John Duns Scotus's reflections on the motive for the incarnation, which shift from these modal debates to an analysis of the order of divine intentions, marks a new moment in the history of considering the motive for the incarnation.[21]

Following Hunter,[22] this summative third moment can thus be summarised: firstly, no necessary reasons for the incarnation can be given; secondly, the hypothetical question whether God would have assumed the human nature if Adam did not sin is therefore generically insoluble; thirdly, reasons from divine attributes are congruous or fitting, not deductive. Hence, all in all, the debate led to a stalemate: the refutation of the deductive character of the arguments resulted in agnosticism as regards supralapsarianism. In this phase of the debate, Scotus breaks fresh ground.[23]

---

18. Hunter, *If Adam Had Not Sinned*, xiv–xv, see also 214–20.

19. Hunter, 120–22.

20. Courtenay, cited by Hunter, 119.

21. Hunter, xiv–xv, see also 214–22.

22. This rendering is for several reasons not comprehensive; especially the primacy question returns in the following paragraph. Hunter, 220–22.

23. For the further fate of supralapsarianism after the thirteenth century, see Edwin Chr. van Driel, "'Too Lowly to Reach God Without a Mediator': John Calvin's Supralapsarian Eschatological Narrative," *Modern Theology* 33, no. 2 (April 2017): 275–92; Trent Pomplun, 'The Immaculate World: Predestination and Passibility in Contemporary Scotism,' *Modern Theology* 30, no. 4 (October 2014): 525–51, https://doi.org/10.1111/moth.12115; van Driel, *Incarnation Anyway*.

98 *Chapter 6*

6.4: SCOTUS'S RATIONALE OF SUPRALAPSARIANISM

Scotus must have agreed with Bonaventura that Grosseteste's aspiration of amassing deductive proofs was doomed to failure. While addressing the dilemma of the communication of properties though, he launches a new approach (*Ord.* III, d7). One of the questions of this distinction was whether 'Christ was predestined to be the Son of God' (*Ord.* III, d7, q3, §55). Traditionally, the positive answer was derived from Romans 1: 3–4: 'He was made of the seed of David, who was predestined to be Son of God in power.' From there, Scotus expounds the supralapsarian thesis (§58, out of which I select the key steps):

- Predestination is the preordination of someone before all else to glory; and then to all that is required for that glory[24]
- Christ's human nature is predestined to supreme glory
- The incarnation is fitting to the end of bestowing supreme glory to his human nature and is therefore included in the predestination of his human nature to supreme glory
- Such glory wouldn't be fittingly conferred to his human nature if it weren't united to the Word

Here, Scotus invokes God's perfect and therefore *well-ordered* willing. God acts 'ordinate volens' along what is 'primum in intentione' because 'universally, well-ordered willing first intends what is nearer to the end' (§61). Cross summarised this in these two interconnected axioms:

a. in any well-ordered action, the end is willed before the means.
b. in any well-ordered action, a greater good is willed before a lesser one.[25]

These two axioms are at work in §58: the preordination of Christ to supreme glory, to the beatific vision, is willed explanatory first. In the next structural moment, all that is required for that end is willed. Perhaps to our surprise, the incarnation is classified as a fitting means too: the incarnation is instrumental to foreordaining Christ's human nature to supreme glory. I will return to this in due time.

The difference with the first necessitarian moment of the debate becomes apparent: whereas Scotus starts from God's free act of predestination, the first moment of the debate attempted to deductively prove the supralapsarian

---

24. Hence, the concept 'predestinatio' can also be translated with 'election' because reprobation is not a kind of predestination. Veldhuis, 'Zur hermeneutischen Bedeutung der supralapsarischen Christologie des Johannes Duns Scotus,' 86.

25. Cross, *Duns Scotus*, 128.

Supralapsarian Christology

view: 'If the highest good did not diffuse itself in creatures, one could think of a greater diffusion than that of God.'[26] However, the greater the desire for compelling reasons, the higher the level of necessity imposed on the divine acts. Scotus, on the other hand, starts from divine free will: the highest Lover *chooses* to share His love for himself with others. This motive is also voiced in the *Reportatio Parisiensis*:

> I argue in this way: First, God loves himself; in the second place, He loves himself for others, and this is pure love; in the third place, He wants to be loved by another who can love him to the highest degree, inasmuch as that is possible to a being outside himself; and finally, He foresees the [hypostatic] union of that nature which ought to love him to the highest degree even if man had not fallen.

Here, Scotus again distinguishes according to explanatory priority: first the end, then the means. And he adds a new and perhaps unexpected aspect of God's love, one in between the love for himself and the love for himself through the assumed human nature in Christ: 'He loves himself for others' ('diligit se aliis'). From all eternity, God not only loves himself, but He also opens this self-love for others. Perhaps we could call this primordial divine *hospitality*. From eternity, His love is internal, but not in a secluded, private manner. Love itself is indeed 'diffusive' because He intends it as hospitable: 'He loves himself for others.' This is reflected in this second structural instant: He opens the door of the heavenly tabernacle, so to speak. In the next structural instant, this openness is consummated: a human person—not a human persona—'outside himself,' who can love him to the highest degree, is elected.[27] He, therefore, foreordains the hypostatic union. Then, in the next moment, others are elected to join in His love. It is like three concentric circles: God's love for himself, a love already open to others; then He loves himself in and through an assumed human nature 'outside himself'; and, thirdly, a mighty 'heavenly court' of human and angelic co-lovers participating in this glory.

In a 'dubium' in the *Ordinatio* (III, d7), Scotus then engages the authorities to the contrary: 'many authorities seem to declare that the Son of God would never have been incarnate if man did not fall.' Hence, does this predestination necessarily require the fall of the human nature (§60)? Scotus refutes this with the axiom of 'ordinate volens.' Firstly, he argues that the supreme glory of Christ must be willed explanatory first as compared to the glory of his brothers and sisters:

---

26. Schumacher, *Early Franciscan Theology*, chap. 10.

27. In §59 Scotus answers the objection whether predestination has not always the persona as its object instead of an (individual) human nature (a person in the modern sense). See also van Driel, 'God and God's Beloved'; see also my objection to van Driel's view in chap. 2.6, note 28.

100 *Chapter 6*

- Therefore, among those to whom He has foreordained glory, it is well-ordered to first intend glory for the one He wants to be nearest to the end, and therefore to Christ's soul. (§61)

But then, it follows:

- It seems that God not just for the redemption predestined that soul [Christ's] to such glory, because that redemption, that is, the glory of a soul to be redeemed, is not as great a good as this glory of the soul of Christ. (§63)
- Nor is it likely that such a maximal good among beings is only occasioned because of a lesser good. (§64)
- Nor is it likely that He would preordain Adam to so great a good before Christ, which nevertheless would follow. (§65)

And as a final argument he pointedly concludes that the infralapsarian view would give us reason to rejoice in the fall of another (§67). And thus, we may conclude that holding 'that God wills the Incarnation for our redemption alone is tantamount to arguing that God wills the means before the end. It is tantamount to arguing that God does not will in an orderly fashion.'[28]

In sum, new ground is broken as Scotus starts from a single, scripturally attested, *benevolent election* of God: 'Christ was predestined to be the Son of God.' Next, predestination is defined as the preordination of someone before all else to glory; and then to all that is required for that glory. From here, it follows that the redemption cannot be the primary reason for the incarnation, because that would imply that God 'does not will in an orderly fashion.'

6.5: FURTHER DISCUSSION

On the background, the aforementioned conflicting philosophical paradigms are at work: on the one hand Neoplatonism, asserting that the highest principle *cannot* enviously keep being for itself. On the other hand, faith-seeking-understanding, upholding that God cannot in any way *be obliged* by his creatures—as stressed by the second and third moment of the debate and by Scotus. Everything He does *ad extra* is a free gift, free grace, *sola gratia*. The former paradigm ultimately leads back to a kind of necessary Neoplatonic emanation, the latter emphases divine will and freedom. Grosseteste was caught between these two 'tectonic plates' in trying to argue that God, due to his goodness, simply *cannot* withhold the incarnation. This

---

28. Pomplun, 'The Immaculate World,' 533.

Supralapsarian Christology

allegedly deductive reasoning was unmasked by the theologians of the second and third moment. Divine freedom was thus safeguarded, although it came at the cost of agnosticism as regards supralapsarianism. Scotus, however, no longer based the argument for supralapsarianism on the old Anselmian and Grossetestean modal strategies. Instead, he reasons from God's free and benevolent choice to share his love with others, amplified by the axiom of well-ordered, again, *willing*. The refutation of the infralapsarian view is based on this landmark principle of well-ordered action, not on deductive reasoning curbing God's actions.

Scotus's focus on the predestination to glory seems to further debar latent Stoic and Middle Platonist tendencies concerning ontological mediation. In Grosseteste's work and the *Summa* figure all kinds of considerations concerning Christ as an *ontological* mediator. Clearly, that would constitute a supralapsarian cause for the Incarnation. For example, the incarnate Son is the 'archetype' of all creation. 'He is at the centre of everything because the basis for every being comes from him.'[29] Though the precise ontological implications are difficult to pin down, rudiments of the *Great Chain of Being* are in the air. The thought of some kind of ontological mediation is biblical as well. In Colossians 1: 15–17 it is said of Christ:

> He is the image of the invisible God, the firstborn of all creation; for in him all things in heaven and on earth were created, things visible and invisible, whether thrones or dominions or rulers or powers—all things have been created through him and for him. He himself is before all things, and in him all things hold together.[30]

This terminology of 'in him, through him and for him,' named 'prepositional metaphysics,' conveys a certain Middle Platonist[31] ambiance. Yet Scotus passes over a text as Colossians 1: 13–20. Is it perhaps because he is not in favour of these 'prepositional metaphysics' with the air of ontological mediation?[32] It is tempting to connect this with Scotus's view that predestination to the highest glory is explanatory prior to the hypostatic union. Let me repeat:

---

29. Schumacher, *Early Franciscan Theology*, 228–29; Adams, *Christ and Horrors*, chap. 7.

30. By the seventeenth century, standard Scotist prooftexts for Christ's primacy were Proverbs 8: 22–23, Colossians 1: 13–20, Ephesians 1: 3–10; for the priority of His predestination Romans 8: 29–30; 1 Corinthians 3: 22–23. Pomplun, 'The Immaculate World.'

31. Geurt Henk van Kooten, 'The Pauline Debate on the Cosmos: Graeco-Roman Cosmology and Jewish Eschatology in Paul and in the Pseudo-Pauline Letters to the Colossians and the Ephesians' (Doctoral Thesis, Leiden, 2001), 314–15.

32. Habets claims that Scotus does mention Col. 1, but he provides no evidence; Myk Habets, 'On Getting First Things First: Assessing Claims for the Primacy of Christ,' *New Blackfriars* 90, no. 1027 (May 2009): 351, https://doi.org/10.1111/j.1741-2005.2008.00240.x.

102   *Chapter 6*

- The incarnation is fitting to that end of bestowing supreme glory to his human nature and is therefore included in the predestination of Christ to supreme glory. (§58)

To put it briefly, the hypostatic union serves the category of love.[33] Firstly, this 'explanatory priority of predestination over incarnation' reminds us of Scotus's vision of theology as a *practical* science: its end is to love God (chap. 1.1). The dissemination of supreme glory is the end, the incarnation the means. And then, returning to the present subject of ontological mediation: this explanatory priority of 'agapy' further discourages the Neoplatonist tendencies of ontological mediation; this 'Scala Naturae' as a cascade of being of which the highest, comprising all else, is the incarnation.[34] Not that the beauty of 'prepositional metaphysics' of Colossians is dispensed with: true, 'all things have been created through him and for him.' But this is stripped of the last remains of a Neoplatonic grid. Neoplatonic and Aristotelian ontological undercurrents are dismantled: instead of the hierarchy of substantial being and the Greek parallelly of being and thought, the sharing of love prevails.[35]

6.6: HERMENEUTICAL IMPLICATIONS

This ultimate end of sharing love pervades the hermeneutical ramifications of Scotus's supralapsarian Christology. Though Scotus was undoubtedly sceptical as regards the demonstrative force of the Grossetestean arguments in favour of supralapsarianism, once the truth of supralapsarianism was newly established, these arguments, now taken as 'fitting' reasons, got a new life. Think of the thought that, in beatitude, we will contemplate the Son with our own *bodily* eyes as well.

The late Dutch Scotus-scholar Henri Veldhuis devoted much attention to this theme; it made him epitomize systematic theology as 'caritas quaerens

---

33. Trent Pomplun remarks as regards this passage and §69: 'Indeed, it very much looks as though Scotus argues that God wills the hypostatic union not as an end in itself, but indeed as a means to the end of glorifying souls. The Scotist tradition, however, generally interprets this passage in light of texts that appear to say otherwise . . .' Pomplun, 'The Immaculate World,' 532.

34. I am critical of the negative portrayal of Scotus by Radical Orthodoxy. Regrettably, their depiction of Scotus is not adequate. See Richard Cross, 'Where Angels Fear to Tread: Duns Scotus and Radical Orthodoxy,' *Antonianum* Annus LXXVI, no. 1 (January–March 2001): 7–41; Thomas Williams, 'The Doctrine of Univocity Is True and Salutary,' *Modern Theology* 4, no. 21 (2005): 575–85; Daniel P. Horan, *Postmodernity and Univocity: A Critical Account of Radical Orthodoxy and John Duns Scotus* (Minneapolis: Fortress Press, 2014).

35. See Ludger Honnefelder, *Ens inquantum ens: der Begriff des Seienden als solchen als Gegenstand der Metaphysik nach der Lehre des Johannes Duns Scotus*, Beiträge zur Geschichte der Philosophie und Theologie des Mittelalters, n. F., Bd. 16 (Münster: Aschendorff, 1979); Vos, *The Philosophy of John Duns Scotus*.

Supralapsarian Christology

intellectum.'[36] One of the essential anthropological and spiritual consequences is that God's condescending love is primarily motivated by itself, not by the need to repair debt, sin, and destruction. Veldhuis: 'God does not need sin in order to love us through his human eyes.'[37] Divine love does not need our misery as a precondition for its supreme flourishing. Compare it to marriage: you do not love the other because the other is in need of help. True, when the other is in need, for instance due to a debilitating cerebral stroke, your love is put to the test. Though our love will be purified in that situation, it is not the case that love *essentially needs* the misery to become what it is in itself.

The infralapsarian opposition often brings into play that, because the incarnation is no longer triggered by the fall, supralapsarian Christology tends to mitigate the depth of our depravity and the concomitant need for salvation. Arguably, however, the depravity is fathomed even more acutely, because this supralapsarianism further exposes the abhorrent true nature of sin as a revolt against our election to glory in Christ.

Moreover, supralapsarians can point out that, because along the infralapsarian standpoint the incarnation is viewed as a remedy for sin, its aim tends to be merely viewed as the *absence* of sin. Obviously, we should not make a caricature out of infralapsarian Christology; true, this tradition exaltedly speaks not just of justification but also of *sanctification*. But surely, the supralapsarian account is a positive impetus as regards this vital spiritual theme of sanctification, because it underscores that redemption is, in the end, not about the absence of sin but about the presence of glorifying love for God.

A further connected theme is our natural desire for God, the 'desiderium naturale.' If the purpose of our creation is anchored in God's desire for a co-lover, firstly in the incarnation and then in a mighty choir of human and angelic co-lovers, it is clear that the only goal which can fulfil our natural, created existence is God himself. Or, as it is said, we all have 'a God-shaped hole' in our hearts. It was Pascal who, following Augustine, famously said in that vein:

> What else does this craving, and this helplessness, proclaim but that there was once in man a true happiness, of which all that now remains is the empty print and trace? This he tries in vain to fill with everything around him, seeking in things that are not there the help he cannot find in those that are, though none can help, since this infinite abyss can be filled only with an infinite and immutable object; in other words, by God himself. (*Pensees*, X, 148)

---

36. Veldhuis, 'Zur hermeneutischen Bedeutung der supralapsarischen Christologie des Johannes Duns Scotus,' 82.

37. My translation: Veldhuis, 94. 'Gott benötigt nicht die Sünde, um uns auf menschliche Weise zu lieben.'

104 *Chapter 6*

This 'craving and helplessness' is by no means restricted to supralapsarian Christology. Yet it is obvious that Scotus's supralapsarian stance is an exemplary foundation for it. And it implies that Aristotle's ontology is definitely abandoned: according to Aristotle's hylomorphism all entities are brought to their full actuality, that is, the true flourishing of their essence, through their *inherent* and *essential* 'form.' Hence, the Christian view of the true flourishing of human life breaches this ontological scheme, because here an essence is brought to completion through an *external* power, an accidental gift, not through its own essential power. That is literally 'unthinkable' in Aristotelian hylomorphism.

On the brink of the next part on atonement, I finally address the relation between supralapsarian Christology and atonement theory. Though it is true that for, for example, Faustus Socinus, supralapsarianism and his polemic against penal substitution theory went hand in hand, this is by no means the overall picture. Supralapsarianism can be joined to a variety of atonement theories. For instance, 'its combination with penal substitution in the early Franciscan context is worth noting . . .'[38] However, as I will show in the next chapter, Scotus connects his supralapsarianism with a merit-centred view of the atonement.

---

38. Schumacher, *Early Franciscan Theology*, 238.

PART II

Theory of Atonement

An Analysis with Scotistic Tools

Chapter 7

Scotus on Atonement

For the love of Christ urges us on, because we are convinced that one has died for all.

—2 Co 5: 14 (NRSV)

7.1: INTRODUCTION

The belief that Jesus was crucified for our sins is central to the Christian faith.[1] In its long history, the Church, sustained by grace, groped to more deeply understand what she worships as perhaps her deepest mystery. About its multifaceted richness, William Craig justly remarks: 'Theologians have often remarked on the multiplicity of metaphors and motifs characterizing the atonement found in the New Testament. The doctrine has been aptly compared to a multi-faceted jewel.'[2] On the realm of theological reflection, Oliver Crisp outlines four facets of this jewel: (1) the kerygmatic imagery of a ransom—also called the 'Christus Victor' view; (2) a satisfaction theory based on the notion of substitutionary merit (Anselm, Swinburne, and, I add, Scotus); (3) moral exemplar or 'transformative' theories (Eleonore Stump, eventually[3]); and (4) penal substitution theories (Calvin, Owen).[4] As facets of

---

1. This is a reworked version of Guus H. Labooy and P. M. Wisse, 'Duns Scotus on Atonement and Penance,' *Heythrop Journal* 63, no. 5 (September 2022): 940–51.

2. William Lane Craig, *Atonement and the Death of Christ: An Exegetical, Historical, and Philosophical Exploration* (Waco: Baylor University Press, 2020), chap. 2.

3. Eleonore Stump, *Atonement*, Oxford Studies in Analytic Theology (Oxford: Oxford University Press, 2018); for a critique, see William Lane Craig, 'Eleonore Stump's Critique of Penal Substitutionary Atonement Theories,' *Faith and Philosophy: Journal of the Society of Christian Philosophers* 36, no. 4 (1 October 2019): 522–44.

4. Oliver D. Crisp, 'Original Sin and Atonement,' in *The Oxford Handbook of Philosophical Theology*, ed. Thomas P. Flint and Michael C. Rea (Oxford: Oxford University Press, 2011), 430–51; published later as 'The Union Account of Atonement' in Oliver Crisp, *The Word Enfleshed*, chap. 7. Crisp himself defends a union account of atonement, a category of its own. However, this view is premised on 'Augustinian realism,' a view not intuitively plausible.

108 *Chapter 7*

a jewel, these views were by no means doomed to be rivals; though preferences and even long strives have occurred, especially in the Enlightenment era, they have often been treated as complementary, a viewpoint I take on exegetical grounds.[5]

I suggest understanding the genre of the ransom view not strictly as systematic but rather as homiletic and kerygmatic. It is the language of our Easter hymns—and as such undisputed.[6] If presented as complementary, the moral exemplar theory is undisputed as well: we all confess that the cross has to transform us. Hence systematic reflection is bound to focus on the two remaining, more contested theories: the satisfaction theory (2) and the penal substitution theory (4). Is Christ's passion a supererogatory and therefore meritorious act? In the literature, this is often dubbed as the 'Anselmian view'—for efficiency, I adopt this characterisation though I still doubt whether it is historically adequate.[7] Or, instead, is the moral rationale of atonement that our debt and guilt are imputed to Christ, who is then punished in our place—as John Calvin or John Owen for instance held? Hence, what is meritorious: the perfect devotion of his life and death (2) or his substitutionary punishment (4)? And it seems that substitutionary punishment would probably include substitutionary merit, but that is not obvious the other way around: a protagonist of substitutionary merit could be committed to rejecting substitutionary punishment.

In this chapter, I investigate Scotus's views on these matters. I will start with the assessment of his analysis of atonement (*Lect.* III, d18-20).[8] This seems to be a nonpenal view that depends on meritorious supererogatory acts of love. However, doubts may remain. Johnson, for instance, remarked that, due to Enlightenment bias, we tend to see theories as 'unique and mutually exclusive explanations.'[9] So perhaps Scotus's attitude to penal atonement theories is actually inclusive? This possibility is supported by recent

---

5. Apart from Crisp's own union view, I know of at least one more model that cannot easily be placed in this taxonomy: Adams's view of horror-participation in her *Christ and Horrors*. According to her, Christ is a horror-defeater. This seems to me a valuable insight, compatible with the other facets. Taken as the main template, however, the same objection arises as in the case of the other facets: in isolation they will be difficult to square with the biblical richness. Adams, *Christ and Horrors*.

6. 'In Augustine's poignant slogan Victor quia Victima we find the best expression of a systematic view of these diverse motifs. Christ conquers by his self-giving sacrifice. Augustine's synthesis illustrates effectively the truth that Christus Victor is not a stand-alone theory but an aspect or facet of a fuller account.' See Craig, *Atonement and the Death of Christ*, chap. 6.

7. Andrew V. Rosato, 'The Interpretation of Anselm's Teaching on Christ's Satisfaction for Sin in the Franciscan Tradition from Alexander of Hales to Duns Scotus,' *Franciscan Studies* 71 (2013): 411–44.

8. See Oliver D. Crisp, 'Original Sin and Atonement'; Adam J. Johnson, ed., *T&T Clark Companion to Atonement* (London/Oxford: T&T Clark, 2017); Cross, *Duns Scotus*; Thomas M. Ward, 'Voluntarism, Atonement, and Duns Scotus,' *The Heythrop Journal* 58, no. 1 (January 2017): 37–43, https://doi.org/10.1111/heyj.12315.

9. Adam J. Johnson, 'Atonement: The Shape and State of the Doctrine,' in *T&T Clark Companion to Atonement*, ed. Adam J. Johnson (London/Oxford: T&T Clark, 2017), 9.

Scotus on Atonement 109

scholarship. Andrew Rosato highlighted the substantial medieval interaction between atonement theory and penance, arguing that Franciscans before Scotus sought to harmonise key concepts from both doctrines.[10] Rosato describes a development starting with Anselm's supererogatory, nonpenal view of atonement in *Cur Deus homo* (1098). He then argues that Franciscans came to progressively adapt this Anselmian nonpenal view of satisfaction to the *penal* understanding of satisfaction operative in the theory of penance. Although Rosato rightly stresses that, according to Scotus, God could have provided satisfaction in many ways, nonpenal ones included, he nevertheless claims that Scotus follows this penal tendency.[11] However, I will show that Scotus's view as regards atonement is *nonpenal*, though he probably regarded penal substitution views as conceptually coherent (chap. 9).

To corroborate this conclusion, I have to include a partial investigation of his analysis of penance (*Ord.* IV, d14-15). We there discover that certain topics we tend to discuss within atonement theory, notably the analysis of punishment, pertained to the subject of penance for Scotus. I describe his extensive analysis of the virtue of penance, defined as *voluntary self-imposed punishment*. Now if Scotus really holds a penal substitution view of Christ's atoning work, it is incomprehensible that he, while scrutinising atonement in book III, did not refer to this extensive analysis of the virtue of voluntary enduring punishment in book IV. I call this the 'no reference' argument. I next consider the concept of *satisfaction*: Could that concept, part and parcel of penance, be responsible for infusing the logic of atonement with penal undertones? It turns out, however, that 'satisfaction' for Scotus does not logically entail punishment. This leads to what I call the 'no transmitter' argument: there is no concept from the realm of penance that inevitably transmitted penal connotations to atonement theory. I thus put to rest any lingering doubts and conclude that Scotus's view of atonement is nonpenal.

7.2: SCOTUS ON ATONEMENT: MERIT IS SOMETHING TO BE REWARDED

Scotus's conceptual analysis of atonement gradually unfolds in the distinctions 18–20 in the *Lectura* III. It starts with an analysis of the concept of *merit* (d18).[12] What stands out is that a meritorious act is not a *monadic* but a *relational* property: it is 'a well-ordered relation between any praiseworthy work in the one who merits and the one who accepts in order to reward' (d18,

---

10. Rosato, 'The Interpretation.'
11. Rosato, 435.
12. *Lect.* III, d18; pp. 1–23.

110 *Chapter 7*

§15). So what 'makes an act of love meritorious primarily is God accepting it as a ground for giving eternal life to the one who performs this act.'[13] Hence, meritoriousness is a relational property: it is bestowed on the act by God, it is in the eye of the divine beholder. Next, merit does not exclude substitutionary cases, because one can also 'merit for another by prayers or other afflictions accepted by God.' Thirdly, as merit is the reward for 'whatever praiseworthy work,' merit does not entail the bearing of punishment because, for instance, a supererogatory act of love could count as 'a praiseworthy work' as well. Finally, because merit, as regards the human side of the relation, consists of performing a 'praiseworthy work,' it entails 'the right willing' of the will (§17).

What constitutes 'right willing'? Here Scotus introduces again (see chap. 5.3) the Anselmian distinction between 'affectio commodi' and 'affectio justitiae':

> And I say that the root of all merit, speaking about merit proper, consists in the affection for justice of the will, not in the affection for the advantageous . . . (§18)

Why is this the root of all merit? Because the affection for justice is directed towards God for his sake, whereas the affection for the advantageous is directed towards ourselves:

> merit is a well-formed movement towards God, by willing all that is good for him, and especially by willing oneself and others to be united to him in whatever particular circumstances. (§19)

This Anselmian understanding of 'right willing' is at the heart of Scotus's view about merit and, hence, atonement. It implies that *all* acts of Christ are meritorious because Christ 'wills himself and others to be united to God' in all his acts. Thus, Scotus endorses the common medieval view that Christ merited during his whole life through *all* his acts. Hence, He did not merit exclusively in his passion. However, would not this entail that all the heavenly saints merit because they all 'will what is good for God' (§33)? They do not merit because they cannot have an affection for the advantageous that is simultaneously *thwarted* by their affection for justice, because everything in them is at total peace. This does not hold for Christ as a wayfarer. Therefore, 'Christ merited by acts contrary to the affection for the advantageous, wherefore the merit of Christ is placed generally in his passions' (§24). In sum, the 'root of all merit' consists in the affection for justice of the will, especially if it compels one to endure a situation 'contrary to the affection for the advantageous.' This bears on atonement theory because this 'root of all merit' is

---

13. Vos et al., *Duns Scotus on Divine Love*, 116.

Scotus on Atonement   111

clearly neutral as regards penal aspects: conceptually, penal notions are neither implied nor excluded.

7.3: THE SCOPE OF CHRIST'S MERIT

Scotus then scrutinises the *scope* of Christ's merit (d19).[14] The common medieval position as reflected by Lombard was that merit as to its sufficiency is infinite due to the Persona of the Word (d19, §9); but as regards efficacy, merit is restricted (§11). However, Scotus denies that the sufficiency of Christ's merit could be due to the Persona of the Word. For he argues that Christ merited by virtue of his *human* acts and, consequently, his merit must be at least *formally* finite, in keeping with the finite human will (§12–16, §23). Here, Scotus's sharp distinction between the causal and the denominative aspect of Christ's human acts cuts deep into the theory of atonement (see chap. 5.2). For the meritoriousness of an act is a quality of Christ's human will which causes the act; it is then denominatively ascribed to the second Persona, but the Persona neither causes the act nor, consequently, its meritoriousness. And therefore, Christ's merit is finite. Notwithstanding this finite character, Scotus still secures that Christ's merit is sufficient. Firstly because, contrary to Anselm, the debt of human evil is finite as well. For all the acts of finite human beings cannot generate a formally infinite debt. So, both our debt and Christ's merit are formally finite due to the finite human will.[15] Secondly, because, as we saw, merit is a *relational* concept: what primarily makes an act of love meritorious is God accepting it as a ground for giving eternal life to the one who performs this act. This perhaps 'voluntaristic bend'[16] in Scotus's view of merit also pertains to the dilemma of what kind of substitution is at stake, meritorious or penal—or both. For if God freely and graciously grants meritoriousness to human acts, it seems that God could

---

14. *Lect.* III, d19; pp. 25–38.

15. Though Scotus notes that both debt and merit are still infinite as regards a *relational* aspect: due to the relation to the infinite Good they are in that relational sense infinite: "infinitus ex ratione termini 'a quo'," 'infinite due to the ultimate end to which it is related' (§33).

16. Scotus is often called a 'voluntarist.' This is mistaken if that label meant that there are no logically necessary ethical propositions; that instead, everything is freely chosen by God's will. It fits, however, if it means that Scotus severs all unfounded necessary connections. Obviously, if there are no constraints other than logical, the scope for Divine free action is enlarged. However, such 'voluntarism' is not to be associated with whimsical arbitrariness because within that widened scope God acts with perfect justice, wisdom, and love. See also Marilyn McCord Adams, 'Duns Scotus on the Goodness of God,' *Faith and Philosophy: Journal of the Society of Christian Philosophers* 4, no. 4 (1 October 1987): 486–505; see also Andrew V. Rosato, 'The Teaching of Duns Scotus on Whether Only a God-Man Could Make Satisfaction for Sin Within the Context of Thirteenth-Century Franciscan Theology,' *The Thomist: A Speculative Quarterly Review* 79, no. 4 (2015): 551–84, https://doi.org/10.1353/tho.2015.0030; see also Ward, 'Voluntarism.'

112   *Chapter 7*

also accept a supererogatory act of love as meritorious satisfaction without exacting a concomitant act of substitutionary punishment.

As regards restricted efficacy, Scotus opposes the established view that the restriction of Christ's merit is because some individuals are not disposed rightly whilst some are (§11). This is false because, according to Scotus, having a faithful disposition is the result, not the ground of receiving grace (§17). His axiom is, again, that a perfect will always wants 'the end prior to the means to that end':

> Because all well-ordered willing wants the end prior to the means to that end, God wanted beatitude for a determined number of the elect prior to whatever merit as a means to that end. And thus, the passion of Christ was foreseen as regards its meritoriousness only for a determined number of the elect. And hence, God foresaw the redemption for these divinely predestined particular persons, not because they were united with God previously (as the other view holds), but because they were predestined to glory previously. (§22)

This response exploits, again, the tool of 'structural instants' in the divine will: the end is loved first, and next, in a *structural* or *explanatory* but not *temporal* sense, the means to that end (chap. 6.1). Thus, God first loves himself, the *summum bonum*. In the next structural instant, He predestines Christ's human nature to 'maximal glory, not because others were foreseen to fall, but that He might enjoy God' (§20)—Scotus's by now familiar supra-lapsarianism, which has a profound influence on atonement theory at this point. In the next structural instant, God predestines a determined number of humans to share in that goal. And, foreseeing that they will fall, He took measures for their restoration. Among those measures are the passion and the fact that the elect gracefully accept that. But the fact that the elect accept the passion can never be the reason for their beatitude. Because their beatitude is wanted first, as an end! 'Why does God elect? Not *for the sake of* the good use of our free will.'[17] But to let us share in Christ's glory! Or, in terms of modern logic: what Scotus denies is that having a faithful disposition could ever be a *sufficient* condition for the election. However, that does not preclude it from being a *necessary* condition.[18]

Note that this view does not collapse into a theory of 'double predestination,' in the sense that the act-structure of God's election would be exactly parallel to that of his reprobation. This is because reprobation is not an end in itself and hence not chosen explanatory first. For God does *not* wish to reprobate, unless a person sins to the end.[19] Remember the distinction between

---

17. Vos et al., *On Divine Love*, 161.
18. https://plato.stanford.edu/archives/sum2017/entries/necessary-sufficient/.
19. Vos et al., *On Divine Love*, chaps. 3 and 4.

Scotus on Atonement 113

God's preceding and his following or consequent will: with his preceding will God creates every human being in order to let it share in his Trinitarian presence, but if the human will refuses to co-act righteously, this is integrated in the divine 'voluntate consequente' (chap. 5.4; *Lect.* II, d34-37, §152). So much as regards the question of the sufficiency and efficacy of merit: Scotus endorses the standard views, yet transforms their justification.

7.4: WAS THE PASSION NECESSARY?

Siding with Augustine, Lombard, and Thomas, Scotus maintains that the passion was not necessary in order to redeem mankind.[20] There must have been other routes to redeem because 'everything is under God's command.' Anselm, however, in *Cur Deus homo*, argued for its necessity.[21] Consequently, Scotus devoted much attention to Anselm's purported necessities (see chap. 6). Firstly, he summarises *Cur Deus homo* in four points:

1. it was necessary to redeem mankind;
2. it is impossible to redeem mankind without satisfaction;
3. the required satisfaction had to be done by a *God*-man;
4. the required satisfaction had to be done by a God-*man*.

As regards the first point, Scotus argues that the redemption cannot be necessary because the goal of the redemption is itself a contingent fact, namely, predestination. There is only a 'necessitas consequentiae': if God predestines someone to glory, then, given the fall, redemption is necessary by implication, though not absolutely (*Lect.* III, d20, §28).

Next, Scotus endorses Anselm's second demand that it is impossible to redeem without satisfaction. Yet he postpones a thorough analysis: he refers to book IV where he will assess the logic of *punishment* and *penance* (*Ord.* IV, d15, q1, §29–34). The discussion of satisfaction belongs there because it is a broader issue which encompasses the logic of penance as well. Along with Scotus, I therefore postpone the discussion of satisfaction too (chap. 7.10). I will there show that Scotus accepts Anselm's second claim, though in a qualified way.

Given this—qualified—requirement of satisfaction, Scotus turns to the third point, whether the required satisfaction had to be done by a *God*-man. This is in fact the first half of Anselm's famous dictum concerning

---

20. *Lect.* III, d20; pp. 39–55.
21. Anselm, *Cur Deus homo*, 5. Aufl; Lateinisch und Deutsch (München: Kösel, 1993); for an extensive discussion, see Rosato, 'The Teaching of Duns Scotus'; see also Craig, 'Eleonore Stump's Critique of Penal Substitutionary Atonement Theories.'

114 *Chapter 7*

satisfaction: '*what only a true God could do and only a true man was obliged to do.*'[22] As aforesaid, Scotus refuted the infinity of human debt and evil and, consequently, the infinity of the required merit. Therefore, a mere finitely good act would suffice:

> Wherefore if Adam, by the gift of grace and love, would have had one or many acts of loving God for the sake of God, out of a greater striving of free will than he strived in sinning, such a love would have sufficed for the redemption and remittance of his sin and would have been satisfaction. (*Lect.* III, d20, §31)

He thus concludes that a 'true God' is not necessary: a mere human being could satisfy if he was conceived without sin and God would have given him maximal grace—as He gave Christ (d20, §33, see also *Ord.* III, d13). Note how decisive the aforementioned point is here (chap. 4.6): 'God's self-presentation to the powers of a creature seems to be an action quite separate from his hypostatic indwelling in the essence and powers of an assumed nature.'

As regards the fourth point, the second half of Anselm's dictum stating that the redeemer needed to be a 'true man,' Scotus argues that 'this does not seem to be absolutely necessary, because one who is not a debtor can satisfy for another, like praying for another' (d20, §32). Hence, why could not an angel intercede for mankind? Moreover, 'all created offerings carry just as much weight as God attributes to them, and not more, as said above.' In sum, Scotus refutes all of Anselm's allegedly necessary deductions, except the second. Allan Wolter called this sifting of necessary connections the Scotistic 'elimination of impersonalism' in ethics.[23]

In the preceding chapter, we pondered the compatibility of supralapsarian Christology and specific types of atonement theory. I think that Anselm's necessitarian theory is hardest to square with the supralapsarian view, yet not due to its element of satisfaction—in whatever form—but precisely due to its necessity: if the incarnation is necessary in order to redeem Adam, supralapsarian motives for the incarnation tend to be preempted.

---

22. *CDH* II/VII: 'eam facere nec potest nisi verus deus, nec debet nisi verus homo.'

23. 'If the will of God underpins it [the law of nature], then the law of nature, especially as regards the second table, loses something of its impersonal and inflexible character. Its personal dimension cannot be ignored. Where other scholastics, following Augustine, who in turn was influenced by the Stoics, link it with the *lex aeterna*, Scotus eliminates this last vestige of impersonalism.' Wolter and Frank, trans., *Duns Scotus on the Will and Morality*, 25.

Scotus on Atonement

7.5: WHAT CAUSED THE PASSION?

So what caused the passion? Scotus gives an exegetical answer and we can easily see why. Anselm wanted to prove by 'necessary reasons' that God must become man, thus hoping to persuade the unbeliever. He wanted to reason *'remoto Christo,'* 'leaving Christ out of view as if nothing had ever been known of him.'[24] However, because such a deductive proof is impossible as Scotus argued, we have to rely on historical evidence instead. That is exactly what Scotus did at this moment of his enquiry:

> However, we must believe that the passion of this man was for the sake of justice. For He had seen the bad things done by the Jews, and through what an inordinate and distorted inclination they were disposed towards his law, as they for instance did not allow a man to be cured on the Sabbath while they themselves have pulled a sheep and a cow from a well on the Sabbath and many more of such things. And Christ sought to recall them from this error by works and sermons; and He rather preferred to die than to keep silent when it was required that the truth was said to them, which He declared to them against their unjust religious undertakings. Therefore, He died for the sake of justice. (*Lect.* III, d20, §37)

Obviously, this view leans on 'the root of all merit,' the distinction between the affection for the advantageous and for justice (*Lect.* III, d18, §18). And Scotus proceeds:

> He in fact freely, through his grace, arranged and offered his passion to the Father for the sake of us. Hence, we are very much obliged to him: because human beings could have been redeemed in another way and yet He redeemed us in this way, out of free will. We owe him therefore very much, and more than if we were redeemed necessarily—so that other ways were impossible. Therefore, to induce us to love him, He especially (as I believe) did this. And like this He wanted human beings to be maximally obliged to God . . . (d20, §38)

I consider this one of Scotus's most precious spiritual insights. It is the pinnacle of what Wolter called the Scotistic 'elimination of impersonalism' in ethics. And Scotus shows himself deeply touched by the love of the Messiah: exactly because God could have redeemed by for instance an angel, this gift of his own life on the cross all the more 'induces us to love him.'

Note that Scotus nowhere mentions penal substitution. True, the phrase 'offered his passion to the Father for the sake of us' could very well encompass it. But if he were its advocate, why not embark on a path of analysing

---

24. Anselm, *Cur Deus homo*, 2: 'remoto Christo, quasi numquam aliquid fuerit de illo.'

116   Chapter 7

penal substitution right here? Moreover, Scotus joyfully highlights which
motive he does endorse: this more 'Abelardian' transformative view of atonement—alongside the already mentioned meritoriousness of the passion.

7.6: PENAL PASSAGES?

I found two passages where Scotus seems to interpret the passion as penal
substitution; they both occur in the 'replies to the initial arguments.' Rosato's
claim that Scotus mingled penal categories into his theory of atonement
depends on one of them. It reads:

> And when it is argued that acts are more laudable than passions, we argue
> that this is true speaking of a virtuous act as distinct from passions that do
> not happen due to virtue, just like the Philosopher maintains. *Nevertheless,
> punitive passions (passiones poenales), and especially death, if accepted and
> commanded by a virtuous act, are more laudable than a virtuous act towards
> something delectable.* Therefore, a virtuous act towards something that causes
> sorrow is more meritorious than an act towards the delectable, because virtue is
> about what's arduous; . . . Hence that Christ wanted to suffer ensued out of his
> intense love of the ultimate end and his love for us by which He loved us for the
> sake of God. (*Lect.* III, d 20, §43; p. 53, italics added)

Rosato cites (in Latin) the italicised sentence as proof that Scotus 'claims that
[Christ's] suffering has a penal dimension and that it is better to bring about
redemption through a penal act than some way that did not involve voluntary
suffering.'[25] True, the punitive aspect is explicitly mentioned concerning the
atonement: 'punitive passions.' Yet to evaluate this properly, we need to consider the context. In the present passage, Scotus refers to an initial argument
(d20, §7) where 'the Philosopher' is invoked to buttress the view that the
passion was not necessary to redeem:

> the Philosopher says: 'because of our passions we are neither praised nor
> blamed.' Hence it is evident that a passion is not meritorious, but to act. (d20, §7)

This clarifies what Scotus is up to in §43: he defends the passion against
the Philosopher who argued *categorically* that 'acts are more laudable than
passions.' Scotus answers that this is only true speaking of 'passions *that
do not happen due to virtue.*' Hence, the main thrust of §43 is to vindicate
the potential importance of passions that *do* happen due to virtue. Rosato's

---

25. Tamen passiones poenalis, et praecipue mors, quando est per actum virtutis acceptata et impe-
rata, laudabilior est quam actus virtutis circa delectabile; Rosato, 'The Interpretation,' 435.

Scotus on Atonement 117

interpretation that this passage aims at penitential suffering seems premature. Its proper context is the need of maintaining the significance of suffering *as such*, which was completely rejected by the opponent. The real thrust of the argument is, therefore, more accurately revealed in the following sentence: 'a virtuous act towards something that causes sorrow is more meritorious than an act towards the delectable because virtue is about what's arduous.' And this conclusion is, of course, neutral as regards penal substitution. In accordance with this, it is quite possible that Scotus thought of 'poenales' (in 'passiones poenales') in its loose sense of 'painful.'[26]

In another passage (*Lect.* III, d19, §34; p. 38), Scotus responds to the following initial argument which asserts the infinity of indebted punishment:

> He did not merit the deletion of punishment for the infinite guilt of the others, because the indebted punishment for such a sin is infinite, as it is eternal, and the merit of Christ was finite, therefore . . . [He did not merit for all] (d19, §4)

The difficulty in §4 for Scotus resides in this claim of the infinity of the guilt, which he himself rejected, as we saw. In his response Scotus says:

> But the indebted punishment is in fact merely infinite as to its *extension* (not that it is impossible to satisfy in another way), and maximally in this person [Christ] where, in the temporal punishment of this person, He did not commute it. And this sufficed. (d19, §34)

Here, Scotus seems to take penal substitution for granted: the indebted punishment is laid on Christ, in the form of an unmitigated temporal punishment. But this does not entail that he endorses it. Wanting to rebut the infinity of the guilt, he merely accepts the penal framework of §4 for the sake of the argument. This interpretation is endorsed by his reminder 'not that it is impossible to satisfy in another way.' He thus seems to warn his readers that he does not favour this penal interpretation. The real challenge of §4 is its claim that the debt is formally infinite, which was denied by Scotus. Worse yet, his interlocutor brings up a fresh argument: the debt is infinite because the *punishment is eternal* and, consequently, infinite. Scotus's line of defence is that the concept of infinity in question is ambiguous: for the infinity appropriate of time is *quantitative* infinity; he calls it '*extensive*' infinity here. On the other hand, God's infinity is '*intensive*' or *qualitative*. In addition, the extensive infinity of the punishment is contingent as well, for God could have annihilated the sinner (§34). In sum, Scotus's defence is to uncover an equivocation: an extensive, contingent infinity does not entail the kind of formal infinity of the

---

26. Lemma 'poenalis' in *Dictionary of Medieval Latin from British Sources* (DMLBS).

118 *Chapter 7*

debt that Scotus rejected. Consequently, this reply is taken out of context if interpreted as an endorsement of penal substitution by Scotus.

Moreover, if Scotus held a penal view, he would not just allude to it, as he does here, but he would elaborate on it when developing his own view in the 'solutio propria'—which he does not. Therefore, we conclude that these two passages cannot bear much weight. Yet they do remind us that Scotus indeed nowhere argued that penal substitution is incoherent or, for that matter, morally suspect. Yet, while explicating his own position, he does not invoke punitive concepts. He confidently develops his own view next to the penal vision present in the 'initial arguments.'

7.7: FIRST OVERVIEW

I now provide a first overview, in which all the analytic interconnectedness impresses even more: (1) merit is 'a well-ordered relation between any praiseworthy work in the one who merits and the one who accepts in order to reward'; (2) merit does not exclude substitutionary cases because one can also 'merit for another by prayers or other afflictions accepted by God'; (3) merit pivots around the difference between the affection for the advantageous and the affection for justice; (4) therefore, on the conceptual level, merit could, but must not be, penal; (5) and therefore Jesus merits during his whole life, not exclusively in the passion; (6) the human debt is not formally infinite; neither is the meritorious redeeming act of the human will of Christ; (7) hence, though meritorious satisfaction is required, it is not necessarily on the shoulders of a *God*-man or God-*man*, that remains a divine choice; (8) exactly due to that divine choice we are induced to love God even more; because (9) He freely died for us for the sake of justice, apparently a nonpenal supererogatory act of love.

Consequently, the initial question seems to be resolved for the time being: contrary to Rosato's claim, Scotus does not invoke vicarious punishment in his 'theory of atonement,' although, contrary to many modern convictions, he probably saw it as a coherent route. Let us now reexamine this outcome by considering the logic of penance. After developing the 'no reference' argument I move on to the 'no transmitter' argument. My assessment of penance is of course tailored to the research question.

7.8: SCOTUS ON PENANCE: INTRODUCTION

During this study, I became convinced that contemporary assessments of medieval atonement theories would profit from broadening the scope to

Scotus on Atonement 119

include the religiously so adjacent practice of penance.[27] Especially the analysis of punishment is a clear example of a topic which for us belongs to penal atonement theory, whereas for Scotus to penance. Penance pervaded the medieval mindset as the 'second board' for shipwrecked sinners—baptism being the first one, cleansing us from original sin. If one gravely sinned after being baptised, penance was required as the 'baptism of tears.' This sacrament of penance consisted of, on the one hand, a virtuous act of *contrition, confession*, and *satisfaction* and, on the other hand, the sacramental ritual conducted by the priest. I leave this latter aspect out of consideration. In the *Ordinatio* IV, Scotus first examines what penance is. According to him, penance is *voluntary self-imposed punishment* (d14, q1). He then meticulously assesses the kind of *virtue* involved in penance (d14, q2).

7.9: ON THE VIRTUE OF PENANCE, THE 'NO REFERENCE' ARGUMENT

All medieval philosophers adhered to the Aristotelian framework of virtue-habits. A virtue is an accidental quality or 'form' belonging to the soul.[28] They distinguished the four natural, *acquired* virtues: prudence, justice, fortitude, and temperance. And next the three theological, *infused* virtues: hope, faith, and charity. Scotus understands all these virtues as generic virtues, each with a host of species and subspecies under it.[29]

According to Scotus, penance is *voluntary self-imposed punishment.*[30] He argues that this 'avenging of sin' or 'applying punishment to oneself' belongs to the virtue of 'moral uprightness' or *justice* (§85, §99–101).[31] Especially within the context of atonement, though, the demand for punishment (or to avenge, 'vindicare,' which Scotus uses as an equivalent) has met with vehement opposition in modern theology. This demand allegedly depicted God as a raging feudal landlord whose honour is injured. Yet Scotus's assessment of punishment is illuminating, also regarding the modern discussions on

---

27. See Abigail Firey, ed., *A New History of Penance*, Brill's Companions to the Christian Tradition, Vol. 14 (Leiden; Boston: Brill, 2008); Arrai A. Larson, *Master of Penance* (Washington, D.C.: CUA Press, 2014).

28. Richard Cross, Duns Scotus, *Great Medieval Thinkers* (Oxford: OUP, 1999), 107.

29. Wolter and Frank, 47–53 and 75–88.

30. *Ord.* d14, q2; pp. 21–32.

31. Scotus distinguishes four hierarchically ordered aspects of voluntariness, the first one including all the others: (1) avenging sin (to apply punishment to oneself); (2) detesting the committed sin; (3) accepting the punishment thankfully; (4) enduring the punishment courageously (§62). Scotus devotes almost all his attention to this first one (§85–§120). In this context, Scotus also discusses the objection that one cannot voluntarily will punishment, as for instance Kant argued; see Stump, *Atonement*, 78.

120   *Chapter 7*

atonement. For the rationale of punishment is a long way off how an enraged, narcissistic landlord would react; instead

> the divine Law is on behalf of the common good of mankind, to whom it is given; and punishment is for whosoever sins against the Law. And that [punishment] is for the observance of the Law, and more remotely for the common good of those to whom the Law is given, ultimately then truly on behalf of the Legislator himself. (§107)

Hence the first goal of the law is the common good, and preserving that common good is God's honour as the Legislator. This appraisal of the virtue of punishment would have served to improve our understanding of penal theories: this isn't 'feudalism, run riot in the field of doctrine,'[32] but rather a Lawgiver whose honour it is to preserve justice so that all may flourish and thrive.

Scotus then asks whether just penance is a kind of friendship: 'Since friendship falls under justice, . . . then surely this act of doing penance or punishing is an act of friendship' (§102)? For 'if there is only punishment in order to be avenged or that the avenger is satiated, that would be a cruelty. Therefore, to avenge is only according to right reason if the one on whom vengeance is taken is to be corrected. But that is friendship' (§104). He finds this view in Aristotle:

> The Philosopher says that reproof (correptio) differs from punishment . . . herein that 'reproof is for the sake of the ones reproved,' so in order to be bettered; 'punishment, however, is for the sake of the one who punishes, that he may be satiated'; but the second is clearly altogether cruel. (§105)

However, Scotus eventually does not follow this lead:

> I respond: to avenge, even if it is a well-ordered act, is not an act of friendship towards the one who undergoes it, because a vindictive action properly refers to a corresponding punishment of a committed offence in accordance with the law, even if it were not accompanied by a reproof of the punished one himself. . . . Nor is it cruelty as the second objection [§104] proceeds, because its proximate goal is the preservation of the law, and the more distant goal is He who is the goal of the law. (§106)

Surprisingly, according to Scotus, well-ordered punishment is not *eo ipso* an act of friendship aimed at the betterment of the perpetrator. Instead 'a vindictive action properly refers to a corresponding punishment of a committed

---

32. Katherine Sonderegger, 'Anselmian Atonement,' in *T&T Clark Companion to Atonement*, ed. Adam J. Johnson (London/Oxford: T&T Clark, 2017), 182.

Scotus on Atonement 121

offence in accordance with the law.' And the law is on behalf of the 'common good' (§106, proof §108). So the connotation of what Scotus calls 'correptio'[33] (here consequently translated with 'to reprove') is *not* included in the concept of 'to avenge' or 'to punish.' A reproof is for the betterment of the reproved, but that is not required for morally upright punishment. This mirrors the contemporary return to retributive theories of punishment.[34]

If, accordingly, friendship is not a *formal* cause of penance—it is not the 'form' of the virtue of punishing—then maybe it is its *final* cause, its goal? He rejects that too:

> If someone is reconciled to God through penance, God still does not avenge on him principally to reconcile him to himself, calling 'reconciliation' to restore to pristine friendship . . . (§109)

Hence, penance is demanded according to the law on behalf of the common good, not to restore friendship. One could wonder why punishing is no longer a *precondition* for restoring friendship. The aforementioned passage in the *Lectura* (chap. 7.3) allows us to reconstruct the answer: again, a perfect will wants 'the end prior to the means to that end.' Consequently, the highest goals are chosen 'first.' Hence, friendship is the *basis* of the other acts. It is not the *result* of God's *instrumental* acts like providing penitential satisfaction. So to what kind of justice does penance belong, if it does not belong to the justice of friendship? It's *a punitive act* of justice, concludes Scotus.

He goes on to further classify the grade of nobleness of these punitive acts, especially as compared to *rewarding* acts: 'And maybe this [punitive] act is nobler than some other act of justice generally, except for the act of rewarding, because that is appropriate for the Legislator' (§112). Here Scotus classifies 'rewarding' as the highest and noblest virtue among the subspecies of justice, an act 'that obviously only fits the master' (§113). So according to Scotus, the act of rewarding is most excellent and surpasses the virtue of voluntary self-punishment, though both reside under the virtue of justice. This rather mediocre classification of the virtue of voluntary self-punishment is also because voluntary self-punishment is directed at 'evil as potentially avenged' (§116). Consequently, 'penance is not only not a theological virtue (see also §81), but neither a virtue simply supremely noble among those directed towards created objects' (§117).

Though I was forced to bypass many intricacies, it was still palpable with how much care Scotus handles the logic of punishment. This adds up to our 'no-reference' argument: if Scotus really regarded penal substitution as an

---

33. See note 71, p. 27, *Ord.* IV, d14. See also the use of 'corripere' in Mt. 18: 15.
34. For theories of punishment, see chap. 9.2 note 6.

122   *Chapter 7*

additional cause of Christ's merit, it is inexplicable that he did not refer to this extensive analysis of punishment. All the more so, because he *does* refer to the discussion of penance in book IV when analysing the necessity of satisfaction in book III. I now turn to that last topic.

7.10: ON SATISFACTION: THE 'NO TRANSMITTER' ARGUMENT

Examining satisfaction as a feature of penance, Scotus distinguishes between satisfaction in a general and a strict sense.[35] As regards the strict sense, we must recall that doing penance consisted of contrition, confession, and *satisfaction*. As such, 'satisfaction' refers to the *exterior* tasks imposed by the priest as part of penance: 'three difficult works, namely fasting, prayer and almsgiving.' This is satisfaction in its strict sense and it entails by definition the aspect of punishment (§44–45). Obviously, one cannot apply this strict meaning of 'satisfaction' to the passion of Christ, because that was not an instance of penance as a sacrament. The definition of satisfaction in its *general* sense is: 'satisfaction is a voluntary restoring, to an equal value, which is otherwise not indebted' (§11). So 'satisfaction' in this sense neither excludes nor includes a connotation of punishment (also §16).[36] This passage corroborates this:

> Thirdly I say that satisfaction in this understanding [the general] more often consists in [self-imposed] punitive acts or voluntary passions than in other good non-punitive acts, although sometimes it is possible that through some kind of good non-punitive act satisfaction is provided because God could very well accept an act of great love as retribution for an indebted punishment of a particular offence. Though it is not strictly punishment, it is nevertheless a greater good and it restores honour to God to a greater extent than through that which would be its proper punishment. However, since guilt is usually regulated through punishment and not through a greater good than the guilt, the satisfaction we now speak of consists of actions or passions having the rationale of punishment. (§32)

Besides reminding us of what I called the 'mediocre' status of punishment, this passage clearly deploys 'satisfaction' neutrally as regards penal implications: there is satisfaction with and without the aspect of punishment. Consequently, if the term 'satisfaction' is applied in the context of atonement, as Scotus does indeed, it does not necessarily entail a penal aspect. Hence, we

---

35. *Ord.* IV, d15, q1; pp. 59–75.
36. See Rosato, 'The Interpretation,' 434.

Scotus on Atonement

disagree with Patout Burns who argued that Scotus's concept of satisfaction did entail penal connotations. He, therefore, perceived a sharp contradistinction between Scotus's use of 'merit' and 'satisfaction,' because, in his view, Scotus used 'merit' without punitive meaning.[37] Because he claimed that Scotus's view on atonement was nonpenal, he tried to show, though to no avail,[38] that Scotus refrained from applying the concept of satisfaction to the atonement. We, however, contend that Scotus regarded satisfaction as a certain *kind* of merit, instead of using these concepts in contradistinction to each other. Here Scotus took the lead of Bonaventure,[39] and the previous passage (§32) bolsters this understanding.

Rosato showed that before Scotus the penitential logic of sacramental theology influenced atonement logic; be that as it may, the previous definition of satisfaction manifests that Scotus's use of this concept was not responsible for infusing Scotus's own view of atonement with penal undertones. As Rosato himself noted too, this concept was not the transmitter, because it did not entail any penal features.[40] But Rosato does not identify any other transmitter and neither can we. Moreover, the assertion that a nonpunitive meritorious act could 'restore honour to God to a greater extent than proper punishment' could easily be deployed as an argument in favour of nonpenal substitutionary satisfaction. As could the assertion in the former section that 'to reward, as the highest and noblest virtue among the subspecies of justice, *surpasses* punishment.' Yet Scotus himself does not exploit these outcomes to overtly argue for nonpunitive substitutionary satisfaction over against a penal substitution theory.

Analysing satisfaction in its general sense, Scotus eventually delivers on his promise in book III to assess Anselm's second claim that it is impossible to redeem mankind without satisfaction (chap. 7.4). Here he indeed defends that God cannot justly beatify the sinner without satisfaction (§23, §29–34). But whereas for Anselm this meant that the crucifixion was a moral necessity, Scotus argues that this is only true given God's *decision* to provide satisfaction through the cross; hence 'de potentia ordinata.' However, God could still have decided to redeem otherwise, for instance through penitential satisfaction offered by the sinner himself—still endowed by grace, of course. So satisfaction is indeed absolutely required, but there are many contingent means to that goal.[41]

---

37. J. Patout Burns, 'The Concept of Satisfaction in Medieval Redemption Theory,' *Theological Studies* 36, no. 2 (June 1975): 301–3.

38. Cross provides textual evidence that Scotus does use satisfaction within the context of atonement. Cross, *Duns Scotus*, chap. 10. Our enquiry further confirms this (*Lect.* III, d19, §34; d20, §31–35).

39. Rosato, 'The Interpretation,' 440.

40. Rosato, 434.

41. The difference is between 'potentia ordinata' and 'potentia absoluta.' See Ward, 'Voluntarism,' 42.

7.11: CONCLUSION: SCOTUS'S SUPEREROGATORY NONPENAL VIEW OF MERIT

In the first part of this chapter, I obtained an overview of Scotus's theory of atonement. It centred on merit and reward and the difference between the affection for the advantageous and for justice. Thus, Scotus defends an atonement view of supererogatory acts of meritorious dedication which yield satisfaction. This abounding love evokes, through the Spirit, our loving response: the transformative motive. Penal substitutionary features were absent.

One could object that Scotus nowhere contends that his meritorious, supererogatory view should be preferred. He only provides its logical analysis and presents that as his solution, endorsed by just *one* exegetical reason: 'Jesus died for the sake of justice.' So maybe Scotus's outlook as regards penal theories is actually inclusive? The two examined penal passages could be interpreted as pointing in this direction. And true, the central concepts of his atonement theory, merit and reward, in no way contradict penal undertones. Nevertheless, I am convinced that his silence on penal substitution reflects Scotus's *preference*: though he does not argue against vicarious punishment, probably because in his view it does not harbour any logical difficulties, he did not adhere to it. For if Scotus thought that Christ freely accepted vicarious punishment, he would have *referred* to his profound analysis of the virtue of self-imposed punishment in book IV. Just as he did while analysing the need for satisfaction. And if sacramental theology really pervaded his atonement concepts, one should be able to identify a 'transmitter.' Satisfaction, the only candidate, is innocent though. Hence, I argue that Scotus did not adhere to a penal view of atonement: his analysis in book III is about meritorious supererogatory acts of justice, not about vicarious punishment, and this assessment is corroborated by the 'no-reference' and 'no-transmitter' argument.

Notwithstanding that Scotus does not adhere to penal atonement theories, his analytic contributions, not least from the realm of penance, can be fruitfully applied to them. And I consider that as highly important because, contrary to Scotus, I became convinced that atonement theory should encompass vicarious penance. This conviction, which ripening took several decades in my case, rests on biblical grounds (see chapter 8). In chapters 9 and 10 I will set out to enrich penal atonement theory by combining it with Scotistic analytic elements.

Chapter 8

The Meaning of the Passion, an Exegetical Excursion

8.1: EMULATING SCOTUS'S EXEGETICAL TURN

'We must believe that the passion of this man was for the sake of justice.' Scotus's refutation of the 'Anselmian necessities' in *Cur Deus homo* paved the way for this admittedly rather imprecise exegetical argument. Imprecise, yet full of burning love for his Messiah (chap. 7.5; *Lect.* III, d20, §38). Emulating Scotus's exemplar, I will now exegetically probe into some aspects of the meaning of Christ's sacrifice. Let me briefly reiterate: I support all four views, namely the 'Christus Victor' view, the substitutionary merit view, the moral exemplar, and the penal substitution view. These are all aspects of the many faceted jewel of atonement. A jewel, infinitely richer than these four abstract, systematic angles can express! As I said, I take this complementary standpoint on exegetical grounds (chap. 7.1). This intermezzo is dedicated to exegetically endorse that the most controversial systematic view, namely 'penal substitution,' has to be included in the quadruplet too, *pace* Duns Scotus. I rely therefore on the work of, for example, N. T. Wright, C. A. Eberhart, and D. M. Moffitt.

8.2: FELLOWSHIP

I offer this brief exegetical digression to highlight that Scotus's oeuvre contains a sign of the ultimate *fellowship* between systematic thought and historical research—in this case, research on first-century Judaism. True, systematic ideas easily become blinkers, but just leaving it at that would be hopelessly one sided. We have reiterated that Enlightenment feud far too long. I showed

126   *Chapter 8*

that Scotus accommodates exegesis due to his critique on allegedly necessary deductions. This stems from his contingent ontology, based on God's
will which, according to Scotus, does not necessarily follow the intellect
as in Greek thought but acts as an independent principle, though always
according to goodness and love. That implies that we cannot *deduce* how the
first Principle expresses itself in our 'sublunar' reality, nor can we therefore
immediately *understand* ancient cultures. Therefore, we have to look; with
regard to the past by meticulous historical investigation, continually being
on the alert for preconceived notions. Hence, blinkers lurk everywhere, but
one of them is failing to acknowledge how Christian philosophers like Scotus
decisively *contributed* to opening a contingent ontology, which in turn is a
precondition for genuinely historical research.[1] Thus this excursion, not least
in honour of new developments in the study of first-century Judaism, aims
at celebrating this ultimate fellowship of systematic and historical research.
Constructing a dichotomy between the two leads to a blinkered view.

8.3: ABRAHAM

I will first briefly portray the grand Israelite narrative in which all the biblical
sacrifices were embedded. Israel's entire story is contained in the program-
matic name 'Abraham,' meaning 'father of many nations' (Gen. 17: 4–6).
God promised to bless all the nations of the earth in Abraham. He therefore
establishes a covenant with Abraham and his offspring. To further prepare
them for this solemn vocation, He delivers Abraham's offspring from Egypt
and grants them the Thora. Yet Israel, called to be God's servant (עֶבֶד) to
redeem the world, is persistently unfaithful to this covenantal vocation. This
eventually led to the enactment of all the dire curses in Deuteronomy. For
there it was written that if they obeyed the Lord their God, then 'The Lord
will cause your enemies who rise against you to be defeated before you'; but
if they did not obey Him, then 'The Lord will cause you to be defeated before
your enemies; you shall go out against them one way and flee before them
seven ways' (Dt. 28: 25). This curse, so the prophets proclaimed, fell upon the
people when Jerusalem was sacked by Nebuchadnezzar and the upper strata

---

1. See Ewald Mackay, *Geschiedenis bij de bron, een onderzoek naar de verhouding van
christelijk geloof en historische werkelijkheid in geschiedwetenschap, wijsbegeerte en theologie*
(Sliedrecht: Merweboek, 1997); see also G. H. Labooy, 'Theologie van het Oude Testament en historisch denken,' *Kerk en Theologie* 65, no. 3 (2014): 249–73; actually, the Enlightenment *philosophes*
could not truly appreciate detailed historical research. Voltaire detested 'cette science vague et stérile
des faits et des dates.' This focus on detail 'c'est une vermine qui tue les grands ouvrages.' See Sandra
Langereis, *Geschiedenis als ambacht: oudheidkunde in de Gouden Eeuw: Arnoldus Buchelius en
Petrus Scriverius*, Hollandse studiën 37 (Hilversum: Verloren, 2001), 57–58.

The Meaning of the Passion, an Exegetical Excursion

of society were deported: the Babylonian exile (587 BCE).[2] Deutero-Isaiah, as an example, explicitly regarded the exile as God's punishment:

> Who among you will give heed to this,
> who will attend and listen for the time to come?
> Who gave up Jacob to the spoiler,
> and Israel to the robbers?
> Was it not the Lord, against whom we have sinned,
> in whose ways they would not walk,
> and whose law they would not obey?
> So he poured upon him the heat of his anger
> and the fury of war;
> it set him on fire all around, but he did not understand;
> it burned him, but he did not take it to heart. (Is 42: 23–25)

Deutero-Isaiah even called the Babylonian exile metaphorically 'the cup of the Lord's wrath':

> Rouse yourself, rouse yourself!
> Stand up, O Jerusalem,
> you who have drunk at the hand of the LORD
> the cup of his wrath,
> who have drunk to the dregs
> the bowl of staggering. (Isaiah 51: 17)

But as the covenant was broken by Israel, how could God still fulfil His promises to Abraham? How could He remain faithful to the covenant and bless all the nations of the earth, now His vital instrument, Abraham and his offspring, had proved dysfunctional again and again? N. T. Wright succinctly answers this question: "when Israel was languishing in the prolonged exile that resulted from sin, the necessary 'new Exodus' could only come, as Isaiah 40–55 states so clearly, by sins being dealt with."[3] This 'dealing with sin' God accomplished by raising one of Abraham's offspring as the Messiah. Like Paul wrote: "Now the promises were made to Abraham and to his offspring. It does not say, 'And to offsprings,' referring to many, but referring to one, 'And to your offspring,' who is Christ" (Gal. 3:16).

---

2. N. T. Wright, *The Day the Revolution Began: Reconsidering the Meaning of Jesus's Crucifixion* (New York: HarperCollins, 2018), 117.

3. N. T Wright, 'God Put Jesus Forth: Reflections on Romans 3: 24–26,' in *In the Fullness of Time: Essays on Christology, Creation, and Eschatology in Honor of Richard Bauckham*, ed. Daniel M. Gurtner (Grand Rapids, MI: William B. Eerdmans Publishing Company, 2016), 151.

128   *Chapter 8*

8.4: ABRAHAM'S OFFSPRING

In the garden of Gethsemane, Abraham's offspring, Jesus the Messiah-King, vicariously representing his 'languishing people in the prolonged exile,' was asked to drink the cup, the bitter cup of the exile.[4] He thus vicariously bore the punishment for Israel's trespasses. Other parts of Deutero-Isaiah immediately come to the fore: the suffering servant in Isaiah 52: 13–53:12 and the subsequent statement in 54: 7–8 that God's anger against his people will turn to mercy.[5]

> But he was wounded for our transgressions, crushed for our iniquities; upon him was the punishment that made us whole, and by his bruises we are healed. All we like sheep have gone astray; we have all turned to our own way, and the Lord has laid on him the iniquity of us all. (Is. 53: 5–6)

Evidence of this vicarious role of Jesus in the New Testament is, for example, found in Galatians 3: 1–14. This passage "focuses on the achievement of the cross in undoing the Deuteronomic 'curse of the exile.'"[6]

So Isaiah's songs of the Lord's servant were personified by Jesus. But there is something peculiar about this suffering servant, the עבד יהוה: reading Deutero-Isaiah, we discern that this servant is both plural *and* singular—just like the Son of Man in Daniel 7. He stands for the faithful remnant of Israel *and* for a single individual personifying this remnant. This is the typically Jewish concept of a 'corporate personality': many and one! Hence Jesus, according to the servant songs, is both the King *and* his people at once. He represents his people in a very strong but non-Western sense: He is *one* with them. What happens to the King, happens to his people as well. Think of David and Goliath in single combat, each representing their own army. Like David, the Messiah represents his people as He, in single combat, slays the final enemy, the Goliath of evil. Now God, through Jesus, Abraham's offspring, has finally dealt with sin and corruption. Thus, Israel was restored and God's covenant faithfulness established[7] 'in order that in Christ Jesus the blessing of Abraham might come to the gentiles, so that we might receive the promise of the Spirit through faith' (Gal. 3: 14, see also Rom. 4).

In this context of penal substitution, it is highly important to recall a distinctive feature typical of the Levitical sacrifices. I think of their *origin*: it is

---

4. Cup is ποτήριον in LXX (ποτήριον τοῦ θυμοῦ ἐκ χειρὸς κυρίου) as in the Gospels.

5. David M. Moffitt, *Rethinking the Atonement: New Perspectives on Jesus's Death, Resurrection, and Ascension* (Grand Rapids, MI: Baker Academic, a division of Baker Publishing Group, 2022), chap. 4. There also applicated to the Maccabees.

6. Wright, *The Day the Revolution Began*, 240.

7. N. T. Wright, *Paul and the Faithfulness of God*, 2 vols, Christian Origins and the Question of God, Vol. 4 (London: Society for Promoting Christian Knowledge, 2013).

The Meaning of the Passion, an Exegetical Excursion

God himself who provides the sacrificial means to amend and restore the relation with himself.[8] See Lev. 17: 11: 'For the life of a creature is in the blood, and I have given it to you to make atonement for yourselves on the altar; it is the blood that makes atonement for one's life.' This merciful, divine origin could be interpreted as prefigurating the incarnation: on the theoretical level, the hypostatic union safeguards the belief that God *Himself* came to our rescue and offered His human life. Against the background of the caricature of an angry god lashing out to a human victim, this cannot be stressed enough. God himself, in Christ, fulfils his covenantal promises: the Deuteronomic one of human accountability *and* the grace and blessings promised to Abraham's offspring in Christ, Jews and gentiles alike.

8.5: PENAL SUBSTITUTIONARY ROLE OF ANIMALS?

Thus far, I tried to exegetically demonstrate that an element of 'penal substitution' must be included in the quadruplet of atonement theory. There is, however, another alleged exegetical bedrock for penal substitution: the Levitical sacrifices. After all, Romans and for instance Hebrews, do portray these rituals as prefigurations of Jesus's self-oblation on the cross. Here, however, preconceived notions of penal atonement could easily be read into the texts. The rationale of the Levitical offerings (קרבן, חטאת, עלה, אשם) points in a different direction because the killing of the animal seems *not* to be at the heart of the Levitical ritual. One of the reasons is that if a substitutionary death penalty were its kernel, the *priest* would have performed the killing and not the offeror (Lev. 4: 13–35). Actually, the blood is central, not the killing: 'when purification was required, this was accomplished not by the act of killing itself but by making available the animal's life-blood, which then functioned as the purifying agent to cleanse the holy place and its furniture—and in some cases the worshipers themselves—from the ongoing pollution either of sin or of impurity.'[9] Thus, recent research has increasingly buttressed that the killing of animals in the temple was not a kind of substitutionary punishment[10]—

---

8. Walter Brueggemann, *An Introduction to the Old Testament: The Canon and Christian Imagination*, first edition (Louisville, KY: Westminster John Knox Press, 2003), 68–69.

9. N. T. Wright, foreword to Moffitt, *Rethinking the Atonement*; see also Jacob Milgrom, trans., *Leviticus 1–16: A New Translation with Introduction and Commentary* (New Haven; London: Yale University Press; Bloomsbury Publishing, 2021), 253–56.

10. See Roland de Vaux, *Ancient Israel: Its Life and Institutions*, The Biblical Resource Series (Grand Rapids, MI: W. B. Eerdmans, 1997; French original 1958); Milgrom, trans., *Leviticus 1–16*; Christian A. Eberhart, *Kulturmetaphorik und Christologie: Opfer- und Sühneterminologie im Neuen Testament* (Tübingen: Mohr Siebeck, 2013); Moffitt, *Rethinking the Atonement*; N. T. Wright, *The Day the Revolution Began*.

130   *Chapter 8*

though there still is diversity of opinion among scholars on this subject.[11] I follow the view that there is no element of substitutionary punishment in the Levitical offerings in the eyes of first-century jews; instead, they served to *purge* the altar—not primarily the sinner—so that the God of Israel could dwell in the temple in the midst of his people. Thus, the Levitical offerings rather point in the direction of the substitutionary *merit* view. Yet these Levitical offerings *presuppose* the covenant, which, once broken, had to be restored by the suffering servant: 'the servant's vicarious death reboots the covenant relationship when it is so broken that no sacrifices can be offered.'[12] Hence, vicarious penance certainly is an element of the passion but to invoke the Levitical offerings in support of that is, I think, invalid.

8.6: A LAST DOUBT

A last disquieting question remains: Isn't substitutionary punishment just scandalous? Isn't that just a remnant of antiquity, with its thunderous gods seeking to retaliate? An era full of wrathful deities which, with any luck, you could bribe? Did not ancient philosophy justly ridicule these gods, along with their gullible devotees? So even if one concedes that penal substitution is present in the New Testament, one might still say that this could be a last figment of first-century Hellenised[13] Jews. True, all the really distorted pagan illusions about corrupted gods are already debunked, by Athens as well as by Jerusalem. But perhaps philosophy has to rise to the challenge and finally erase this last scandalous residue of penal substitution? To this question we now turn, whilst again standing on the shoulders of our giant, Scotus. Exegetics has had its say, what does Scotus's logic tell us? Is penal substitution morally sound or even logically coherent?

---

11. Calvin, Turrettin, and, for example, Wenham use the analogy to Leviticus 16 to explain the hand-ritual in Leviticus 4. Gordon J. Wenham, *The Book of Leviticus*, The New International Commentary on the Old Testament (Grand Rapids, MI: Eerdmans, 2009); there are however many reasons to doubt a similarity between the hand-ritual on Yom Kippur, which meant the transmittance of sin, and the hand-ritual in connexion with sin offerings (חטאת) as described in Leviticus 4. See Rolf Rendtorff, *Leviticus*, Biblischer Kommentar 3 (Neukirchen-Vluyn: Neukirchener Verlag, 2004), 34; see also Rene Peter, 'L'imposition Des Mains Dans l'Ancien Testament,' *Vetus Testamentum* 27, no. 1 (January 1977): 48–55, https://doi.org/10.2307/1517355.

12. Moffitt, *Rethinking the Atonement*, chap. 4.

13. See for the concept of a 'noble death' in a Hellenised culture, Wright, *The Day the Revolution Began*, chap. 3.

Chapter 9

The Coherence of Penal Substitution

9.1: PENAL SUBSTITUTION MORALLY OBJECTIONABLE?

In the previous chapters I argued that Scotus's view on atonement is built on meritorious, supererogatory, nonpenal, substitutionary acts.[1] I also showed that Scotus refutes nearly all the Anselmian necessities in atonement theory. Hence, a theory of atonement cannot be the result of strictly deductive reasoning. I therefore, just like Scotus, turned to exegesis. On that basis, I argued that there are vicarious penal aspects in the death of the Messiah Jesus.

However, particularly since the twilight of early modernity, the theory of penal substitution is contested. Can someone be punished for the sins of another person? Is this conceptually coherent? And if so, is it just? Brian Hebblethwaite is by no means alone when arguing: 'What sort of judge can impose death on another or even on himself as a substitutory punishment, thus letting me go free? Such ideas are morally objectionable in their analogical base—the purely human context—before ever they get transferred, by analogy, to the divine-human context; and a fortiori, they make no moral sense when predicated of a God of love.'[2]

Faced with such criticism, it is time to return to Scotus's analytic clarity. Certainly, he is not a defender of penal substitution—or 'vicarious penance' which I use as a less abstract synonym. All the same, his analysis of the relation between guilt and punishment has been of great importance in the

---

1. This is an improved version of G. H. Labooy and P. M. Wisse, 'The Coherence of Equivocal Penal Substitution: Modern and Scholastic Voices,' *International Journal for Philosophy of Religion* 86, no. 3 (1 December 2019): 227–41, https://doi.org/10.1007/s11153-019-09709-y.

2. Brian Hebblethwaite, *Ethics and Religion in a Pluralistic Age: Collected Essays* (Edinburgh: T&T Clark, 1997), 79.

132   *Chapter 9*

subsequent scholastic search for the conceptual coherence of penal substitution. In this chapter, I will describe Scotus's analysis of guilt in its relation to punishment, including its fate: the way his heirs did or did not applicate these logical tools.

I will start with two contemporary analytic contributions: Stevin Porter's defence of substitutionary punishment and Mark Murphy's opposed plea that substitutionary punishment is conceptually incoherent.[3] Having thus become more acquainted with the modern debate, we turn to Reformed and medieval scholasticism: first Petrus van Mastricht (1630–1706), then John Owen (1616–1683), and finally Duns Scotus. I will demonstrate that this scholastic manoeuvre sheds additional light on the same, perennial, analytic difficulties. Scotus's analysis—and Owen's who seems to be dependent on him—clarifies van Mastricht's analysis and the two contemporary ones, integrating their best elements into a coherent whole. Following Owen and Scotus in their use of a relational analysis of guilt and its punishment, I argue that penal substitution is conceptually coherent, albeit not univocally vis-à-vis ordinary punishment. Absent in the case of penal substitution is personal deservedness; herein I follow Murphy. However, this leaves open the conceptual possibility of *representative deservedness* (pace Murphy). Put succinctly: even though punishment implies deservedness, deservedness does not analytically imply *personal* deservedness.

9.2: PORTER'S DEFENCE OF PENAL SUBSTITUTION

The background to Porter's defence of penal substitution is Richard Swinburne's atonement theory.[4] Swinburne's position resembles that of Anselm and Scotus because he understands satisfaction as the provision of great merit. Siding with the likes of Augustine, Thomas, and Scotus, he furthermore contends that God could have redeemed in another way, using an angel or an ordinary human being.[5]

Porter objects that Swinburne's theory fails to account for the cross: If Christ could have brought satisfaction just by living a perfect life, does that

---

3. Steven L. Porter, 'Swinburnian Atonement and the Doctrine of Penal Substitution,' *Faith and Philosophy* 21, no. 2 (2004): 228–41; Mark C. Murphy, 'Not Penal Substitution but Vicarious Punishment,' *Faith and Philosophy* 26, no. 3 (2009): 253–73; see further Ryan W. Davis, 'The Authority of God and the Meaning of the Atonement,' *Religious Studies* 50, no. 4 (December 2014): 405–23, https://doi.org/10.1017/S0034412514000134; William Lane Craig, 'Is Penal Substitution Unjust?,' *International Journal for Philosophy of Religion* 83, no. 3 (1 June 2018): 231–44, https://doi.org/10.1007/s11153-017-9654-x.

4. Richard Swinburne, *Responsibility and Atonement* (Oxford; New York: Clarendon Press; Oxford University Press, 1989); see also Steven S. Aspenson, 'Swinburne on Atonement,' *Religious Studies* 32, no. 2 (1996): 187–204.

5. Swinburne, *Responsibility and Atonement*, 160.

The Coherence of Penal Substitution 133

not make the crucifixion foolish or suicidal (see chap. 10.2). Porter seeks to repair this alleged weakness: by supplementing penal substitution he establishes a contingent, fitting rationale for Christ's voluntary sacrifice. Firstly, he argues that human life and society require retributive punishment (chap. 7.9)[6]: 'For to demand that a wrongdoer suffer the loss that he deserves takes the harm done with due moral seriousness; it treats the wrongdoer as a responsible moral agent; and it expresses the value of the victim as well as the value of the personal relationship involved.'[7] Next, he defends that this retributive element is also needed in the relationship between God and sinners. For in this way 'human sin is taken with utter seriousness and sinners are treated as responsible moral agents, and the high value of the Godhead and the divine/human relationship is expressed.'[8] Finally, he defends 'the coherence of transferring punishment from a guilty party to an innocent party' (yet without 'Anselmian necessities,' see chap. 7.4).

We will focus on this last step. Porter argues that although there is oftentimes a moral objection to punishing an innocent person, it does not involve a logical impossibility. Porter cites Anthony Quinton, who claimed that it is part of the meaning of the word 'punish' that the one inflicted must be guilty: the relation between punishment and guilt is *analytic*. Porter retorts:

> But as R.M. Hare points out, even if we mistakenly punish an innocent person, they were nevertheless punished. This is what makes such a situation tragic. So the claim that punishment must only be of the guilty is not a logical claim, contra Quinton, but a moral one. It is not logically impossible to punish an innocent person whom we think is guilty, rather it is morally egregious to do so just because it is logically possible.[9]

In contrast to such morally reprehensible instances of punishing the innocent, there are also just substitutionary examples, so Porter argues. These should meet the following requirements: (1) a retributive view of penal substitution;

---

6. There are two competing modern theories of punishment, namely utilitarian and retributive. The utilitarian theory of punishment holds that offenders are punished merely in order to discourage future wrongdoing and protect society. It is therefore essentially 'consequentialist' in nature; it is forward-looking. Needless to say, this view suffers from all the weaknesses connected with the 'naturalistic fallacy' (G. E. Moore). The retributive or 'absolutist' theory, in contrast, states that wrongdoers morally deserve to suffer a proportionate punishment and that this retribution contains within itself the basis of its morality. Referring to future goods does not constitute the moral quality of punishment. See https://plato.stanf ord.edu/entries/justice-retributive/. Recently Craig has noted: 'Fortunately, there has been over the last half-century or so a renaissance of theories of retributive justice, accompanied by a fading of consequentialist theories, so that we need not be distracted by the need to justify a retributive theory of justice.' Craig, 'Is Penal Substitution Unjust?,' 235.

7. Porter, 'Swinburnian Atonement and the Doctrine of Penal Substitution,' 234.

8. Compare these two arguments with Scotus's view: 'that punishment is for the observance of the Law, and more remotely for the common good of those to whom the Law is given,' chap. 7.9. Porter, 237.

9. Porter, 236.

134   *Chapter 9*

(2) penal transfer is the right of the offended party; and (3) the demand that 'the substitute voluntarily and with sound mind accepts the penalty.'

> Take for instance the football player who is late to team practice. The coach of the team punishes the late player by demanding he run 5 laps around the field. The team captain steps forward and asks the coach if he could run the 5 laps in the other's stead. If the coach agrees to such an arrangement, then there does not seem to be anything unjust about this transfer of penalty.[10]

Now Porter insists that retributive punishment implies that the wrongdoer 'suffers the loss that he *deserves*.' I call this the 'deservedness' of punishment ('dignitas poenae,' van Mastricht). And this deservedness is based on the guilt of the evildoer. But in penal substitution, there is allegedly no 'deservedness' because, as for instance Murphy will argue, the substitute has no guilt—at least, no *personal* guilt. Hence, punishment in these instances seems to be of a different kind than the punishment in ordinary cases because it lacks the *deservedness* essential to standard situations of retributive punishment. This leads one to suspect that the *meaning* of the concept of punishment could change when applied to a vicarious situation. This is a point that Porter does not address head on. As I will show, the atonement debate in Reformed scholasticism revolved precisely around this topic: mainline Reformed scholasticism sought to guarantee that the concept of substitutionary punishment still implied *deservedness*. Grotius, however, advocated a utilitarian or 'consequentialist' concept of substitutionary punishment:[11] on a strictly utilitarian view of punishment, it is not relevant that the substitute may not in fact deserve the punishment.[12] Key for the utilitarian is that the *effect* of punishment, whether inflicted on the perpetrator or the innocent substitute, is just and wholesome for the group—for the redeemed in the case of the cross.

Sometimes, Porter gives the impression that perhaps his retributive concept of punishment fades to a more utilitarian kind of punishment when applied in the substitutionary context. Take for instance: 'What motivates the vicarious form is that the good ends which justify the punishment of the one who deserves it are also served in the punishment of the substitute.'[13] Another proper example would be the mother of the rapist.[14] There Porter highlights the utilitarian goals of 'deterrence and prevention.' I am *not* arguing that Porter is a covert utilitarian when it comes to the substitutionary situation; I

---

10. Porter, 236.

11. Craig argues that Grotius was not a consequentialist. Craig, *Atonement and the Death of Christ*, chap. 8; see however G. A. van den Brink, 'Hugo Grotius,' in *T&T Clark Companion to Atonement*, ed. Adam J. Johnson (London/Oxford: T&T Clark, 2017), 523–25.

12. See note 6.

13. Porter, 'Swinburnian Atonement and the Doctrine of Penal Substitution,' 237.

14. Porter, 237.

The Coherence of Penal Substitution

merely argue that this issue requires further clarification, as Reformed scholasticism did—by standing on Scotus's shoulders, as I will show.

9.3: PENAL SUBSTITUTION
CONCEPTUALLY INCOHERENT?

We now turn to the other faction: Mark Murphy who, like Quinton, argues that penal substitution is conceptually incoherent.[15] His critique, albeit cast in slightly different terms, is aimed precisely at the point I just mentioned, namely that as regards vicarious punishment there is no guilt and hence there is no 'deservedness.' If follows, according to Murphy, that it is no longer punishment. Vital to his refutation is the analysis of punishment. In keeping with recent studies, Murphy claims that punishment is

1. hard treatment upon one
2. for the failure to adhere to some binding law
3. with an authoritative imposition of that law
4. while this punishment expresses condemnation of the wrongdoer.[16]

The fourth element expresses the crucial condition. Murphy exploits it to differentiate between private law and criminal law, between torts and criminal offences: 'Torts and penalties involve authoritatively imposed hard treatment for failures to adhere to a standard, but they are not punishments.'[17] Thus, Murphy also discards Porter's example of the football player: just as with torts and penalties, this is simply not an example of substitutionary *punishment*. Whereas the purpose of a criminal case is to identify and punish someone who has broken the law, the purpose of a civil case is to settle a dispute between parties that can no longer come to an agreement on their own. So in the case of criminal law, there is indeed condemnation of the wrongdoer (4). Or, in other words, punishment implies *deservedness* and *guilt*. Accordingly, punishment is nontransferrable: 'one cannot express condemnation via hard treatment of someone who one does not take to be worthy of condemnation.'[18] Consequently, Murphy, along Quinton, argues

---

15. I will pass over Murphy's own position of 'vicarious punishment' because it takes us too far away from our present topic. His view can be summarised as follows: 'A deserves to be punished; B undergoes hard treatment, which hard treatment constitutes A's being punished; and so A no longer deserves to be punished' (p. 260). Note that I do not use the term 'vicarious punishment' in this sense, but rather as a synonym for penal substitution.

16. Murphy, 'Faith and Philosophy,' 255–56; for another interesting discussion of Murphy, see Craig, *Atonement and the Death of Christ*, chap. 9.

17. Murphy, 'Faith and Philosophy,' 256.

18. Murphy, 256.

136   *Chapter 9*

for the conceptual incoherence of penal substitution: it is logically impossible to punish an innocent person, because there is no *deservedness*. As Murphy puts it: 'The problem is not that penal substitution is immoral, but that it is conceptually defective. Once its incoherence is brought to light, it is plain that recent philosophical defences of penal substitution by Steven Porter and David Lewis are failures.'[19]

But what about Porter's objection that there are cases where we mistakenly punish innocent persons? Is not that an example of punishing the innocent? Murphy retorts that such cases concern *defective* punishment. Regardless of how many examples of defective punishment one offers, they do not in any way downplay the significance of the four criteria of proper punishment: defective cases do not affect the *meaning* of punishment. And even if, in this controversy, we would side with Porter, arguing that defective cases of punishment are nevertheless punishment, one still cannot legitimise God's acts on the basis of these defective human cases. Surely Murphy is correct in tacitly assuming that God will act along the *true* conceptual rules.

However, by proving that defective cases of punishment do not in fact open up logical space for God to punish the innocent, one does not prove that punishing the innocent is conceptually incoherent. The same holds for Murphy's distinction between the logic of punishment within the context of civil law and the context of criminal law. It may be true that one cannot *univocally* transpose punishment idiom from torts and basketball teams to the realm of criminal law, but refuting this argument for coherence once again does not amount to a proof of incoherence.[20]

Murphy's key argument for incoherence seems to be the aforementioned claim that 'one cannot express condemnation via hard treatment of someone who one does not take to be worthy of condemnation.'[21] It should be noted, however, that the topic of nonunivocity or analogy is again not directly addressed. It is true that in penal substitution cases there is no *personal* guilt and hence no *personal* deservedness; consequently, univocal punishment is ruled out. But Murphy quickly glosses over the question of whether we might be able to distinguish between personal deservedness and other kinds of deservedness—he even acknowledges that he has 'given these alternative formulations of penal substitution short shrift.'[22] As the following pages will make clear, this is not true for Reformed scholasticism. Their thought hinges on the belief that guilt, in a certain sense, *is* transferable. Think of Israel,

---

19. Murphy, 255. Murphy adheres to unqualified negative retributivism, see Craig, 'Is Penal Substitution Unjust?'

20. Similar considerations are at stake concerning Murphy's critique of Lewis's account of penal substitution as paying fines.

21. Similarly Stump, *Atonement*, 24.

22. Murphy, 'Faith and Philosophy,' 259.

The Coherence of Penal Substitution

with its deeply ingrained cultural patterns of 'corporate personalities.' As I said in the previous chapter, in Israelite culture, the messianic King *represented* his people in a very robust way: what holds for the King, holds for his people. Accordingly, if the elected covenantal people deserved punishment, the Messiah-King, by representing them, could vicariously make this 'deservedness' his own by completely identifying with them.[23] We then have an instance of a *certain kind* of deservedness divergent from *personal* deservedness, which of course catches the eye in highly individualised Western societies. Consequently, even though I agree with Murphy that punishment demands 'deservedness,' I still insist on the possibility of vicarious punishment of a personally innocent person—a *nonunivocal*, *analogical* way of punishment, on the ground of representative deservedness. In this specific sense, guilt seems to be 'transferable'—or better, *attributable* or *imputable*. The weak spot in Murphy's argument against penal substitution is that it fails to prove that deservedness analytically implies *personal* deservedness.

9.4: REFORMED SCHOLASTICISM: VAN MASTRICHT AND OWEN

In Reformed scholasticism, the previous conceptual questions were intensely debated. Before starting our assessment of Owen and van Mastricht, I need to provide a brief sketch of the main views on penal substitution in Reformed scholasticism. For this overview, I am greatly indebted to the impressive historical study of Gert van den Brink, building on the scholarship of authors as Richard Muller, Antoon Vos, and the late Willem van Asselt.[24]

The Reformed debate was to a considerable degree provoked by a 1594 work of Faustus Socinus in which he unbendingly rejected the thought of penal substitution and insisted that the cross of Jesus was only a 'pure suffering.' This ingenious, heterodox view ignited a high-level academic debate lasting more than a century, in which several different types of Reformed positions prevailed.

As mentioned, while defending the Reformation against Socinus, Hugo Grotius in his *De Satisfactione* (1617) argued that only punishment, not sin or guilt, is ascribed to Christ. Thus, he asserted the attribution to Christ of the *effects* of sin alone, namely punishment, but not of sin or guilt as such. Accordingly, Grotius explicitly defended a consequentialist theory of

---

23. Craig calls this inclusionary place-taking, as opposed to exclusionary place-taking. Craig, *Atonement and the Death of Christ*, chap. 11.

24. G. A. van den Brink, *Tot zonde gemaakt: de Engelse antinomiaanse controverse (1690–1700) over de toerekening van de zonden aan Christus, met bijzondere aandacht voor Herman Witsius' Animadversiones Irenicae (1696)*, (Kampen: Summum Academic Publications, 2016).

138   *Chapter 9*

punishment, as opposed to a retributionist theory. This implies the afore-mentioned shift in the meaning of vicarious punishment: it is no longer hard treatment upon a vicarious person to whom the guilt of others is attributed, but rather hard treatment on behalf of its *effects*, that is, the 'bonum commune.'[25] The later 'neonomians' (Richard Baxter, Anthony Wotton) followed Grotius in this consequentialist sense of punishment.

Many Reformed theologians rejected this position. Among them were Owen and van Mastricht. They argued that Christ in some sense was made guilty: *the guilt of our sins was attributed (imputatio) to him.* As a matter of fact, Murphy echoes Owen in his defence of the conceptual unity of guilt on the one hand and punishment on the other: *punishment without guilt is not punishment.* Unlike Murphy, however, Owen explores nonunivocal meanings of guilt, as we shall see shortly. Van den Brink classifies this position as the 'mainstream Reformed view.'

The last category in Reformed thought is that of the antinomians, who presented themselves as the staunch defenders of free grace (Tobias Crisp, Isaac Chauncy). Sin itself, as a stain *and* as an act, is imputed to Christ; or one could rather say, is *transferred* to him. This means that something like a commutation of the person is effected. Through grace our sins are no longer ours, but Christ's. And thus He, made sin, was punished in our place. He was even hated by the Father, because God hates the sinner. The commutation of the person grants that Christ was punished *univocally*. Reformed theologians in general rejected this univocal view of punishment. Owen, for example, argued that imputation cannot mean 'having done the things themselves; that were not to *impute*, but to *err* in judgement, and indeed, utterly to overthrow the whole nature of gracious imputation.'[26]

In what follows, I will focus on van Mastricht and Owen because their analyses shed important light on our topic. Mainstream theologians like them had to develop a fitting logic of the imputation of guilt to safeguard the *deserved* nature of the punishment inflicted upon the vicarious substitute, because otherwise the punishment would no longer be punishment. Van Mastricht distinguishes five aspects of sin and guilt:[27]

1. the act of transgressing a preceptive part of the law (sin properly)

---

25. ' . . . poenaeque vocabulo utor largius, non quatenus *timoorian* signat, sed quatenus *para-deigma.*' van den Brink.

26. John Owen, *The Works of John Owen*, vol. 5 (London, 1851), 168. Original: J. Owen, *Justification by Faith Through the Imputation of the Righteousness of Christ, Explained, Confirmed, & Vindicated* (London: R. Boulster, 1677).

27. Brink, *Tot zonde gemaakt*, 159–65. It should be noted that van den Brink actually weaves the positions of (primarily) van Mastricht and Owen together, and, by calling that section 'the position of Owen' (4.2.1.), ascribes it primarily to Owen. However, as the following will make clear, this is misguided. What van den Brink describes in that section is actually van Mastricht's view.

The Coherence of Penal Substitution

2. the stain caused by that
3. potential guilt (reatus potentialis): being worthy of punishment, 'dignitas poenae'
4. actual guilt (reatus actualis): actual, extrinsic condemnation, by court
5. the punishment

For the present analysis, (3) and (4) are the most important aspects. Van Mastricht elaborately describes them:

> Guilt (reatus) follows sin, in part because of its intrinsic nature and demerit; as far as this is concerned, it is not neutral or indifferent, but rather by nature evil and urgently demanding punishment, which cannot be denied, unless the nature of things be confused and all distinction between good and evil taken away. And, in part, [guilt follows sin] because of the sanction of divine law. The first is being intrinsically worthy of punishment (intrinsecam poenae dignitatem), Rom. 1: 32; in the second sense, it means an actual order to be punished (actualem ordinationem ad poenam). The former, 'reatus potentialis,' is inseparable from sin; the latter, the '[reatus] actualis,' is, by God's graceful dispensation, even if not separable from sin at least separable from the sinner. So 'reatus' is something in the middle, between fault (culpa) and punishment: for it arises from the fault and leads to punishment, so that the guilt of fault and the guilt of punishment are one [thing], which extends between those two terms like a middle term and is characterised equally by both.[28]

Aspect (3) is being intrinsically worthy of punishment and cannot be separated from the sinner; it is what I called 'deservedness.' Aspect (4) is the actual order to be punished, which can be separated from the sinner. The trouble with this distinction has already been encountered earlier: if there is no 'deservedness' (3) in the case of a vicarious substitute, then there is no longer punishment in a strong enough sense. Van Mastricht is well aware of this. His strategy is to exploit the ambiguity of the two kinds of 'reatus,' that is, the two concepts (3) and (4). On the one hand, 'reatus,' guilt, is a middle term, 'something in between,' of which two contradictory properties can be predicated, namely, separability *and* inseparability from sin. On the other hand, it is one thing.

Yet van Mastricht cannot have it both ways: if 'reatus' is 'one thing,' it cannot be both separable and inseparable from sin. It seems that two conflicting

---

28. The last part: Ille reatus potentialis, à peccato inseparabilis; hic actualis, qui per gratiosam Dei dispensationem, si non à peccato, saltem à peccatore seperari potest. Est ergo reatus medium quid, inter culpam & poenam: ex culpa enim oritur, & ad poenam ducit, adeo ut unus sit reatus culpae & poenae, qui inter istos terminos quasi medius incedit, & ab utroque ex aequo denominatur. Van Mastricht, Theoretico-practica Theologia, Amsterdam 1724. Lib. IV caput secundum; par. 7. p. 444 (translation ours). See also Peter van Mastricht, *Theoretical-Practical Theology*, vol. 3 (Grand Rapids, MI: Reformation Heritage Books, 2018), 450.

140 *Chapter 9*

motives are to be served here. On the one hand, the concept must be really one, because otherwise, in the absence of deservedness (3), the actual order of vicarious punishment (4) is no longer punishment in the required sense. On the other hand, there must be some logical looseness, for how else do you attribute an *inseparable* and *intrinsic* guilt to someone else? Van Mastricht, therefore, seems to be exploiting the ambiguity of 'reatus' to conceal inconsistency.[29]

No wonder that Owen unequivocally rejects this distinction between potential and actual guilt (3 and 4). In fact, he plays the same 'analytically one' card as Murphy and Quinton. The reason for this is plain since in Owen's view punishment demands *dignitas poenae*, deservedness. Owen writes:

> And the distinction of 'dignitas poenae' and 'obligatio ad poenam' is but the same thing in diverse words, for both do but express the relation of sin unto the sanction of the law: or if they may be conceived to differ, yet they are insepa-rable; for there can be no 'obligatio ad poenam' where there is no 'dignitas poena.' . . . And where there is not this 'reatus culpae' there can be no 'poena,' no punishment properly so called.[30]

Although Owen here still admits that the two concepts can be conceived to differ, he strongly emphasises their unity: they denote 'the same thing in diverse words.'[31] His own alternative analysis hinges on, as we will soon see, a *Scotistic* insight: a *relational* analysis of both (3) and (4). That will enable him to keep the 'dignitas poenae' and 'obligatio ad poenam' closely together.

Owen begins his analysis of sin by insisting that the act of sin as the transgression of the law is absolutely nontransferable.[32] He thereby rejects the antinomian view according to which even the act of sinning is taken over by Christ. For to suppose that imputation would mean a transmission of sin in this sense 'is to overthrow that which is affirmed; for, on that supposition, Christ could not suffer for our sins, for they ceased to be ours antecedently unto his suffering.'[33] So too the next element, the stain, cannot be communi-cated to someone else. The *guilt*, however, can:

---

29. Davenant's analysis is quite similar, although he shows less signs of uneasiness. He contrasts 'intrinseco ejus poenae merito' and 'extrinseca ordinatione ad poenam, proveniente à voluntate Dei statuentis & volentis illud punire.' See *Disputatio de justitia,* Disputatio posterior; Praelectiones de justitia habituali et actuali; Cambridge 1631; Cap VIII, p. 241.

30. John Owen, *The Works of John Owen*, vol. 5, 199, cap. viii.

31. One could say: there is a distinction but no separation between the concepts; Duns would prob-ably argue that there is a 'distinctio formalis a parte rei.'

32. Owen, *The Works of John Owen*, 5:199.

33. Owen, 5:201.

The Coherence of Penal Substitution

But the guilt of sin is an *external* respect of it, with regard unto the sanction of the law only. This is separable from sin.[34]

As remarked earlier, Owen's solution resides in the idea that guilt defined as the unity of 'dignitas poenae' and 'obligatio ad poenam' is *not* partly intrinsic, as van Mastricht held, but *entirely relational*. From there Owen moves on to create the logical space required for penal substitution. If there is no personal sin, 'no person can be constituted formally a sinner. However, any one may be so *denominated*, as unto some certain end or purpose . . .' Thus, Christ was made 'alienae culpae reus,' 'debtor by the guilt of others.' Owen's decisive definition of guilt or debt is worthy of close consideration:

> And so guilt, or 'reatus,' is well defined to be 'obligatio ad poenam, propter culpam, aut admissam in se, aut imputatam . . .'

If the Latin in this quotation from Owen is translated,[35] it reads that 'reatus' is 'an obligation to be punished, on the ground of guilt, whether committed by the person himself or imputed [to him].' The strength of this definition is apparent: (1) it holds guilt and punishment firmly together in one concept: *obligatio ad poenam, propter culpam*; and (2) its 'aut . . . aut' construction allows for different senses of guilt or deservedness ('whether committed by the person himself or imputed [to him]'). As to the first point, Owen firmly comes down on the side of Murphy; the fact that one is guilty and the fact that one is liable to punishment belong inextricably together. With the second element of this definition, however, Owen acknowledges that there may be different senses of deservedness. The weak spot in Murphy's argumentation was that he took it for granted that deservedness is *personal* deservedness. Owen, however, recognises that there may be other kinds of deservedness. For example, deservedness, freely accepted, on the ground of being emperor or a messianic King. In that case, you become 'alienae culpae reus,' debtor by the guilt of others; this may be called 'representative deservedness.' Like recently William Lane Craig,[36] Owen furnishes many examples of indebtedness for the guilt of others deriving from civil law, the military (Livius, *de Bello Punico*), and the mystical union between Christ and the church as his body, which he calls 'the foundation of the imputation of the sins of the church unto Christ—namely, that He and it are one person.'[37]

---

34. Owen, 5:202.
35. Owen, 5:199. This definition seems to contain a quotation (the Latin), but we were unable to trace its origin.
36. Craig, 'Is Penal Substitution Unjust?,' 243.
37. Owen, *The Works of John Owen*, 5:178.

142 *Chapter 9*

Taking stock, on the technical level Owen's analysis, based on the insight that guilt is entirely relational, is more successful than van Mastricht's, although it is clear that both reformers, on the doctrinal level, uphold a nuanced doctrine of penal substitution situated in between the two poles of Grotius's consequentialism and Crisp's antinomianism. The analytic key of Owen's solution is that deservedness or 'dignitas poenae' is indeed analytically implied in punishment, but that this *does not analytically imply personal deservedness*. A messianic King, representing his people, can be 'debtor by the guilt of others.' This yields a nonunivocal, analogous concept of penal substitution.

9.5: SCOTUS ON GUILT AND PUNISHMENT

Up to this point, we have enriched Porter's and Murphy's contributions by using the Reformed debate, a controversy which appeared to wrestle with the same conceptual difficulties. I now compare this with Scotus's analysis of guilt and punishment, hoping that this deeper and older 'archaeological stratum' will again bring more clarity. Scotus, the 'doctor subtilis,' offers an analysis of guilt that, like in chapter 7, derives from the context of penance, not atonement. While investigating penance, Scotus first offers an analysis of what exactly *remains* in the sinner after a sin is committed. Van Mastricht took it for granted that something intrinsic remains. As I will show, Duns would have disagreed.

For starters, Scotus is convinced that sin in its formal aspect cannot remain in the sinner because sin is an act—in all his work, Scotus persistently differentiates between dispositions and acts.[38] Because sin is formally an act, it does not remain in the sinner after the deed; what is left in the sinner is only a bad *habit*. That, however, is not formally sin:

> And if it were to be said that something remains of the act, it is not formally sin, since it can remain in someone who is justified, just as an evil habit or an inclination to it remains in someone who is justified all at once. This is manifest since, initially, he will be prone to follow this inclination of the wicked habit; but in fighting against his inclination, he virtuously gains merit and acquires the opposite habit for himself. (*Ord.* IV, d14, §29)

But if the deed does not remain in the soul, and the habit is actually irrelevant, then what remains in the soul after sinning? For, 'that because of which a sinner is called a sinner after the act does not cease to be, no matter how much

---

38. *Ord.* IV, d14, §17. The whole following passage uses §28–34.

The Coherence of Penal Substitution

time passes by, even though similar acts are not added: because one is in infinity a sinner because of what one did.' Scotus's answer focuses purely on divine will and knowledge:

> So, there is nothing absolute or relational, positive or privative, whereby one may be called a sinner after the act has ceased until penance, but only a certain rational relation (relatio rationalis), insofar as it is the object of God's knowledge and will. For, after one has committed [sin], God's will orders punishment for him according to that sin, and his knowledge foresees [it] before all ages until the owed punishment has been paid. (d14, §30)

What is implied by the technical term 'a rational relation' in this key passage? Here it denotes the relation between the divine knowledge-and-will and its object. But why, then, does Scotus reject something 'relational' in the *first* sentence of this passage? I find this difficult to answer. Knowing that Scotus discerned many kinds of relations, I think that perhaps Scotus here loosely dismisses all those other kinds of relations in order to save just the rational one a bit further on in his argument. Anyway, I think it is clear that Scotus understands 'what remains' as something exclusively in God's will and knowledge, a 'relatio rationalis': God *knows* what happened and He *wants* to punish that. Other aspects like stain, guilt, and offence are seen as further aspects of this 'rational relation.'[39] This thoughtful analysis from the context of penance can now be applied to the debate on penal substitution.

9.6: INTEGRATION OF SALIENT INSIGHTS

I will now gather all the salient insights from all these analytic philosophers. Murphy argued that substitutionary punishment conceals a logical contradiction. To the extent that a univocal concept of *personal* deservedness is at stake, this remains the hard conceptual core of any sound debate (*pace* the antinomians). Contrary to the guilt, an *act*—whether sinful or not—is logically nontransferable. That would be 'to err in judgement,' as Owen put it. Instead, a substitute bears the sins of *others*, and hence there is no *personal* deservedness. That guarantees at the same time that He is a sinless, innocent substitute.

Porter is akin to Scotus in that he too prioritises the divine act and hence the *relational* analysis of punishment. After all, Porter argues that if the substitute meets certain conditions, the imputation of punishment is the right of

---

39. *Ord.* IV, d14, §34. Even the stain is seen as part of God's verdict, contrary to Owen, who deemed it intrinsic; I think that Scotus's view is more defendable. This is an intricate subject that we cannot delve into here.

144   *Chapter 9*

the offended party—in this case, God. This insight runs parallel to Scotus's view that guilt and the command to punish are features of the 'relatio rationalis' of divine knowing and willing, though Scotus of course has the ordinary, nonvicarious situation of penance on his mind. How Porter conceived the imputation of guilt remained, I think, not sufficiently clarified. Is the *guilt* also imputed, as, for example, Owen holds?

Like many other mainstream Reformed theologians, van Mastricht tried hard to tie the 'dignitas poenae' and the 'obligatio ad poenam'—deservedness and its punishment—firmly together. Due to his erroneous analytic framework of 'something intrinsic in the sinner' and 'something loose enough from the sinner,' he was not able to surmount the ensuing conceptual obscurities. But his insistence, like Murphy's centuries later, on the unity of deservedness and punishment reveals yet again a conceptual issue of great importance. It implied a repudiation of the utilitarian view that the justification of punishment lies merely in its wholesome effects. Thus, spurred by the witness of Scripture as expounded by the Reformers, mainstream Reformed thought tried to do justice to the retributive core in punishment. I showed that Scotus's relational analysis of guilt managed to harvest this important point in a logically convincing way.

It seems that Owen was influenced by this seminal Scotistic view. Whereas the guilt, according to van Mastricht, is inseparable from the transgressor, Owen maintains that 'the guilt of sin is an *external* respect of it, with regard unto the sanction of the law only. This is separable from sin.' The *external* respect is, of course, nothing but God's verdict: it is He who 'knows of the committed sin' and warrants 'the sanction of the law.' Although Owen does not mention Scotus in this passage, Scotus probably influenced him either directly or indirectly. In general, Scotistic thought was very influential in Reformed scholasticism.[40] And in the context of this topic, both Davenant and Vazquez quote Scotus, describing his use of the 'relatio rationalis' and his consequent rejection of every intrinsic aspect of guilt.[41] Arguably, this suggests that Scotus's 'relatio rationalis' was a standard component of the logical toolkit of the scholastics.

---

40. J. Martin Bac, *Perfect Will Theology: Divine Agency in Reformed Scholasticism as against Suárez, Episcopius, Descartes, and Spinoza*, Brill's Series in Church History, vol. 42 (Leiden; Boston: Brill, 2010); Andreas J. Beck, *Gisbertus Voetius (1589–1676): Sein Theologieverständnis Und Seine Gotteslehre*, Forschungen Zur Kirchen- Und Dogmengeschichte, Bd. 92 (Göttingen: Vandenhoeck & Ruprecht, 2007).

41. Davenant, *Disputatio de justitia*, 241. Gabriel Vazquez, *Commentariorum ac Disputationum in (partes) S. Thomae*, Tom. Secundus, Antwerp 1621; Disp. CCVI, caput 1, pp. 645–46.

The Coherence of Penal Substitution

9.7: REPRESENTATIVE DESERVEDNESS

The weak spot in Murphy's argument against penal substitution is that it fails to prove that deservedness analytically implies *personal* deservedness. I think that Scotus would not have jumped to that conclusion as readily as Murphy. Firstly, as his honorary title 'doctor subtilis' indicates, Scotus is extremely aware of different shades of meaning. Next, the fact that he discusses Christ's vicarious punishment without scruples (chap. 7.6) suggests that he did not see any *logical* difficulties there. And thirdly, his relational analysis of guilt and punishment helps us to understand why substitutionary punishment is not incoherent.

Perhaps on the face of it, though, it is. For it seems that, generally, guilt is felt to be something *intrinsic*, something inseparable from the person who committed the act. Yet there is nothing that remains in the soul after sinning. True, a habit will be built up, but a habit is not an act and therefore not a sin and the act of sinning itself does not remain. Hence, Scotus argues that 'what remains' is something exclusively in God's will and knowledge, a 'relatio rationalis': God *knows* what happened and He *wants* to punish that. Hence, imputation of guilt and punishment is *always* at stake, also in the ordinary cases of guilt and punishment. It is always God who knows and wants to punish. Consequently, the imputation of guilt is *not* a questionable monopoly of the theorists of vicarious punishment. The real question is whether personal deservedness is the *only basis* for imputation, or whether there may be other grounds for imputation, for instance, representative deservedness. I argued that in a culture saturated with notions of 'corporate personality,' a culture where the messianic King *represented* his people, a concept like 'representative deservedness' could form such an alternative basis for imputation. To further explore this matter, we must return to the overarching topic of Scotus's meta-ethical theory (see already chap. 7.3, note 16). This is the task of the last chapter in which I will try to integrate all systematic aspects of atonement theory, vicarious penance included, into a coherent whole.

Chapter 10

Vicarious Penance

A Synthesis with Scotistic Tools

10.1: PULLING TOGETHER THE THREADS

Exegetical considerations resulted in the conviction that all four views, namely, the Christ-Victor, the Anselmian, the moral exemplar, and the penal substitutionary view, are invaluable elements of the one multifaceted jewel of atonement (chapter 8). And still more interpretations could be added, as long as they do not, like the cuckoo, eject all the other legitimate eggs from the nest. Here I think of, for instance, Adams's important view of horror-participation. I further described Scotus's substitutionary merit view (chapter 7) and his analysis of guilt which contributed to the analysis of vicarious punishment in Reformed scholasticism (chapter 9).

Pulling together the threads of all these chapters, I will now provide an account of Christ's vicarious penance. Of course, as I said, this is but one side of the jewel, the others are just as invaluable—and maybe it is wise to resist the temptation to exalt one of the sides of the jewel to the detriment of one of the others, for this could easily be part of a centuries-old reactionary strive.

10.2: META-ETHICAL THEORY: ELIMINATION OF IMPERSONALISM

I start with factors applying equally to substitutionary merit and substitutionary punishment. Firstly, Scotus's meta-ethical theory about the foundation of objective moral values and duties—this was partly relegated to the footnotes until now. Principally, moral duties do not necessarily flow from God's nature, instead, they are chosen by the divine will (see also chapter 6). Allan Wolter called this the 'elimination of impersonalism' in ethics (chap. 7.4). That is not to say that there are no necessary ethical truths; there is a hard core of

148   *Chapter 10*

necessary oughts like 'we must love God above all else.' Or its inverse: 'it is *logically* impossible for God to command me to hate him.'[1] Or, as I described earlier (chap. 7.10), God cannot beatify the sinner without satisfaction—but there are more ways of providing satisfaction than Anselm claimed. Yet apart from this lucid bedrock of necessary oughts, God's will contingently—though possibly for eternity—chooses moral duties. But obviously, these preferred duties are still in concordance with his nature, which is abounding love. In accordance with this, Scotus does not defend a strong version of the divine command theory because moral decisions have reasons which mirror the fact God 'respects the intrinsic values of things.'[2] As Cross states:

> Scotus is quite clear, however, that it is not the case that a divine command is necessary for an action to have moral value. Scotus talks of an action being mor-ally good if it has all the features that are *conveniens* (appropriate) to it; thus, it must be an appropriate sort of action for the agent and its object, in the relevant circumstances. Furthermore, this *convenientia* is discernible by reason.[3]

Based on this meta-ethical theory of the 'elimination of impersonalism,' objections to the sometimes 'mechanistic' character of necessitarian theories of atonement can be met. An obvious example of a necessitarian account is Anselm's; an example of a necessitarian version of a penal substitution theory would be Turrettin's. Eleonore Stump is highly critical of these necessitarian theories. She signals this crucial problem:

> To start with one of the obvious ones, contrary to what interpretations of this kind intend, they do not in fact seem to present God as foregoing anything owed him by human beings or omitting any of the punishment deserved by human beings. God exacts every bit of what is owed or visits the whole punishment deserved; he allows none of the debt to go unpaid or the guilt to be unpunished.[4]

True, I think that we have to admit that, perhaps especially in the pews, there was not seldom a thundering 'no part of what is owed is left unpaid or unpunished.' However, we must be on our guard lest caricature creeps in. This charge of 'he allows none of the debt to go unpaid or the guilt to be unpunished' is beside the mark as regards Turrettin for instance. For he explicitly declares: 'In a pecuniary transaction, the fact of the payment of the sum due frees the debtor . . . but in penal matters the case is different.'

---

1. Cross, *Duns Scotus*, 89–95.

2. Yet these principles are not part of natural law in that they would oblige God in his dealings with his contingent creation. Cross, 92–93.

3. Cross, 90. It seems to me that this meta-ethical theory reflects Scotus's view on the intimate unity of the essentially different powers of intellect and will (chapter 5).

4. Stump uses the label 'the Anselmian kind' in this context; I prefer the designation of 'the neces-sitarian kind' here. Stump, *Atonement*, 24, 77.

Vicarious Penance 149

Because vicarious satisfaction 'is not of that kind, which by the act itself frees the debtor. To effect this there must be an act of pardon passed by the Supreme Judge, because that is not precisely paid . . .'[5] So the idea that everything is 'precisely paid' is explicitly rejected by Turrettin. God foregoes the sinner on the basis of Christ's vicarious satisfaction, but the act of satisfaction does not by itself frees the debtor, for there must be 'an act of pardon.' This conforms to Scotus's relational view of merit; it could very well depend on him. Nonetheless, Turrettin's theory remains necessitarian to the extent that satisfaction is necessarily provided by punishment, by the vicarious penance of God incarnate.[6] Scotus had a different view: (1) satisfaction in itself is necessary, but (2) it could be offered by a nonpenal meritorious act as well and (3) also by an angel or a beatified man. So although Turrettin is by no means totally 'mechanistic' in his thought, the Scotistic meta-ethical theory goes much further in its 'elimination of impersonalism.' Just remember how Scotus connects this personalised meta-ethics with love (chap. 7.5):

> He redeemed us in this way, out of free will. We owe him therefore very much, and more than if we were redeemed necessarily—so that other ways were impossible. (*Lect.* III, d28, §38)

Thus, Scotus avoids the impression of a mechanistic process on a deeper level than, say, Turrettin; the latter's staunch claim that satisfaction must necessarily be punished is perhaps enough to evoke associations of a mechanistic process in which, indeed, 'he allows none of the debt to go unpaid or the guilt to be unpunished.'

This meta-ethical view is also pivotal as regards Porter's question: 'if Christ could have brought satisfaction just by living a perfect life, does that not make the crucifixion foolish or suicidal' (chap. 9.2)? Certainly, Porter commits himself explicitly to a nonnecessitarian meta-ethic.[7] Still, the question suggests that, as to the cross, we must secure that 'other ways are impossible' (§38). Several Reformed theologians in the wake of the Socinian controversy did indeed fell back on an increased 'Anselmian' grade of moral necessity of penal substitution. The present meta-ethical theory, however, seeks the justification of the cross in a—whether supererogatory or penal—*free* act of love: if Christ did this freely, it follows that 'we owe him very much, and more than if we were redeemed necessarily—so that other ways were impossible.' This is, indeed, a theology of love: 'caritas quaerens intellectum' (chap. 6.6).

---

5. François Turrettin, *The Atonement of Christ* (Grand Rapids, MI: Baker Book House, 1978), 16–17.

6. Turrettin, 25.

7. Porter, 'Swinburnian Atonement and the Doctrine of Penal Substitution,' 235.

150   *Chapter 10*

This meta-ethical theory is of great relevance to every aspect of atonement. To call attention to just one more consequence: according to Scotus, Christ's torture by crucifixion was not a necessary condition for our redemption. Hence, we could have refrained from killing and torturing him while being redeemed all the same. For instance, God could have granted Jesus to be our saviour while He nevertheless experienced a natural death. Hence, the *responsibility* for Jesus's torture and death remains fully ours; him being tortured is not a *necessary* condition for our salvation. This bears upon the Enlightenment critique that atonement theory attributes *violence* to God. From this Scotistic perspective, all the violence is *ours*. True, it is God's plot, right from the start: He governs, He permits. Nevertheless, we are truly free—wicked—actors in his drama; compare the chess grandmaster integrating my future free moves in his plot.

10.3: ENDS BEFORE MEANS

Then, because God acts perfectly, the ends are willed before the means. I have demonstrated how vital this is in atonement theory, for this implied that love is the *basis* of God's redeeming acts. Consequently, merit is not required to *earn* his love—not for oneself, nor for others (chap. 7.9). In other words, satisfaction is not propitiation if by that term we mean what in German is called 'Umstimmung,' that is, provoking a *change* of God's inner attitude, provoking him to love us. That is indeed an utterly pagan intuition. The basis of God's acts is his love and his concomitant wish to reward us with everlasting life in his presence. Hence, everything, including his demand for satisfaction as a means, is based on that love—I will elaborate on that shortly (chap. 10.5). He even provides those means himself: the Levitical offerings and, eventually, his *self*-oblation on the cross; wherein the element of 'self' is adequately expressed by the hypostatic union (chap. 8.4).

10.4: THE LAWGIVER

But why would God want to exact satisfaction for committed sins? Because He is offended? But what does it mean that He is offended? And does that compel him to ask for compensation or, much worse, does He, therefore, want to see blood? I showed, however, that the first goal of the law is the common good; and preserving that common good is God's honour (chap. 7.9). Exacting satisfaction is not 'feudalism, run riot in the field of doctrine,' but rather the task of a lawgiver whose honour it is to preserve justice so that all may flourish and thrive. Craig pointed this out lucidly, vis-à-vis Stump:

Vicarious Penance 151

Like far too many contemporary atonement theorists, Stump neglects legal analogies of the atonement and turns instead to private, personal relationships to motivate or criticize theories of the atonement, thereby overlooking God's status as Ruler and Judge. Taking God to be like the offended party in a personal dispute between two friends, she criticizes Anselm's insistence on our need to satisfy the demands of God's justice on the basis of the inappropriateness of demanding satisfaction as a precondition of personal forgiveness.[8]

This is an important observation. Firstly, when we overlook God's status as a ruler and lawgiver, we miss the point that it is his 'honour to preserve justice so that all may flourish and thrive.' So when Stump charges Anselmian theories that 'they fail to address the issue of the suffering of the victims of human wrongdoing,'[9] she thereby exactly confirms Craig's point: her objection arises from the fact that his role as ruler and lawgiver is apparently in oblivion. We all know how absolutely vital it is for victims of suffering that the perpetrators receive their due punishment. Hence, this conflation of friendship with the ruler-subject relationship deranges our grasp of atonement. By contrast, I showed how carefully Scotus distinguishes between friendship and God's duty as a lawgiver (chap. 7.9). A ruler's virtue of implementing legal punishment is a different virtue than that of friendship, though it could be anchored in friendship, as in the case of God; punishment, however, is required for maintaining the proper observance of the law alone.

And secondly, mixing up friendship with the lawgiver status could all the more induce us to take a phrase as 'He is offended' in an emotional sense. This danger of highly anthropomorphic language being prevalent anyway, it is of fundamental importance to realise that a just lawgiver does not exact satisfaction because he is himself emotionally offended or insulted, but because he wants the community to thrive—and *that* is his honour. So God being offended means that He, out of his sheer goodness and love, wants to put things right and He, therefore, commands punishment—or rather, in Latin, 'poenitentia.' Penance, which is even a graceful *sacrament* of course (*Ord.* IV, d14). Ominous, that modernity is completely oblivious of the tact that once the divine 'penitentiary institutions' were sacramental?

10.5: MERIT

I showed that the relational concept of merit was central in Scotus's atonement theory (chap. 7): merit is 'a well-ordered relation between any praiseworthy work in the one who merits and the one who accepts in order to

---

8. Craig, *Atonement and the Death of Christ*, chap. 9.
9. Craig, 'Eleonore Stump's Critique of Penal Substitutionary Atonement Theories,' 542.

152   *Chapter 10*

reward.' Or, put loosely, like beauty is in the eye of the beholder, meritoriousness is bestowed on our praiseworthy acts from the side of the one who accepts. Hence, the meritoriousness of a human act is not, as we perhaps tend to think, a monadic quality, a certain amount of goodness we somehow have to achieve, albeit through the power of the Holy Spirit operating in us.[10] Instead, accepting a suitable act as meritorious flows from the generosity of God and is a means to the end of rewarding someone with everlasting life. Hence, the Father, fountain of all goodness, has as his *aim* to reward us with the sharing of his Triune love—and to confer merit to suitable acts is a means to reward us properly. For there can be no true reward without the graceful gift of merit. Thus, an autonomous, self-righteous concept of merit is cut off at the root (see also chap. 5.4).

We thereby touch upon what is perhaps a partial misunderstanding of those opposing satisfaction theories: they perhaps do not appreciate that meritorious satisfaction, at least in its Scotistic mode, reaches out for *more* than just God forgiving human sin and then letting them enter his Kingdom. God not only forgives us and then admits us; He wants our entry into the Kingdom to be a just reward! The response to the legitimate question 'why couldn't God just forgive us?' is therefore twofold: firstly, as already mentioned, He demands satisfaction out of his respect for the law and the common good (chap. 7.9). Secondly, God is also far more generous than that He 'just forgives' us. He desires that Adam and Eve's readmission in the Kingdom is a fitting reward, not the result of merely waiving our debts. Due to Christ's merit, He therefore accepts our acts in Christ as meritorious, which is much more generous than just letting somebody off the hook. This imputation of merit is a *means* to the end of properly restoring Adam. God elects us, and one of the means for that end is making his pilgrims 'holy and blameless before him in love' (Eph. 1: 4). These praiseworthy works are not autonomously generated by us but given by the Spirit and accepted by God as meritorious. They are not a man-made *sufficient condition* for election but a God-made *necessary condition* for election.

And next, according to Scotus, merit hinges upon acts stemming from the affection for justice, in contradistinction to merely striving for the advantageous; therefore, on the conceptual level, merit could, but must not, be penal. As an example of a nonpenal understanding of the cross, I paraphrase Scotus's view: Jesus died because He, by speaking up for justice, opposed the Jews—as well as the Romans, we add, after World War II. So He died because of his affection for justice. Such a supererogatory act of love is meritorious; and,

---

10. Hence, I do not argue that the contested views always ignore that Jesus's devotion and sacrifice are themselves the *result* of divine grace; theirs is not a modern autonomous view of human freedom (chap. 5.3). A very good example in this respect would be Calvin (Inst. Bk. 2, Ch. xvii).

as I argued, its meritoriousness is a means to the end of rewarding. Thereby, God freely but justly rewards the Messiah and, subsequently, rewards the elect partaking in the Messiah.

10.6: VICARIOUS PENANCE: INTRODUCTION

Having considered issues which pertained to substitutionary merit and substitutionary punishment alike, I now proceed to the issue of penal substitution per se. To further analyse this theme, Scotus's analysis of penance (chap. 7.8–9) will prove helpful. It is easy to see why: penance is defined as voluntary self-imposed punishment. It could therefore be applied to someone who voluntarily endures punishment on behalf of others; that could be called *vicarious penance*—a label I prefer, because it sounds less technical than 'penal substitution.' So although Scotus himself does not defend vicarious penance, his meticulous analysis of penance as voluntary self-imposed punishment amounts to a fresh contribution to penal substitution theories.

Firstly, I provide an appealing contemporary example of vicarious penance; next, a summary of the preceding chapter which demonstrated the coherence of vicarious penance, focussing on the concept of representative deservedness; thirdly, the rationale of punishment; and finally, I discuss an intriguing variant which I labelled 'Australian penance.'

10.7: THE 'WARSCHAUER KNIEFALL'

I argued that it is not unreasonable to expect that his wisdom and perfect love could be detected and admired by us too (chap. 10: 2). Hence, can we also detect the beauty of vicarious penance? For instance, can we find any credible contemporary examples? Craig scrutinises a whole series of modern analogies and many of them are quite compelling to my mind, like the ones concerning the vicarious liability of employers.[11] I just add one true story, the 'Warschauer Kniefall.' On December 7, 1970, German chancellor Willy Brandt unexpectedly fell to his knees at the memorial to the Warsaw Ghetto. This 'Warsaw Genuflection' meant a first step, however small, on the long way towards reconciliation.

> On the morning of December 7, chancellor Willy Brandt laid a wreath at the memorial to the Warsaw Ghetto. It commemorates the courage of the thousands of Jews who lost their lives in the ghetto in a desperate bid to free themselves

---

11. Craig, *Atonement and the Death of Christ*, chap. 11.

from their German oppressors. Brandt straightened the ribbon attached to the black-red-gold funeral wreath. He took a couple of steps back. Seconds passed. And then he fell to his knees, his head tipping forwards slightly. Remaining still on the cold granite.[12]

Figure 10.1.   German chancellor Willy Brandt, Warsaw, December 7, 1970. *Dpa picture alliance/Alamy Stock Photo.*

---

12. https://www.dw.com/en/germany-poland-reconciliation-willy-brandt/a-55828523.

Vicarious Penance 155

This is how Brandt recorded the moment in his memoirs: 'Faced with the abyss of German history and the burden of the millions who had been murdered, I did what we humans do when words fail us.'[13] He went down on his knees like a penitent sinner. Yet he himself was relatively innocent: Brandt had actively resisted the early Nazi regime, spending most of Hitler's reign in exile. This gesture of penance, therefore, amounts to *substitutionary* penance. For he did it on behalf of his people which he, as its chancellor, properly represented.[14] Of course, a random German individual would not have been able to represent the German people the way Brandt did as its chancellor. And he did not deserve this penance, at least not personally. But, as their representative, there was this *representative deservedness*. And this representative quality was *acknowledged* that day by almost all Germans: they all had to opt-in or opt-out! A German firsthand witness recorded the polarised reactions at the time: 'Brandt did it for me, I knelt there too,' or . . . 'how dared he!?' These reactions of the Germans are a mirror image of what, on the realm of Christ's historic genuflection for us all, is contrite conversion or obdurateness.

Of course, one could retort that there is no need to think of penance in this case, penance as a voluntary self-imposed punishment. For could not this be understood as merely a confession of sin and a supplication for forgiveness? But all real supplication borders on penance. Moreover, this argument does not require that Brandt's gesture can only be understood as penance; just the *possibility* of a penitential interpretation suffices. The argument just requires the acknowledgement that, along with supplication, there is possibly also penance or a willingness to endure substitutionary penance. That would intensify his action deeply. For instance, Brandt could have tenaciously fasted nearby the memorial.

Another objection is the incommensurability of Brandt's gesture and the actual guilt—evidently, his penance will never *quantitatively* suffice! This reflects the fact that merit is a *relational* concept: God bestows merit on a praiseworthy act in order to freely reward. It is like the five loaves and the two fishes: He generously multiplies our small contribution.

In sum, Brandt's impressive gesture is, I hope, ethically convincing and serves as another analogy of Christ's vicarious penance.

---

13. 'Am Abgrund der deutschen Geschichte und unter der Last der Millionen Ermordeten tat ich, was Menschen tun, wenn die Sprache versagt.' Willy Brandt, *Erinnerungen: mit den 'Notizen zum Fall G,'* Neuausg., 1. Aufl, Ullstein-Bücher 36497 (München: Ullstein, 2003).

14. In G. H. Labooy, 'Als een keizer die knielt,' *Kerk en Theologie* 49 (1998): 209–21, I used the imaginative example of a kneeling emperor.

156   *Chapter 10*

10.8: REPRESENTATIVE DESERVEDNESS

In the former chapter, I argued that the decisive question is whether personal deservedness is the *only basis* for the imputation of guilt or that there may be other grounds for imputation. True, the demand for an analytic unity of punishment and deservedness should be acknowledged, but this does not logically imply *personal* deservedness. For it could also be *representative* deservedness, like when God imputes Israel's guilt on its Messiah. And, furthermore, Scotus's 'relatio rationalis' elucidated that such an imputation of guilt is *not* a questionable monopoly of the theorists of vicarious punishment (chap. 9.7).[15] Hence, vicarious penance is voluntarily undergoing the implementation of the deserved punishment of others made possible by the fact that one can lawfully represent those others.

Pondering this possibility of lawfully representing others, the theme of meta-ethics resurges. True, there is representative deservedness because God so decides: He imputes it on Jesus. But according to Scotus, God 'respects the intrinsic values of things,' as Cross argued. Hence, we may expect a creational feature which somehow is appropriate for representative deservedness. I think of the fact that He created us as utterly social beings. I suppose that God could have chosen to only imprint purely individualistic values and duties in the fabric of our creaturely existence. Think of a creation without parenthood, where each individual is created 'ex nihilo' and is completely self-supporting at that. We then would never have coined the concept 'individualistic'—for it would have been the air we breathe. In that possible world, representative deservedness would have been an oxymoron. But God chose to do otherwise: in our present reality, we are all fundamentally connected as fathers, mothers, siblings, families, groups, heads, and peoples. These relations belong to the 'intrinsic values of things' and are appropriate for the gift of representative deservedness. Especially the relation between king and people is an 'intrinsic value of things' which is appropriate for this great gift of representative deservedness. In that gift, the highest beauty of his divine Kingship is revealed. He voluntarily endured deserved penance in the capacity of a representative: the Messiah-King freely offering his life for his people.

---

15. Craig has further refined this analysis by distinguishing positive and negative retributive justice, contending that penal substitution theorists could argue that God is only 'qualifiedly a negative retributivist.' I, however, do not need this distinction for my argument. Just like Craig himself signals, given the doctrine of the imputation of sins on Christ, this manoeuvre is purposeless: 'But for penal theorists like the Protestant Reformers, who affirm the imputation of our sins to Christ, there is no question in Christ's case of God's punishing the innocent and so violating even the prima facie demands of negative retributive justice. For Christ in virtue of the imputation of our sins to him was legally guilty before God.' Craig, *Atonement and the Death of Christ*, chap. 10; Craig, 'Eleonore Stump's Critique of Penal Substitutionary Atonement Theories,' 531.

10.9: THE RATIONALE OF PUNISHMENT

What is, however, the rationale for punishing? Is it for instance—a much dreaded and even abhorred answer to that question—to appease God? Yet, as stated already (chap. 10.4), according to Scotus, satisfaction is required 'with respect to the law.' Whether satisfaction is offered through a supererogatory act of love or through punishment makes no difference at this point. So the first goal of punishment is the observance of the law, which in its turn serves 'the common good; and preserving that common good is God's honour.' Hence, to depict penal substitution as involving an enraged, narcissistic landlord who demands satisfaction because his honour is somehow offended is deeply mistaken. The 'Warsaw Genuflection,' though indistinctly, demonstrated that too: Brandt did not kneel before an angry, narcissistic God. Far from the mark! His consciousness was crushed by the thought of all those millions tortured and killed. He was horrified by this atrocious violation of the law, the law whose purpose is to preserve the common good. Therefore, 'he did what we humans do when words fail us.' And everyone senses, the trembling demons most, that such fundamental laws are neither relative nor man-made—a strong argument against naturalism.[16] These eternal truths are dear to God: their observance is his honour, the punishment of their violation his duty.

Next, Scotus argued that punishment is *not* supremely noble as compared to the act of rewarding. 'To reward, as the highest and noblest virtue among the subspecies of justice, *surpasses* punishment' (chap. 7.9). I called this a 'moderate ranking of the virtue of punishment.' As God always wills the end before the means, He first wills to reward the elect. And as a means to that end, He wants vicarious penance, accepting that as substitutionary merit. This idea repairs those penal substitution theories which present punishment as the 'moral axis' of atonement. What I mean by 'moral axis' is that sometimes, atonement seems to solely revolve around punishment. Substitutionary punishment is what 'does all the heavy lifting,' while God's act of accepting that as meritorious is pictured as the natural consequence of that penal process—obviously, here the present theme partly merges with the meta-ethical theme of necessitarianism (chap. 10.2). Eleonore Stump criticised this aspect of penal substitution theories unceasingly; this is one passage out of many:

> According to the penal substitution theory, God exacts the full extent of the punishment due for human sin; God allows none of it to go unpunished. It is true that, on this theory, it is God who fully endures the punishment which sinful

---

16. Mark D. Linville, 'The Moral Argument,' in *The Blackwell Companion to Natural Theology*, ed. William Lane Craig and J. P. Moreland (Chichester: Wiley-Blackwell, 2012), 391–448.

158   *Chapter 10*

human beings deserve. This part of the story is perplexing; but what it shows is only that God has borne the punishment, not that God has agreed to forego any part of the punishment.[17]

I argued that her charge that God does not forego anything is not always accurate, as with respect to Turrettin: he states that God *pardons* the sinner. However, it is true that atonement often entirely revolves around punishment: satisfaction is offered by enduring substitutionary punishment, while God's acceptance and reward are just the logical outcomes of that. But then, God's goal of rewarding is no longer the gracious *fountain* of atonement—with all its necessary means in due order. Instead, the sole fountain is the bearing of punishment. Yet punishing is not supremely noble. Is it this incongruity which is sensed by the modern critique of penal substitution? In vicarious punishment, God imposes the punishment. But to impose punishment is, though a virtue, not a supremely noble virtue. This should be, I think, acknowledged. It only becomes supremely noble when the one imposing it is *also* the one who vicariously suffers the punishment—as in the incarnation. 'And being found in appearance as a human, he humbled himself and became obedient to the point of death—even death on a cross' (Phil. 2: 8).

In sum, Christ's enduring vicarious punishment is a fountain of grace and mercy, but not as a necessary *and* sufficient condition, only as a necessary condition (and even then '*de potentia ordinata*'[18]). The danger I sense—and which seems to trigger Stump's critique—is that the vicarious bearing of punishment, even when it is justly understood as being only a necessary condition for God's acceptance, becomes in itself the moral axis of redemption. Otherwise stated: there is a tendency, perhaps especially in Reformed thought, that the divine free gift of graciously rewarding the merit He himself bestows on a human praiseworthy act is preempted by a more quantitative understanding of the efficacy of Christ's penitential suffering.

I prefer Scotus's lead: what makes an act of love meritorious is God accepting it as a ground for rewarding someone with eternal life. The 'moral axis' of atonement is God's predestination to glory and the ensuing desire to reward—compare Matthew 20: 1–16 the parable of the workers in the vineyard: 'Or are you envious because I am generous?' And vicarious penance is the means for this fountain of goodness. For it still is true that rewarding is only proper if there are praiseworthy acts to be rewarded. Whose acts? As I argued, causally seen the acts of Christ's human nature, sanctified by grace; denominatively spoken, the acts of the Son of God (chap. 5.2; chap. 7.3). And as the tradition said, Christ's whole life counts as something to be rewarded

---

17. Stump, *Atonement*, 77.
18. See chap. 7.4: it is not an absolutely necessary condition, this concerns a necessity of another kind: it is a necessary condition because God so decided, 'de potentia ordinata.'

(chap. 7.2): it is full of 'praiseworthy acts.' But especially his passion: there, Christ offers vicarious penance to reward all those participating in the body of the Messiah. Thus, penal substitution theory could benefit from these Scotistic tools derived from the realm of penance. Whether and how precisely our own acts, performed in Jesus Messiah, are also meritorious is not the subject of this book (see chap. 5.4).

10.10: AUSTRALIAN OR VICARIOUS PENANCE?

For a decade, I adhered to alternative theory of atonement, a view I coined 'an Australian way of bearing punishment.'[19] It is helpful to ponder the strength and weaknesses of this alternative as well. I have argued that the cup Jesus drank was an allusion to the Babylonian exile (chap. 8.4). This exilic nature of the Messiah's punishment is of course well caught by using an exilic analogy: between 1788 and 1868, a multitude of convicts was transported from Britain and Ireland to various penal colonies in Australia. It meant a lifetime exile. Now suppose that there have been priests and pastors who truly identified with the convicts and, driven by the Spirit of Jesus, wanted to provide the pastoral care these image-bearers so desperately needed. Therefore, they freely decided to go into exile along with them. And so they met exactly the same hardships and tribulations as the convicts. Yet for these priests and pastors, these hardships were not a punishment. For them, all the trials were pure sufferings. Craig discusses this option as well:

> On such an understanding, Christ bore the suffering that, had it been inflicted upon us, would have been our just desert and, hence, punishment. In other words, Christ was not punished but he endured the suffering that would have been our punishment had it been inflicted on us.[20]

Could we interpret Isaiah 53 like this: 'upon him was the punishment that made us whole'? What to think of this 'Australian' option? Craig eventually rejects this view, because:

> If the punishment for an offense were, say, deportation, how could justice be satisfied by someone else's voluntarily going or even being sent into exile unless it were intended to be a punishment for the wrongdoing in question?

---

19. G. H. Labooy, 'Christus' toewijding als verzoenende verdienste. Over zijn Australisch strafdragen,' *Kerk & Theologie* 2, no. 67 (2016): 146–60.

20. Craig, *Atonement and the Death of Christ*, chap. 9.

160   *Chapter 10*

But this objection presupposes that justice could only be satisfied through substitutionary punishment. Therefore, it overlooks the Anselmian kind of meritorious satisfaction by supererogatory acts of love from a nonpenal kind. I do not support this Australian metaphor anymore, but not on the basis of an alleged impossibility of providing satisfaction as Craig does. Along Scotistic lines I would rather argue that both the Anselmian and the penal substitutionary view could pass that test. I reject this Australian metaphor, if meant exclusively, for exegetical reasons alone (chap. 8).

10.11: CHRISTOLOGY AND ATONEMENT: ON GOD'S SHOULDERS

In this book, I analysed Christology and atonement, using a wide array of Scotistic tools, an apparatus stemming from a theology typified as 'caritas quaerens intellectum.' A brilliant analytic jewel as regards Christology was Scotus's groundbreaking analysis of the hypostatic union. Like the James Webb space telescope offered us a first-ever glimpse of the formation of the earliest stars, just so John Duns Scotus offered us the first glimpse of a mystery far deeper than that of the stars: the union of God and man in Jesus Christ. Not to thereby reach to the stars, but to grow in humility, worship, and service. And as regards atonement, Scotus's subtlety shone in his contingent meta-ethics, not to mention his careful analysis of guilt and its imputation, of punishment, of merit and reward. I argue that all these elements contribute to a more convincing account of atonement. Atonement which Scotus himself seems to see as substitutionary, supererogatory acts of love through which Christ is vindicated as Victor and we, in him, are changed and reborn— perhaps the heart of what is dubitably called the 'moral exemplar theory.' However, I argued that, on exegetical grounds, the 'breadth and length, height and depth' of atonement are even greater: there is also vicarious penance in it—which Scotus neither denies nor affirms. Thus, the Messiah carried Israel's penal exile upon his own shoulders:

> He said, 'Surely they are my people,
> children who will be true to me';
> and so he became their Savior.
> In all their distress he too was distressed,
> and the angel of his presence saved them.
> In his love and mercy he redeemed them;
> he lifted them up and carried them
> all the days of old. (Isaiah 63: 8–9 niv)

'He lifted them up and carried them': the Word carried the individual human nature on his shoulders in the incarnation, and He, Christ, Son of God, carried us on his shoulders on the cross—and in his resurrection.

And we gentiles are all invited to share in this redemptive love; for Israel was restored 'in order that in Christ Jesus the blessing of Abraham might come to the gentiles, so that we might receive the promise of the Spirit through faith' (Gal. 3: 14). John Duns Scotus, the gentile from Scotland and Oxford, Paris and Cologne, he was found by that love as well. And he testified thereof, not only by serving the Almighty with his most subtle mind, but also when he most movingly exclaimed:

> He in fact freely, through his grace, arranged and offered his passion to the Father for the sake of us. Hence, we are very much obliged to him: because human beings could have been redeemed in another way and yet He redeemed us in this way, out of free will. We owe him therefore very much, and more than if we were redeemed necessarily—so that other ways were impossible. (*Lect.* III, d28, §38)

Glossary

Analytic-Synthetic distinction: an *analytic* sentence: all surgeons are doctors. A *synthetic* sentence: all surgeons are brave.

Compositionalist metaphysics: said of a metaphysical account of the incarnation when the human nature, depending accidentally on the divine nature, is itself a substance, an *individual* human nature.

Compatibilism: the view that genuine human freedom is compatible with determinism being true.

Contrary-Contradictory distinction: two propositions are *contrary* if they cannot be simultaneously true but can be simultaneously false: John is glad, John is sad. Propositions are *contradictory* if they cannot be simultaneously true nor simultaneously false. John is glad, John is not glad.

Haecceitas: is the this-ness (or 'individual-nature') of something (for example: 'Daniëlitas' of Daniel).

Human persona: is *the independence* of an individual human nature.

Hypostatic union: the union between the Word and the human nature in Christ.

Incommunicability: one of the discriminating properties of a divine Persona. It means 'attributed, and attributable, to only one.'

Independence: this concept is not about the negation of *existential* or *causal* or *psychological* dependence. Instead, it is the negation of 'metaphysical' dependence: think of the relation of an accidental property to its substance as a kind of 'bearer' (as the redness of a dress depends on the surface of the dress). That kind of dependence is negated in the concept of a human persona. Ordinary human persons are independent. Jesus' human nature, though, is dependent on the Word.

Necessary and sufficient condition: a necessary condition is a condition which must obtain for the result to occur. A sufficient condition is a condition (or set of conditions) in which presence the result will occur.

Personae (divine Personae): are incommunicable, independent modes of being of the divine essence. I distinguish between 'persona' and 'person' (and, applied to the divine, between Persona and Person). I use 'person' in its modern sense: a rational individual nature. I use 'persona' in a technical, scotistic sense: see Human persona.

Quidditas: is the what-ness (or 'kind-nature') of something (Example: being a horse).

Semantics: what is the exact meaning of a term within a specific sentence?

Structural or explanatory priority: over against temporal priority. Ends are chosen 'structurally prior' or 'explanatory prior' to the means to that end, though they might be chosen at the same moment in time—or in the same 'now' of eternity.

Bibliography

Adams, Marilyn McCord. *Christ and Horrors: The Coherence of Christology.* Current Issues in Theology. Cambridge, UK; New York: Cambridge University Press, 2006.

———. 'Duns Scotus on the Goodness of God.' *Faith and Philosophy: Journal of the Society of Christian Philosophers* 4, no. 4 (1 October 1987): 486–505.

Adamson, Peter. *Medieval Philosophy.* First edition. A History of Philosophy without Any Gaps, volume 4. Oxford; New York: Oxford University Press, 2019.

Anselm. *Cur Deus homo.* 5. Aufl; Lateinisch und Deutsch. München: Kösel, 1993.

Aquinas, Thomas. *Catena Aurea: Commentary on the Four Gospels, Collected out of the Works of the Fathers: St. Matthew.* Edited by J. H. Newman. Vol. 1. Oxford: John Henry Parker, 1841.

Aspenson, Steven S. 'Swinburne on Atonement.' *Religious Studies* 32, no. 2 (1996): 187–204.

Asselt, W. J. van, J. M. Bac, and D. te Velde. *Reformed Thought on Freedom: The Concept of Free Choice in Early Modern Reformed Theology.* Texts and Studies in Reformation and Post-Reformation Thought. Grand Rapids, MI: Baker Academic, 2010.

Ayres, Lewis. *Nicaea and Its Legacy: An Approach to Fourth-Century Trinitarian Theology.* Oxford; New York: Oxford University Press, 2004.

Bac, J. Martin. *Perfect Will Theology: Divine Agency in Reformed Scholasticism as against Suárez, Episcopius, Descartes, and Spinoza.* Brill's Series in Church History, Vol. 42. Leiden; Boston: Brill, 2010.

Bäck, Allan. 'Scotus on the Consistency of the Incarnation and the Trinity.' *Vivarium* 36, no. 1 (1998): 83–107.

Barth, Karl. *Die Kirchliche Dogmatik.* Vol. I/2. Zollikon, 1939.

Bauckham, Richard. *Jesus and the God of Israel: God Crucified and Other Studies on the New Testament's Christology of Divine Identity*, Colorado Springs: Paternoster, 2008.

Beck, Andreas J. *Gisbertus Voetius (1589–1676): Sein Theologieverständnis Und Seine Gotteslehre.* Forschungen Zur Kirchen- Und Dogmengeschichte, Bd. 92. Göttingen: Vandenhoeck & Ruprecht, 2007.

166 *Bibliography*

Beek, A. van de. *Lichaam en Geest van Christus: de theologie van de 'kerk en de Heilige Geest.* Spreken over God, 2.2. Zoetermeer: Uitgeverij Meinema, 2012.

Beilby, James K., Paul R. Eddy, and Gregory A. Boyd, eds. *Divine Foreknowledge: Four Views.* Downers Grove, IL: InterVarsity Press, 2001.

Bok, Nico den. *Communicating the Most High: A Systematic Study of Person and Trinity in the Theology of Richard of St. Victor (1173).* Bibliotheca Victorina 7. Paris: Brepols, 1996.

———. 'Eén ding is noodzakelijk.' In *Geloof geeft te denken: opstellen over de theologie van Johannes Duns Scotus*, edited by Andreas J. Beck and H. Veldhuis, 225–81. Scripta Franciscana 8. Assen: Koninklijke Van Gorcum, 2005.

Bok, N. den, M. Bac, A. Beck, K. Bom, G. Labooy, H. Veldhuis, and A. Vos. 'More than Just an Individual. Scotus's Concept of Person from the Christological Context of Lectura III 1.' *Franciscan Studies*, no. 66 (2008): 169–96.

Bok, Nico den, and G. H. Labooy, eds. *Wat God bewoog mens te worden: gedachten over de incarnatie.* Zoetermeer: Boekencentrum, 2003.

Bonaventura. *De Scientia Christi.* Ad claras Aquas Quaracchi, 1882.

Bonaventura, Ewert H. Cousins, and Ignatius C. Brady. *The Soul's Journey into God.* The Classics of Western Spirituality. Mahwah, NJ: Paulist Press, 1978.

Brandt, Willy. *Erinnerungen: mit den 'Notizen zum Fall G.'* Neuausg., 1. Aufl. Ullstein-Bücher 36497. München: Ullstein, 2003.

Brink, G. A. van den. 'Hugo Grotius.' In *T&T Clark Companion to Atonement*, edited by Adam J. Johnson, 523–25. London/Oxford: T&T Clark, 2017.

———. *Tot zonde gemaakt: de Engelse antinomiaanse controverse (1690–1700) over de toerekening van de zonden aan Christus, met bijzondere aandacht voor Herman Witsius' Animadversiones Irenicae (1696),* Kampen: Summum Academic Publications, 2016.

Brueggemann, Walter. *An Introduction to the Old Testament: The Canon and Christian Imagination.* First edition. Louisville, KY: Westminster John Knox Press, 2003.

Coakley, Sarah. *God, Sexuality and the Self: An Essay 'on the Trinity.'* Cambridge; New York: Cambridge University Press, 2013.

———. "What Does Chalcedon Solve and What Does It Not? Some Reflections on the Status and Meaning of the Chalcedonian 'Definition'." In *The Metaphysics of the Incarnation*, edited by Anna Marmodoro and Jonathan Hill, 143–63. Oxford: Oxford University Press, 2011.

Craig, William Lane. *Atonement and the Death of Christ: An Exegetical, Historical, and Philosophical Exploration.* Waco: Baylor University Press, 2020.

———. 'Eleonore Stump's Critique of Penal Substitutionary Atonement Theories.' *Faith and Philosophy: Journal of the Society of Christian Philosophers* 36, no. 4 (1 October 2019): 522–44.

———. 'Is Penal Substitution Unjust?' *International Journal for Philosophy of Religion* 83, no. 3 (1 June 2018): 231–44. https://doi.org/10.1007/s11153-017-9654-x.

Crisp, Oliver. 'Compositional Christology without Nestorianism.' In *The Metaphysics of the Incarnation*, edited by Anna Marmodoro and Jonathan Hill. Oxford: Oxford University Press, 2011.

———. 'Original Sin and Atonement.' In *The Oxford Handbook of Philosophical Theology*, edited by Thomas P. Flint and Michael C. Rea, 430–51. Oxford: Oxford University Press, 2011.

———. *The Word Enfleshed: Exploring the Person and Work of Christ.* Grand Rapids, MI: Baker Academic, 2016.

Cross, Richard. *Duns Scotus*. Great Medieval Thinkers. Oxford: Oxford University Press, 1999.

———. *Duns Scotus on God*. Ashgate Studies in the History of Philosophical Theology. Aldershot: Ashgate, 2005.

———. 'Homo Assumptus in the Christology of Hugh of St Victor: Some Historical and Theological Revisions.' *The Journal of Theological Studies* 65, no. 1 (1 April 2014): 62–77. https://doi.org/10.1093/jts/flu002.

———. 'The Incarnation.' In *The Oxford Handbook of Philosophical Theology*, edited by Thomas P. Flint and Michael Rea, 452–75. Oxford Handbooks. Oxford; New York: Oxford University Press, 2011.

———. *The Metaphysics of the Incarnation: Thomas Aquinas to Duns Scotus*. Oxford: Oxford University Press, 2002.

———. 'Vehicle Externalism and the Metaphysics of the Incarnation: A Medieval Contribution.' In *The Metaphysics of the Incarnation*, edited by Anna Marmodoro and Jonathan Hill. Oxford: Oxford University Press, 2011.

———. 'Where Angels Fear to Tread: Duns Scotus and Radical Orthodoxy.' *Antonianum* Annus LXXVI, no. 1 (January–March 2001): 7–41.

Daley SJ, Brian E. "Nature and the 'Mode of Union': Late Patristic Models for the Personal Unity of Christ." In *The Incarnation: An Interdisciplinary Symposium on the Incarnation of the Son of God*, edited by Stephen T. Davis, Daniel Kendall, and Gerald O'Collins, 164–96. Oxford; New York: Oxford University Press, 2002.

Davis, Ryan W. 'The Authority of God and the Meaning of the Atonement.' *Religious Studies* 50, no. 4 (December 2014): 405–23. https://doi.org/10.1017/S0034412514000134.

Dekker, E. *Middle Knowledge*. Studies in Philosophical Theology 20. Leuven: Peeters, 2000.

Driel, Edwin Chr. van. 'God and God's Beloved: A Constructive Re-reading of Scotus's Supralapsarian Christological Argument.' *The Heythrop Journal* 63, no. 5 (September 2022): 995–1006. https://doi.org/10.1111/heyj.14132.

———. *Incarnation Anyway: Arguments for Supralapsarian Christology*. Oxford; New York: Oxford University Press, 2008.

———. '"Too Lowly to Reach God Without a Mediator": John Calvin's Supralapsarian Eschatological Narrative.' *Modern Theology* 33, no. 2 (April 2017): 275–92.

Duns Scotus, John. *Contingency and Freedom: Lectura I 39*. Edited by A. Vos. The New Synthese Historical Library, Vol. 42. Dordrecht; Boston: Kluwer Academic Publishers, 1994.

Eberhart, Christian A. *Kulturmetaphorik und Christologie: Opfer- und Sühneterminologie im Neuen Testament*. Tübingen: Mohr Siebeck, 2013.

Firey, Abigail, ed. *A New History of Penance*. Brill's Companions to the Christian Tradition, Vol. 14. Leiden; Boston: Brill, 2008.

168 Bibliography

Geach, Peter Thomas. *Logic Matters*. 1. California paperback print. Berkeley, CA: University of California Press, 1980.

Gorman, Michael. 'Christological Consistency and the Reduplicative Qua.' *Journal of Analytic Theology* 2 (2014): 86–100.

Grillmeier, Alois. *Christ in Christian Tradition. From the Apostolic Age to Chalcedon (451) [Vol. 1]*. Second edition, 1975.

Habets, Myk. 'On Getting First Things First: Assessing Claims for the Primacy of Christ.' *New Blackfriars* 90, no. 1027 (May 2009): 343–64. https://doi.org/10.1111/j.1741-2005.2008.00240.x.

Harnack, Adolf von. *Lehrbuch Der Dogmengeschichte*. Vol. II. Darmstadt, 1964.

Hebblethwaite, Brian. *Ethics and Religion in a Pluralistic Age: Collected Essays*. Edinburgh: T&T Clark, 1997.

Hick, John, ed. *The Myth of God Incarnate*. London: SCM Press, 1977.

Hill, Jonathan. 'Introduction.' In *The Metaphysics of the Incarnation*, edited by Anna Marmodoro and Jonathan Hill. Oxford: Oxford University Press, 2011.

Hoeres, Walter. *Der Wille als reine Vollkommenheit nach Duns Scotus*. München: Pustet, 1962.

Honnefelder, Ludger. *Ens inquantum ens: der Begriff des Seienden als solchen als Gegenstand der Metaphysik nach der Lehre des Johannes Duns Scotus*. Beiträge zur Geschichte der Philosophie und Theologie des Mittelalters, n. F., Bd. 16. Münster: Aschendorff, 1979.

———. 'Philosophische Reflexion als Medium theologischer Einsicht im Rahmen der Christologie des Johannes Duns Scotus.' In *Wie beeinflusst die Christusoffenbarung das franziskanische Verständnis der Person?*, edited by Herbert Schneider, 76–90. Veröffentlichungen der Johannes-Duns-Skotus-Akademie für Franziskanische Geistesgeschichte und Spiritualität Mönchengladbach 16. Kevelaer: Butzon und Bercker, 2004.

Horan, Daniel P. *Postmodernity and Univocity: A Critical Account of Radical Orthodoxy and John Duns Scotus*. Minneapolis: Fortress Press, 2014.

Hunter, Justus Hamilton. *If Adam Had Not Sinned: The Reason for the Incarnation from Anselm to Scotus*. Washington, DC: The Catholic University of America Press, 2020.

Hurtado, Larry W. *Lord Jesus Christ: Devotion to Jesus in Earliest Christianity*. Grand Rapids, MI: Eerdmans, 2005.

Johnson, Adam J. 'Atonement: The Shape and State of the Doctrine.' In *T&T Clark Companion to Atonement*, edited by Adam J. Johnson, 1–17. London/Oxford: T&T Clark, 2017.

———, ed. *T&T Clark Companion to Atonement*. London/Oxford: T&T Clark, 2017.

Kelly, J. N. D. *Early Christian Doctrines*. Fifth revised edition. London: A & C Black, 1985.

King, Peter. 'Scotus on Metaphysics.' In *The Cambridge Companion to Duns Scotus*, edited by Thomas Williams. Cambridge Companions to Philosophy. Cambridge, UK; New York: Cambridge University Press, 2003.

Knuuttila, Simo. 'The Psychology of the Incarnation in John Duns Scotus.' *Philosophy and Theology in the Long Middle Ages*, 1 January 2011, 737–48.

Bibliography

Kooten, Geurt Henk van. 'The Pauline Debate on the Cosmos: Graeco-Roman Cosmology and Jewish Eschatology in Paul and in the Pseudo-Pauline Letters to the Colossians and the Ephesians.' Doctoral Thesis, 2001.

Labooy, G. H. 'Als een keizer die knielt.' *Kerk en Theologie* 49 (1998): 209–21.

———. 'Antwoord aan Jeroen de Ridder en René van Woudenberg.' *Tijdschrift voor Filosofie* 72, no. 3 (2010): 557–80.

———. 'Christus' toewijding als verzoenende verdienste. Over zijn Australisch strafdragen.' *Kerk & Theologie* 2, no. 67 (2016): 146–60.

———. '"Duns Scotus" Univocity: Applied to the Debate on Phenomenological Theology.' *International Journal for Philosophy of Religion; Dordrecht* 76, no. 1 (August 2014): 53–73. http://dx.doi.org.vu-nl.idm.oclc.org/10.1007/s11153-014 -9443-8.

———. *Freedom and Dispositions: Two Main Concepts in Theology and Biological Psychiatry: A Systematic Analysis*. Contributions to Philosophical Theology, Vol. 8. Frankfurt am Main; New York: Peter Lang, 2002.

———. 'Freedom and Neurobiology, a Scotistic Account.' *Zygon* 39, no. 4 (2004): 919–32.

———. 'Stepped Characterisation: A Metaphysical Defence of qua-Propositions in Christology.' *International Journal for Philosophy of Religion* 86, no. 1 (August 2019): 25–38. https://doi.org/10.1007/s11153-019-09698-y.

———. 'The Historicity of the Virginal Conception. A Study in Argumentation.' *European Journal of Theology* 13, no. 2 (2004): 91–101.

———. 'Theologie van het Oude Testament en historisch denken.' *Kerk en Theologie* 65, no. 3 (2014): 249–73.

Labooy, G. H., and P. M. Wisse. 'The Coherence of Equivocal Penal Substitution: Modern and Scholastic Voices.' *International Journal for Philosophy of Religion* 86, no. 3 (1 December 2019): 227–41. https://doi.org/10.1007/s11153-019-09709-y.

Labooy, Guus H., and P. M. Wisse. 'Duns Scotus on Atonement and Penance.' *Heythrop Journal* 63, no. 5 (September 2022): 940–51.

Langereis, Sandra. *Geschiedenis als ambacht: oudheidkunde in de Gouden Eeuw: Arnoldus Buchelius en Petrus Scriverius*. Hollandse studiën 37. Hilversum: Verloren, 2001.

Langston, Douglas C. 'Did Scotus Embrace Anselm's Notion of Freedom?' *Medieval Philosophy and Theology* 5 (1996): 145–59.

Larson, Arrai A. *Master of Penance*. Washington, D.C.: CUA Press, 2014.

Leftow, Brian. 'The Humanity of God.' In *The Metaphysics of the Incarnation*, edited by Anna Marmodoro and Jonathan Hill, 20–44. Oxford: Oxford University Press, 2011.

Linville, Mark D. 'The Moral Argument.' In *The Blackwell Companion to Natural Theology*, edited by William Lane Craig and J. P. Moreland, 391–448. Chichester: Wiley-Blackwell, 2012.

Mackay, Ewald. *Geschiedenis bij de bron, een onderzoek naar de verhouding van christelijk geloof en historische werkelijkheid in geschiedwetenschap, wijsbegeerte en theologie*. Sliedrecht: Merweboek, 1997.

Marenbon, John. *Later Medieval Philosophy (1150–1350): An Introduction*. London; New York: Routledge & K. Paul, 1987.

Marmodoro, Anna. 'The Metaphysics of the Extended Mind in Ontological Entanglements.' In *The Metaphysics of the Incarnation*, edited by Anna Marmodoro and Jonathan Hill, 205–27. Oxford: Oxford University Press, 2011.

Mastricht, Peter van. *Theoretical-Practical Theology*. Vol. 3. Grand Rapids, MI: Reformation Heritage Books, 2018.

McGrath, Alister E. *Iustitia Dei: A History of the Christian Doctrine of Justification*. Cambridge: Cambridge University Press, 1989.

McGuckin, John Anthony. *The Orthodox Church: An Introduction to Its History, Doctrine, and Spiritual Culture*. Malden, MA; Oxford: Blackwell Pub. Ltd., 2008.

Michaels, J. R. *The Gospel of John*. Grand Rapids, MI; Cambridge, UK: William B. Eerdmans Publishing Company, 2010.

Milgrom, Jacob, trans. *Leviticus 1–16: A New Translation with Introduction and Commentary*. New Haven; London: Yale University Press; Bloomsbury Publishing, 2021.

Moffitt, David M. *Rethinking the Atonement: New Perspectives on Jesus's Death, Resurrection, and Ascension*. Grand Rapids, MI: Baker Academic, a division of Baker Publishing Group, 2022.

Morris, Thomas V. *The Logic of God Incarnate*. Ithaca: Cornell University Press, 1987.

Murphy, Mark C. 'Not Penal Substitution but Vicarious Punishment.' *Faith and Philosophy* 26, no. 3 (2009): 253–73.

Owen, John. *Justification by Faith Through the Imputation of the Righteousness of Christ, Explained, Confirmed, & Vindicated*. London: R. Boulster, 1677.

———. *The Works of John Owen*. Vol. 5. London, 1851.

Pannenberg, W. *Grundzüge Der Christologie*. Gütersloh, 1964.

Pasnau, Robert. 'Cognition.' In *The Cambridge Companion to Duns Scotus*, edited by Thomas Williams, 285–311. Cambridge Companions to Philosophy. Cambridge, UK; New York: Cambridge University Press, 2003.

Patout Burns, J. 'The Concept of Satisfaction in Medieval Redemption Theory.' *Theological Studies* 36, no. 2 (June 1975): 285–304.

Pawl, Timothy. 'A Solution to the Fundamental Philosophical Problem of Christology.' *Journal of Analytic Theology* 2, no. May (2014): 61–85.

———. *In Defense of Conciliar Christology: A Philosophical Essay*. Oxford Studies in Analytic Theology. Oxford; New York: Oxford University Press, 2016.

———. 'The Freedom of Christ and the Problem of Deliberation.' *International Journal for Philosophy of Religion* 75, no. 3 (June 2014): 233–47. https://doi.org/10.1007/s11153-014-9447-4.

———. *The Incarnation*. Cambridge Elements. Cambridge: Cambridge University Press, 2020.

Pawl, Timothy, and Kevin Timpe. 'Freedom and the Incarnation.' *Philosophy Compass* 11, no. 11 (2016): 743–56. https://doi.org/10.1111/phc3.12362.

Peter, Rene. 'L'imposition Des Mains Dans l'Ancien Testament.' *Vetus Testamentum* 27, no. 1 (January 1977): 48. https://doi.org/10.2307/1517355.

Bibliography

Plaisier, A. J. red. *Om een persoonlijk God*, serie Utrechtse cahiers 1. Zoetermeer: Boekencentrum, 2006.

Plantinga, Alvin. *The Nature of Necessity*. Oxford: Oxford University Press, 1974.

Pomplun, Trent. 'The Immaculate World: Predestination and Passibility in Contemporary Scotism.' *Modern Theology* 30, no. 4 (October 2014): 525–51. https://doi.org/10.1111/moth.12115.

Porter, Steven L. 'Swinburnian Atonement and the Doctrine of Penal Substitution.' *Faith and Philosophy* 21, no. 2 (2004): 228–41.

Rahner, Karl. *Theological Investigations*. Vol. V. London: Darton, Longman & Todd, 1969.

Rendtorff, Rolf. *Leviticus*. Biblischer Kommentar 3. Neukirchen-Vluyn: Neukirchener Verlag, 2004.

Ridder, G. J. de, and R. van Woudenberg. 'Een Scotistisch argument voor dualisme.' *Tijdschrift voor Filosofie* 72, no. 3 (2010).

Rosato, Andrew V. 'The Interpretation of Anselm's Teaching on Christ's Satisfaction for Sin in the Franciscan Tradition from Alexander of Hales to Duns Scotus.' *Franciscan Studies* 71 (2013): 411–44.

———. 'The Teaching of Duns Scotus on Whether Only a God-Man Could Make Satisfaction for Sin Within the Context of Thirteenth-Century Franciscan Theology.' *The Thomist: A Speculative Quarterly Review* 79, no. 4 (2015): 551–84. https://doi.org/10.1353/tho.2015.0030.

Schumacher, Lydia. *Early Franciscan Theology: Between Authority and Innovation*. Cambridge, UK; New York: Cambridge University Press, 2019.

Sonderegger, Katherine. 'Anselmian Atonement.' In *T&T Clark Companion to Atonement*, edited by Adam J. Johnson, 175–93. London/Oxford: T&T Clark, 2017.

Stump, Eleonore. 'Aquinas' Metaphysics of the Incarnation.' In *The Incarnation: An Interdisciplinary Symposium on the Incarnation of the Son of God*, edited by Stephen T. Davis, Daniel Kendall, and Gerald O'Collins, 197–218. Oxford; New York: Oxford University Press, 2002.

———. *Atonement*. Oxford Studies in Analytic Theology. Oxford: Oxford University Press, 2018.

Sturch, R. L. 'God, Christ and Possibilities.' *Religious Studies* 16, no. 1 (March 1980): 81–84. https://doi.org/10.1017/S0034412500011999.

Swinburne, Richard. *Responsibility and Atonement*. Oxford/New York: Clarendon Press; Oxford University Press, 1989.

———. *The Christian God*. Oxford [England]: New York: Clarendon Press; Oxford University Press, 1994.

———. 'The Coherence of the Chalcedonian Definition of the Incarnation.' In *The Metaphysics of the Incarnation*, edited by Anna Marmodoro and Jonathan Hill, 153–67. Oxford: Oxford University Press, 2011.

Tanner, Norman P., ed. *Decrees of the Ecumenical Councils*. London: Washington, DC: Sheed & Ward; Georgetown University Press, 1990.

Timpe, Kevin. *Free Will in Philosophical Theology*. Bloomsbury Studies in Philosophy of Religion. New York; London: Bloomsbury Academic, 2014.

Bibliography

Turrettin, François. *The Atonement of Christ*. Grand Rapids, MI: Baker Book House, 1978.

Unger, Dominic. 'Franciscan Christology: Absolute and Universal Primacy of Christ.' *Franciscan Studies* 2 (1942): 428–75.

Vaux, Roland de. *Ancient Israel: Its Life and Institutions*. The Biblical Resource Series. Grand Rapids, MI: W. B. Eerdmans, 1997.

Veldhuis, Henri. 'Zur hermeneutischen Bedeutung der supralapsarischen Christologie des Johannes Duns Scotus.' In *Menschwerdung Gottes—Hoffnung des Menschen*, edited by Herbert Schneider, 81–110. Veröffentlichungen der Johannes-Duns-Skotus-Akademie für Franziskanische Geistesgeschichte und Spiritualität Mönchengladbach 12. Kevelaer: Butzon und Bercker, 2000.

Vos, A. *The Philosophy of John Duns Scotus*. Edinburgh: Edinburgh University Press, 2006.

Vos, A., H. Veldhuis, N. W. den Bok, and a.o. *Duns Scotus on Divine Love*. Aldershot: Ashgate, 2003.

Ward, Thomas M. 'Voluntarism, Atonement, and Duns Scotus.' *The Heythrop Journal* 58, no. 1 (January 2017): 37–43. https://doi.org/10.1111/heyj.12315.

Ware, Kallistos. 'Christian Theology in the East 600–1453.' In *A History of Christian Doctrine*, edited by Hubert Cunliffe-Jones, 181–226. Edinburgh: Clark, 1978.

Weinberg, Julius R. *A Short History of Medieval Philosophy*. Princeton: Princeton University Press, 1964.

Wenham, Gordon J. *The Book of Leviticus*. The New International Commentary on the Old Testament. Grand Rapids, MI: Eerdmans, 2009.

Williams, Scott M. 'Unity of Action in a Latin Social Model of the Trinity.' *Faith and Philosophy* 34, no. 3 (2017): 321–46. https://doi.org/10.5840/faithphil20178385.

Williams, Thomas. 'The Doctrine of Univocity Is True and Salutary.' *Modern Theology* 4, no. 21 (2005): 575–85.

Wisse, Maarten. *Trinitarian Theology beyond Participation: Augustine's De Trinitate and Contemporary Theology*. London; New York: Bloomsbury T. & T. Clark, 2013.

Wolter, Allan Bernard, and William A. Frank, trans. *Duns Scotus on the Will and Morality*. Washington, D.C.: Catholic University of America Press, 1997.

Wolterstorff, Nicholas. *Thomas Reid and the Story of Epistemology*. First paperback edition. Modern European Philosophy. Cambridge: Cambridge University Press, 2004.

Wright, N. T. 'God Put Jesus Forth: Reflections on Romans 3: 24–26.' In *In the Fullness of Time: Essays on Christology, Creation, and Eschatology in Honor of Richard Bauckham*, edited by Daniel M. Gurtner, 135–61. Grand Rapids, MI: William B. Eerdmans Publishing Company, 2016.

———. *Jesus and the Victory of God*. Christian Origins and the Question of God 2. London: Fortress Press, 1996.

———. 'Jesus' Self-Understanding.' In *The Incarnation: An Interdisciplinary Symposium on the Incarnation of the Son of God*, edited by Stephen T. Davis, Daniel Kendall, and Gerald O'Collins, 47–61. Oxford; New York: Oxford University Press, 2002.

Bibliography

———. *Paul and the Faithfulness of God.* 2 vols. Christian Origins and the Question of God, volume 4. London: Society for Promoting Christian Knowledge, 2013.

———. *The Day the Revolution Began: Reconsidering the Meaning of Jesus's Crucifixion.* New York: HarperCollins, 2018.

Zie Brower, Jeffrey. 'Medieval Theories of Relations.' In *The Stanford Encyclopedia of Philosophy* (winter 2015 edition), ed. Edward N. Zalta. http://plato.stanford.edu /archives/win2015/entries/relations-medieval/.

Index

Anselm, 76, 78, 95–96, 110–11, 113–15, 125, 131, 151

atonement, theories of, 107–9; and Levitical offerings, 129–30; love as reason of, 115; necessity of, 113; penal substitution, viii, 4–5, 107–8, 124–25, 131–45; punishment, rationale of, 157–59; quantitative view of efficacy of penitential suffering, 149, 158; representative deservedness, 132, 137, 141, 145, 153, 155–56; Scotus's view of, 118, 124; utilitarian and retributive views of punishment, 133–34, 144, 156n15

Bok, Nico den, 18, 19n29, 21n33, 22, 32n33, 94n4

Brandt, Willy, 153–55, 157

Brink, Gert van den, 137–38

Chalcedon, creed of, 23; central Christological predicament, 31; Chalcedonian demands, 24–26, 32, 36, 39, 42–43, 75; coherence problem, 41–42; dilemma of, 25

characterisation, 2, 33–34, 42; causal and the predicative aspects of agency, 74–76; communicatio idiomatum, 42; Pawl, 50n32, 81–84;

stepped vs. direct, 42–55, 74–75, 80n22

communicatio idiomatum. *See* characterisation

compositionalist metaphysics, 27, 29, 42, 47, 163

Craig, William L., 137n23, 141, 151, 159

Crisp, Oliver, 31, 38n46, 107

Cross, Richard, 27, 35–38, 44n13, 48, 49n29, 63n11, 74, 98, 148

denominate. *See* characterisation

dependence, characterisation tracking it, 50–52

Driel, Edwin van, 31n28

elimination of impersonalism in ethics. *See* meta-ethical theory

ends before means, 93, 112, 150

explanatory priority, in acting, 93, 99, 112

free will: affection for justice and affection for the advantageous, 78, 110, 115; compatibilist account of, 77; creative art on the new haven and earth, 91; divine preceding and divine consequent wills, 79, 113;

175

176 *Index*

freedom of the human will of Christ, 80–91; Free Will-Defence (FWD), 78; infallible love of the blessed, 86–91; synchronic alternative possibilities, 82; voluntas naturalis and voluntas libera, 76–78

Hunter, Justus, 95
hypostatic union, viii, 2, 16, 70–71, 99, 101–2, 129, 150, 160; actual and dispositional dependences, 35; (in)dependent on the Word, 29, 31–32; instrumental theory of, 36–38; metaphysics of, 23–40, 42, 46–49; monadic and relational properties, 32; summary of Scotus's view of, 39. *See also* characterisation; compositionalist metaphysics

impeccabilitas Christi, 84–86. *See also* free will
inhere, relation of, 49
interior monologue, 59, 75

John Duns Scotus Research Group, vii

knowledge: foreknowledge, 81–84; of human nature of Christ, 57–71; incomprehensibility, 10; intuitive, 66–68; seeing objects relucent in the Word, 64

Leftow, Brian, 80n21

McCord Adams, Marilyn, 3, 34, 42, 45–47, 147
merit, 109–13, 115, 151–53
meta-ethical theory, 147–50, 156; elimination of impersonalism in ethics, 114–15, 148; voluntarism, 111n16
Morris, Thomas V., 43, 52n36
Murphy, Mark, 132, 134–37, 143

Nestorianism and monophysitism, 24–27, 31, 36–38, 58

Owen, 137–44

the passion. *See* atonement
Pawl, Timothy, 44n13, 50n32, 81–84
penal substitution (vicarious penance). *See* atonement
penance, 109, 118–24, 142
Porter, Steven, 132–36, 149
P(p)ersona (hypostasis), concept of, 2, 15; in Christology, 24–27, 30–33, 35, 39; definition of Persona, 22; definition of persona, 31; and incommunicability, 15, 19, 33, 163; and independence, 15, 19–20, 31–32, 35, 39, 58, 163; in the Trinity, 15, 17, 19–20. *See also* hypostatic union
predestination of Christ to highest glory, 93–94
principle of plenitude, 94–97

qua-propositions, 42–64; 'qua ad simpliciter' inference, 44, 53–54

Rosato, Andrew V., 109, 116, 123

scriptural evidence, 68–71, 86, 100, 125–30
sin, relational analysis of, 143
structural, not temporal priority. *See* explanatory priority
Stump, Eleonore, 48n26, 107, 148, 151, 157
substance and accident, 28
supralapsarian Christology, 3, 22, 31n28, 93–104, 114

this-ness (*haecceitas*) and what-ness (*quidditas*), 28, 30
Timpe, Kevin, 87, 91
Trinity: basic terminology, 15, 17; consubstantial, coequal and coeval, 19; economic and essential aspects

of, 11, 22, 94; modalism, 16–19; mono-personal view, 12–14, 16; 'opera ad extra indivisa sunt,' 20–21, 38, 74, 80; social view, 12, 14, 18, 21–22, 94; 'Son' in Jewish sense, 68, 75

Turrettin, François, 148–49, 158

utilitarian view of punishment. *See* atonement

voluntarism. *See* meta-ethical theory

Vos, Antoon, vii, 67, 82n25, 110n13, 137

About the Author

Guus Labooy (1959) was raised in a secular family in The Hague in the Netherlands. He converted to Christianity in his early twenties while studying medicine. He worked for several years as an MD in addicted behaviour care, studying theology at the same time. His PhD is on the interface of psychiatry and theology. His publications include work on Scotism, integration of science and religion, incarnation, and atonement. From 2017 to 2021 he was affiliate researcher at the Protestant Theological University in Amsterdam, and he has been invited as guest lecturer at several universities in the Netherlands. At present, he is working as a pastor in the Protestant Church of the Netherlands. He is married and has three children and one grandson.